THE CLASSIC TINKERTOY™ CONSTRUCTION SET

Building Manual

Graphic Instructions for 37 World-Famous Designs

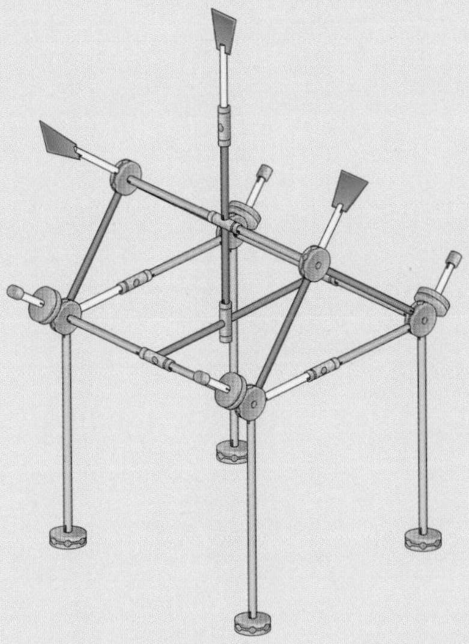

By Dylan Dawson • Illustrations by Robert Steimle

STERLING

New York / London

www.sterlingpublishing.com

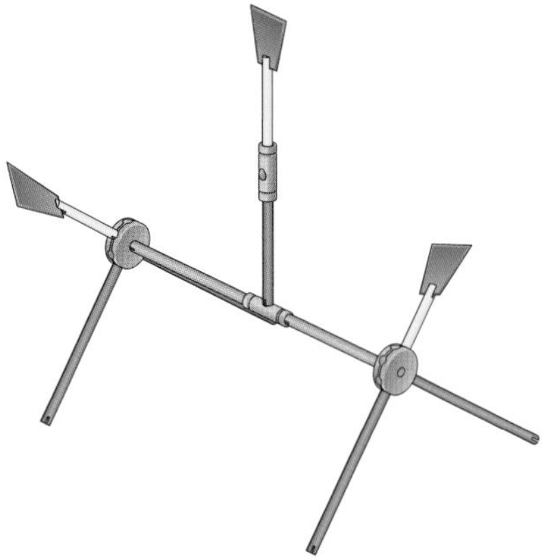

Library of Congress Cataloging-in-Publication Data

Dawson, Dylan.
Tinkertoy building manual : graphic instructions for
37 world-famous designs / Dylan Dawson.
p. cm.
ISBN-13: 978-1-4027-5078-6
ISBN-10: 1-4027-5078-1
1. Wooden toys. 2. Tinkertoys (Trademark) I. Title.
TS2301.T7D39 2007
745.592—dc22 2007004287

2 4 6 8 10 9 7 5 3 1

Published in 2007 by Sterling Publishing Co., Inc.
387 Park Avenue South, New York, NY 10016

Distributed in Canada by Sterling Publishing
c/o Canadian Manda Group, 165 Dufferin Street,
Toronto, Ontario, Canada M6K 3H6
Distributed in the United Kingdom by GMC Distribution Services,
Castle Place, 166 High Street, Lewes, East Sussex, England BN7 1XU
Distributed in Australia by Capricorn Link (Australia) Pty. Ltd.
P.O. Box 704, Windsor, NSW 2756, Australia

Printed in China

Sterling ISBN-13: 978-1-4027-5078-6
ISBN-10: 1-4027-5078-1

Design by Pamela Darcy of Neo9 Design Inc.

For information about custom editions, special sales, premium and
corporate purchases, please contact Sterling Special Sales
Department at 800-805-5489 or specialsales@sterlingpub.com.

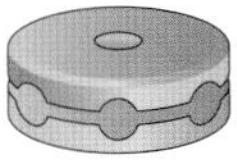

CONTENTS

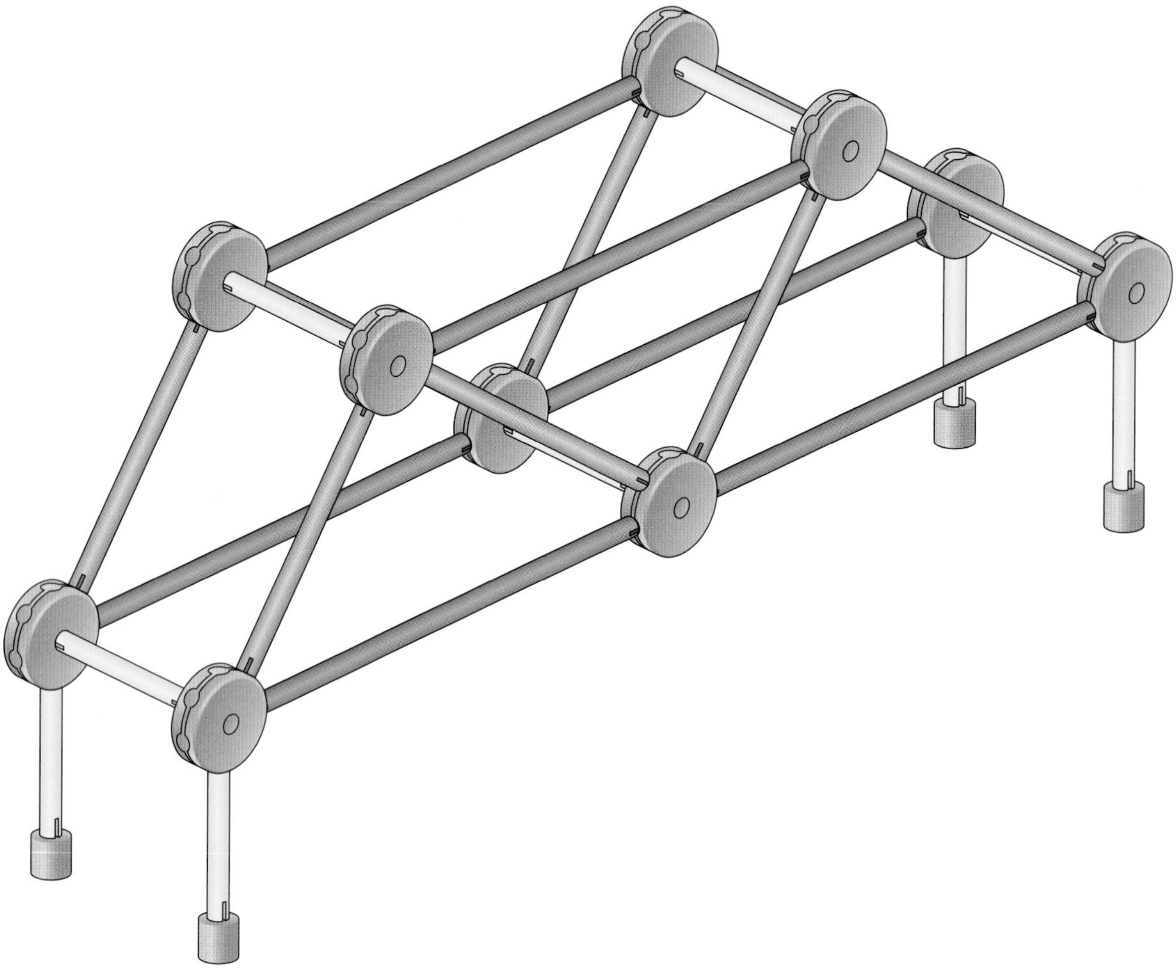

4

INTRODUCTION

TINKERTOY™ construction sets are one of the truly classic toys of all time. Introduced over 85 years ago, they have driven the imaginations of children for generations. These fun and stimulating spokes, spools, rods and reels provide endless construction possibilities.

This book provides vivid illustrations which take you step by step through 37 exciting designs like a Space Alien and Moon Rover. The projects are ordered from easier to more challenging so you can chose which ones you want to tackle. You can start with a cool Airplane and work up to a Cargo Loader! Or maybe you'll want to begin with a Rocket Ship and then see how amazing a Pirate Ship would look!

We've included a CD-Rom which shows how to assemble each project, so you'll be able to follow along on your computer as you put together these exciting designs. You may need more than one set to complete some of these, so make sure you've got some extra pieces before you begin.

Happy tinkering!!

Necklace

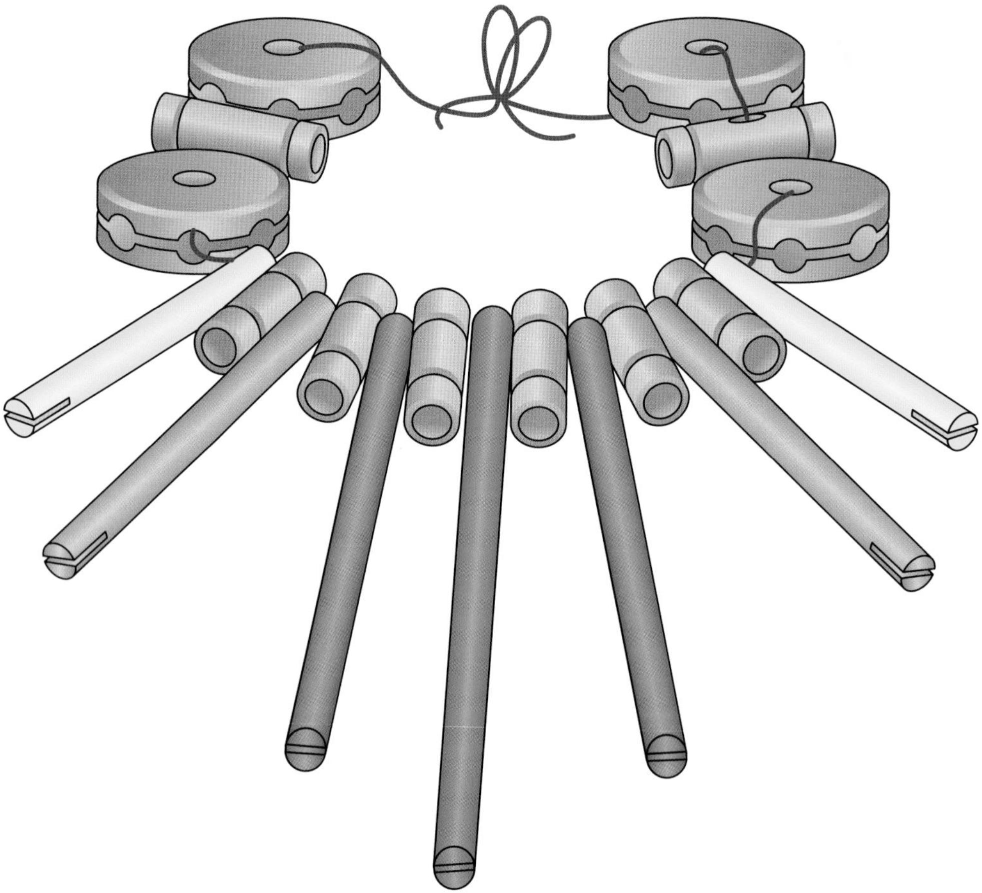

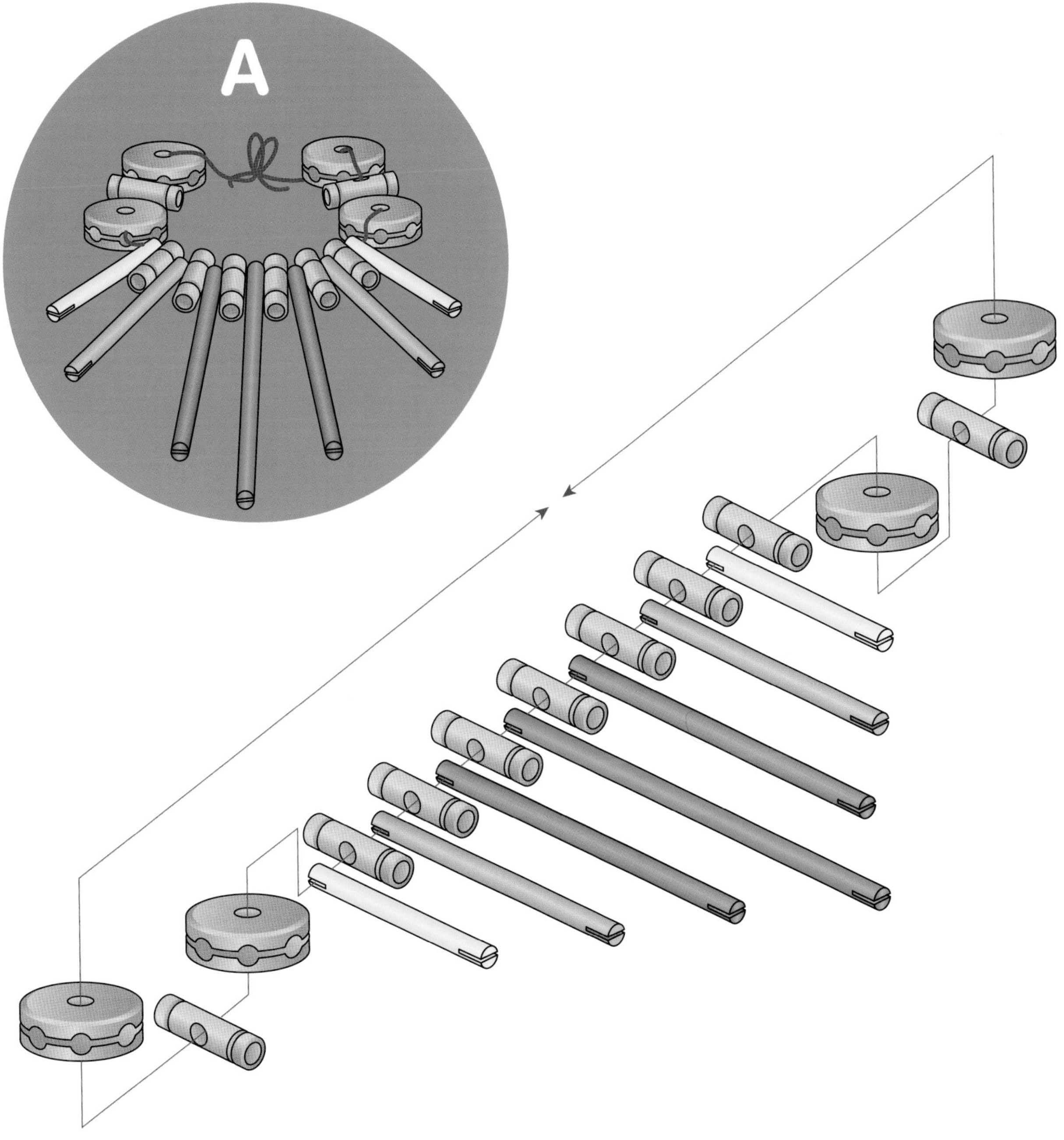
A

Shopping Cart

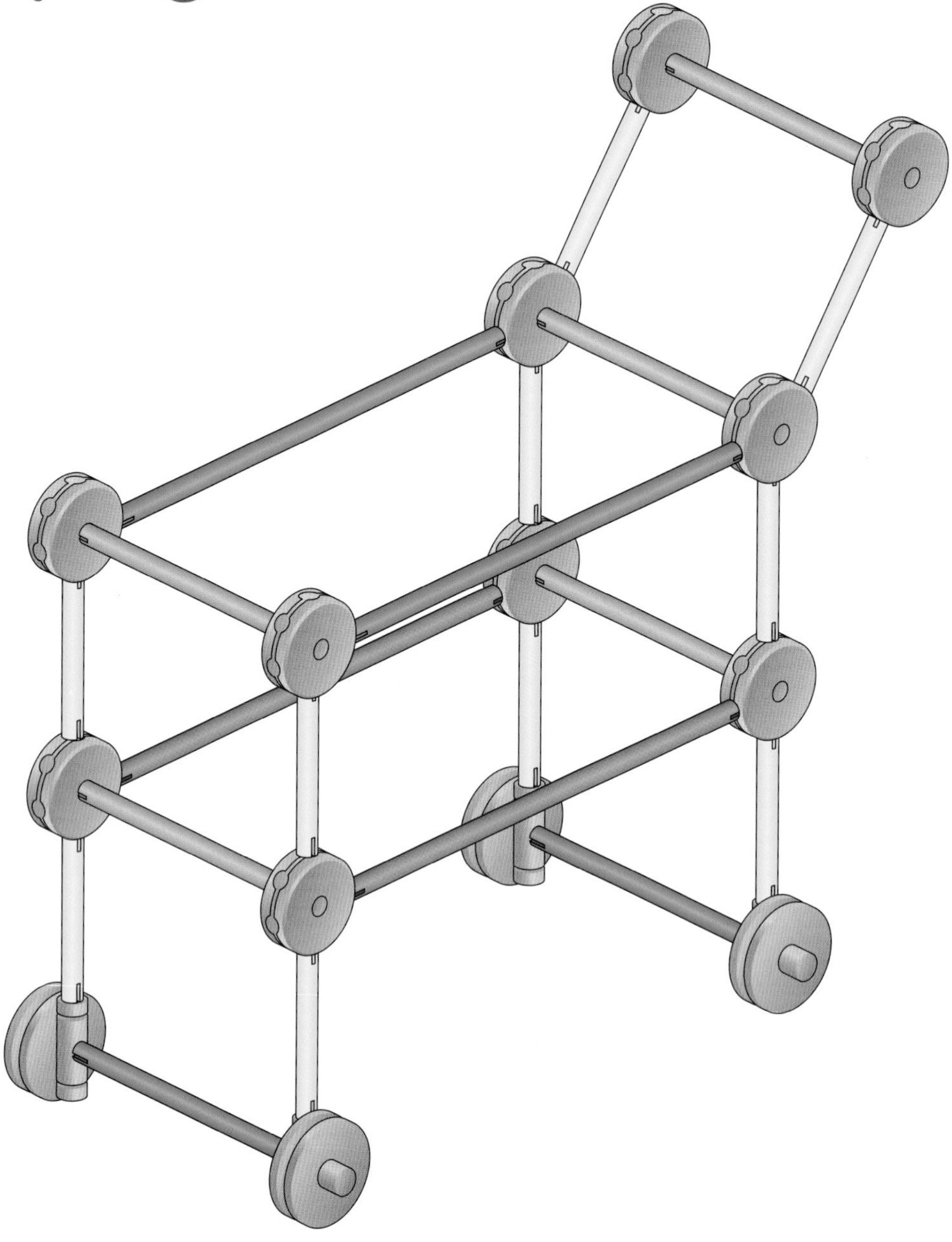

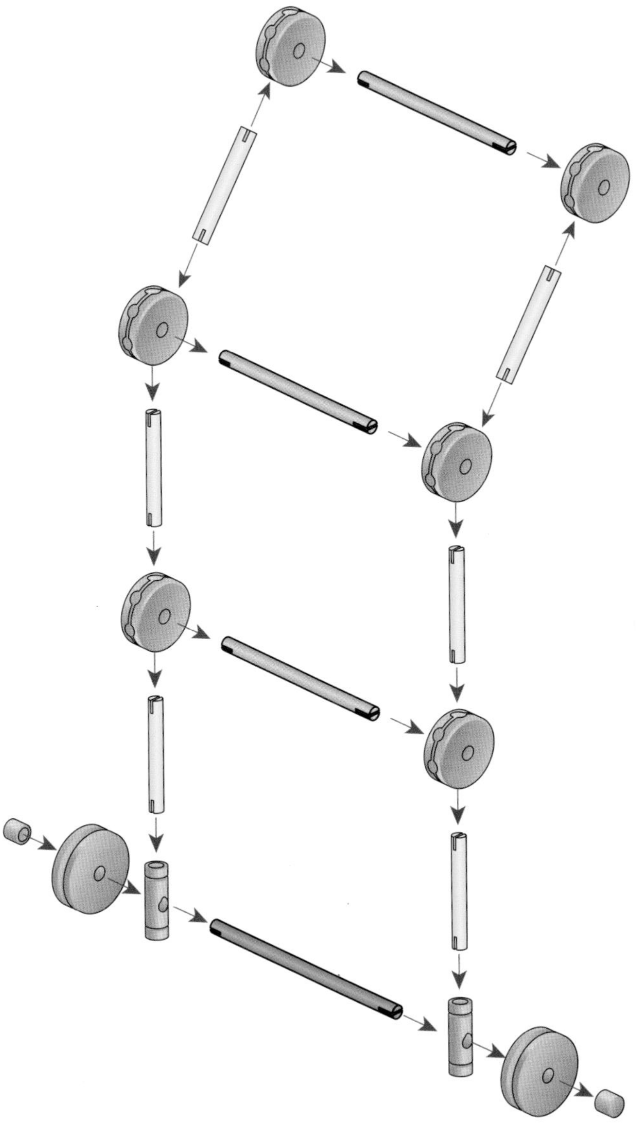

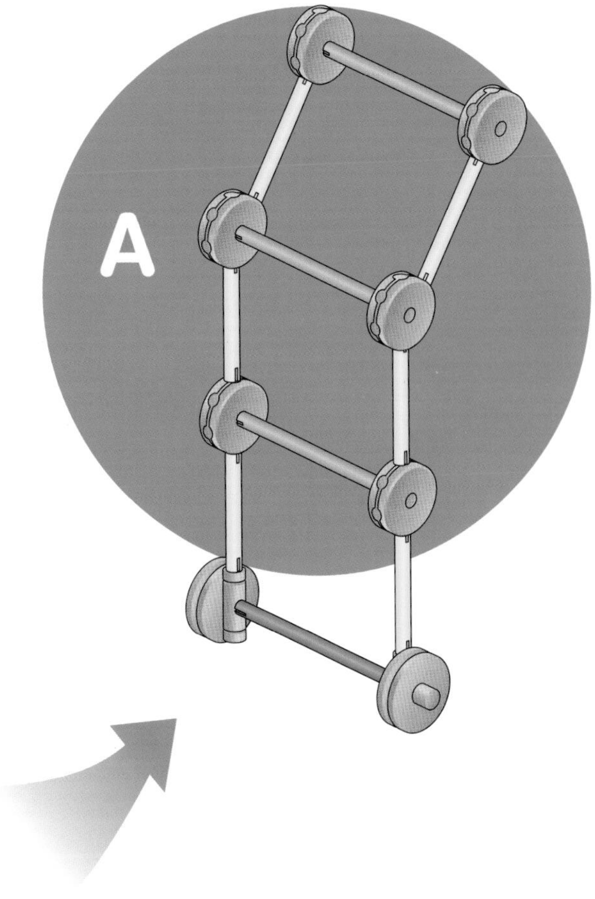
A

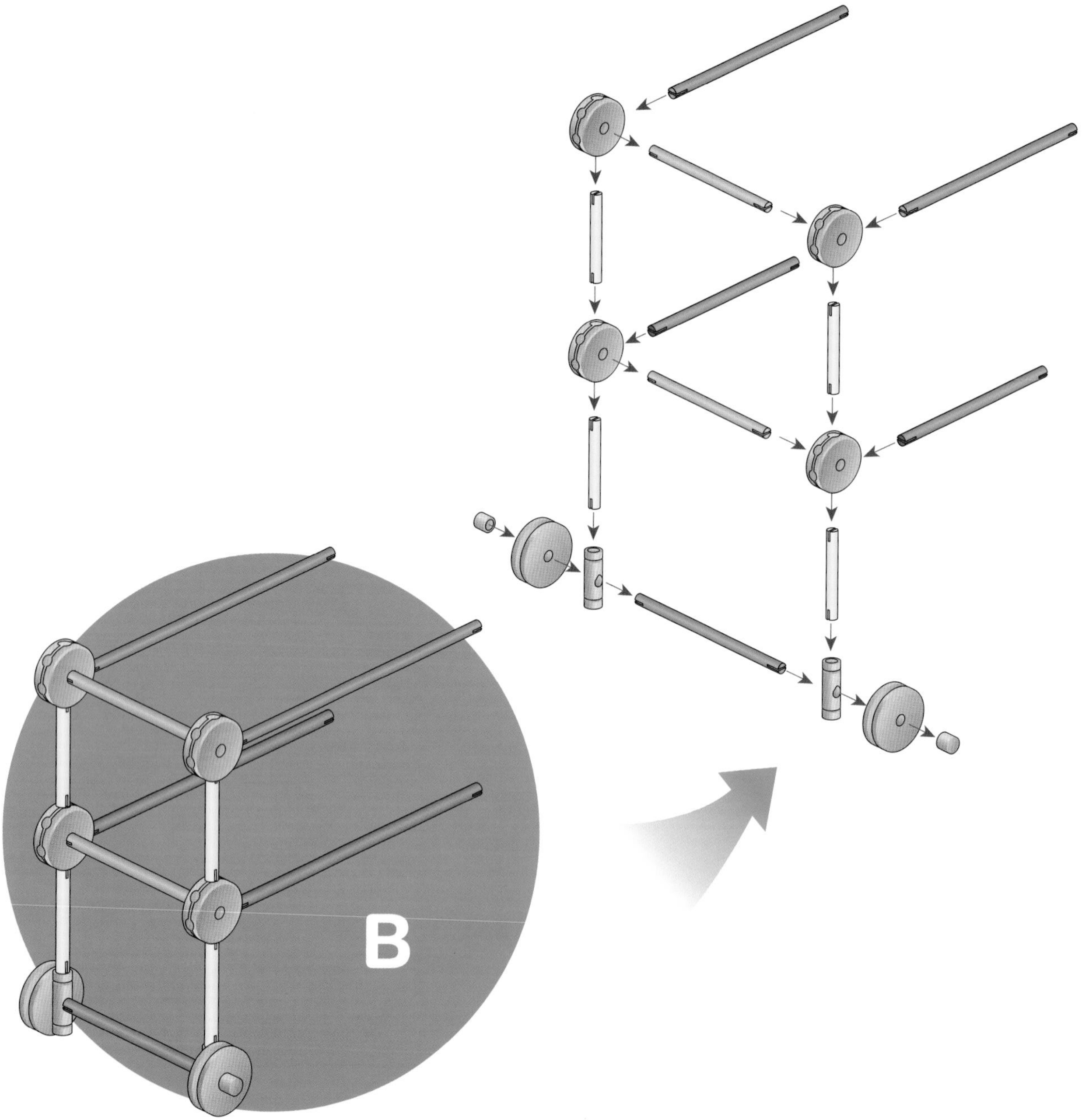
B

Airplane

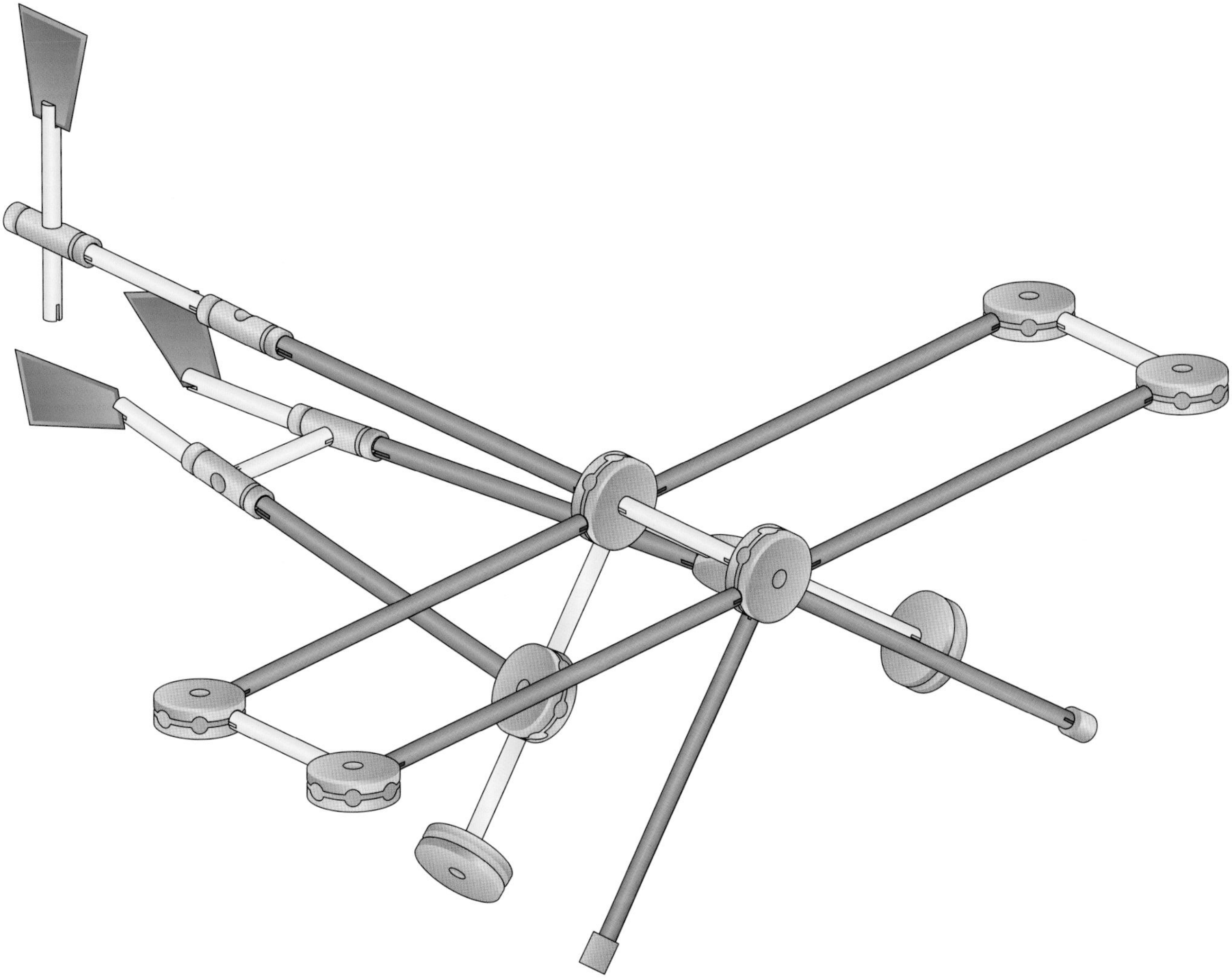

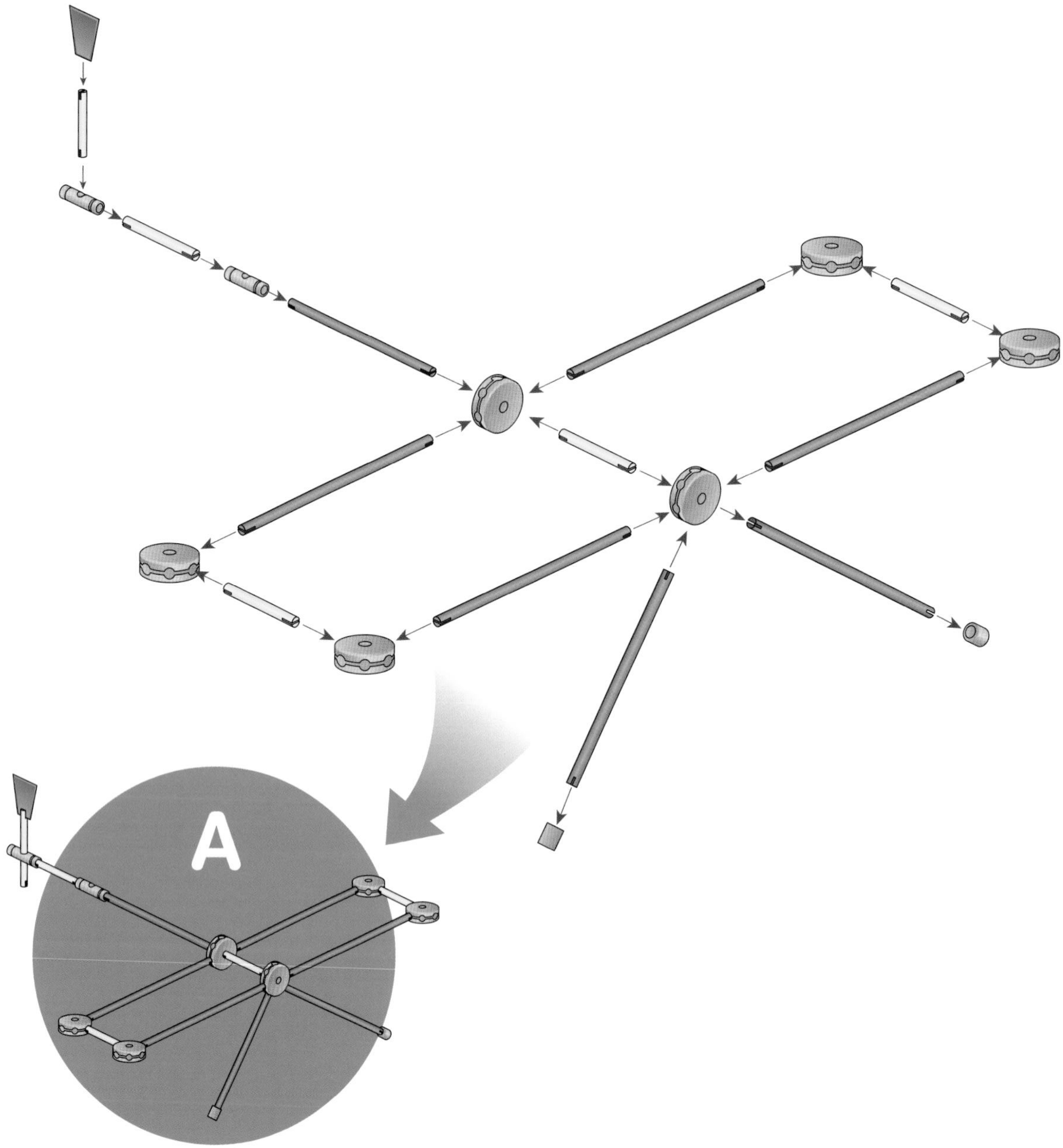
A

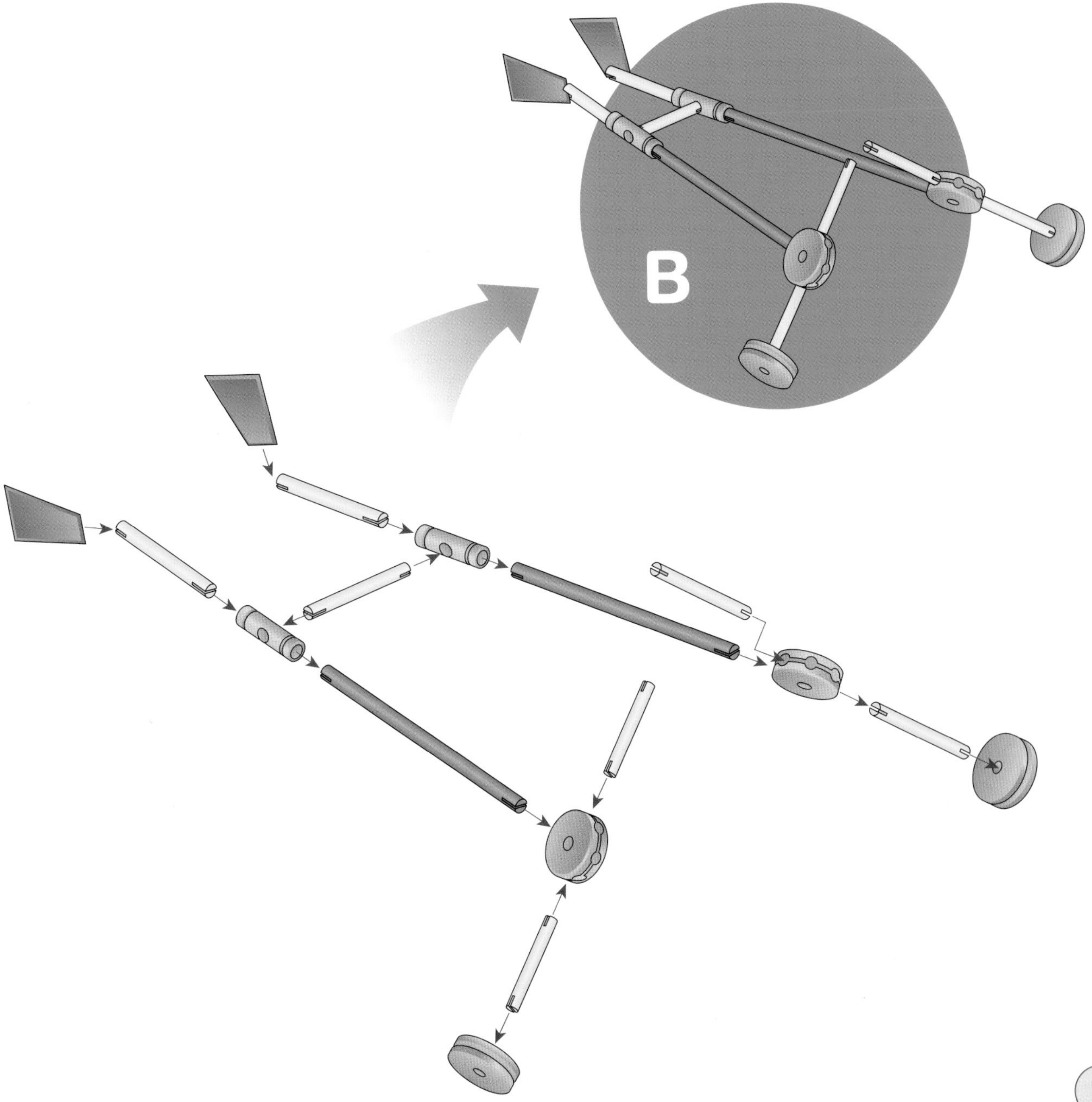
B

House

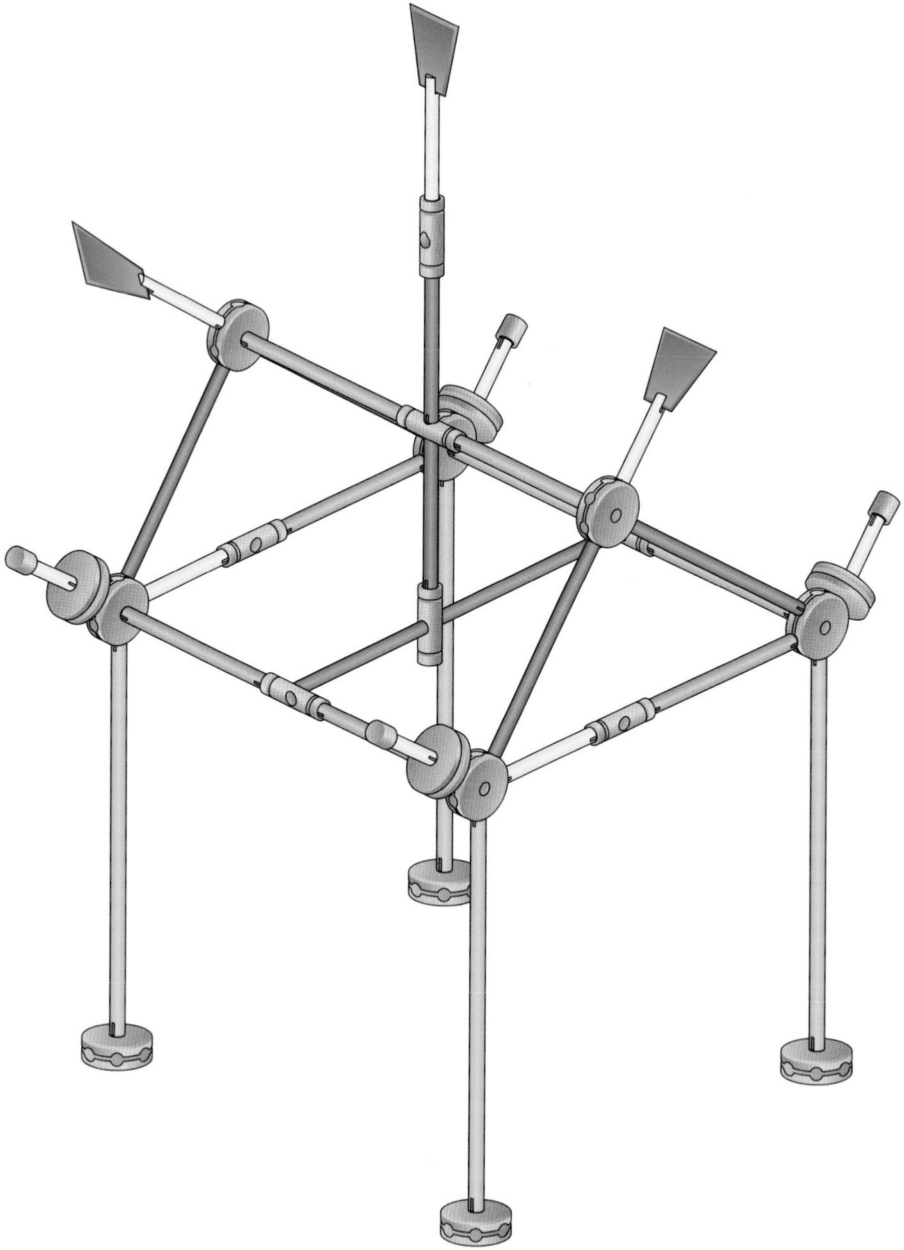

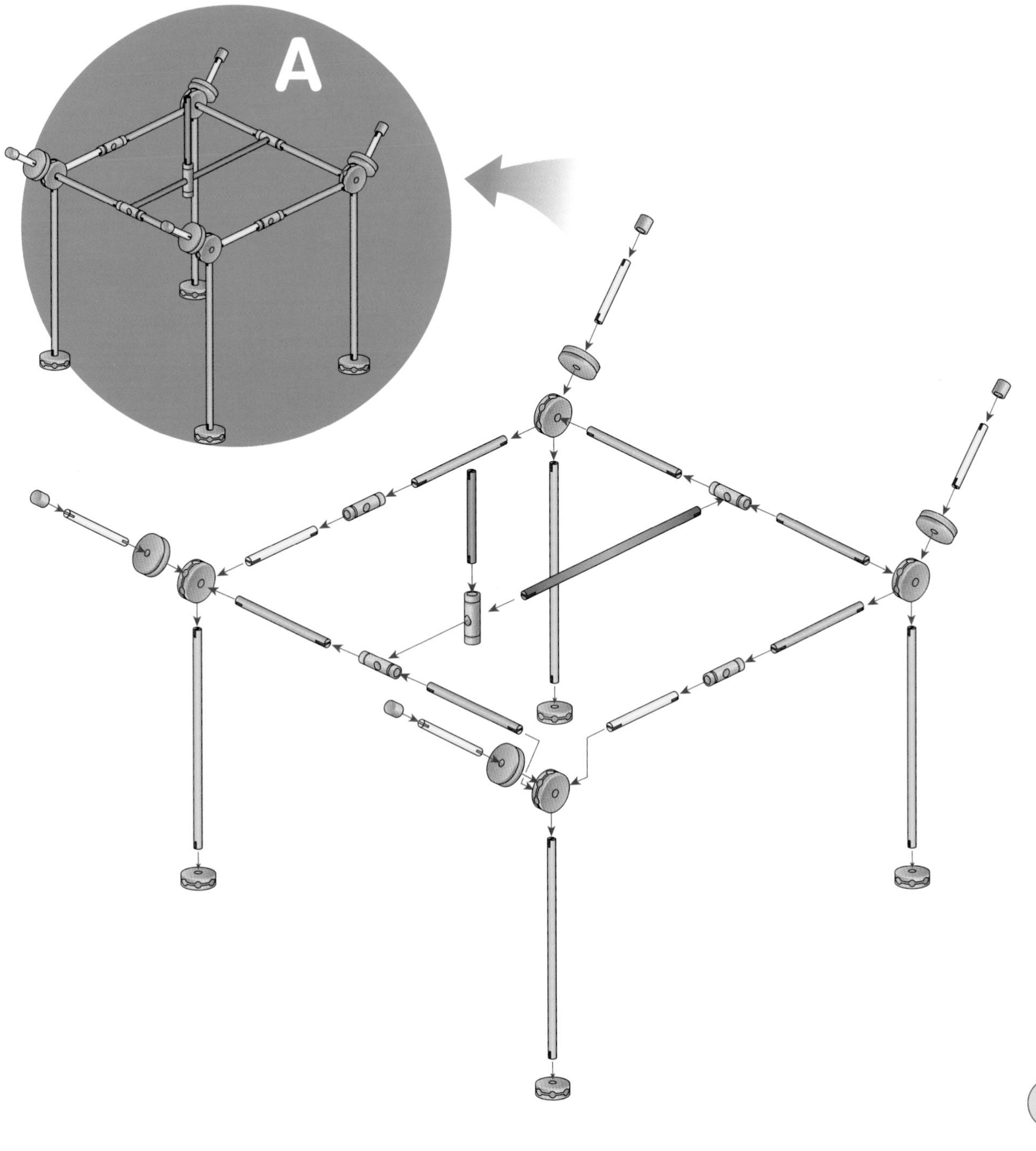
A

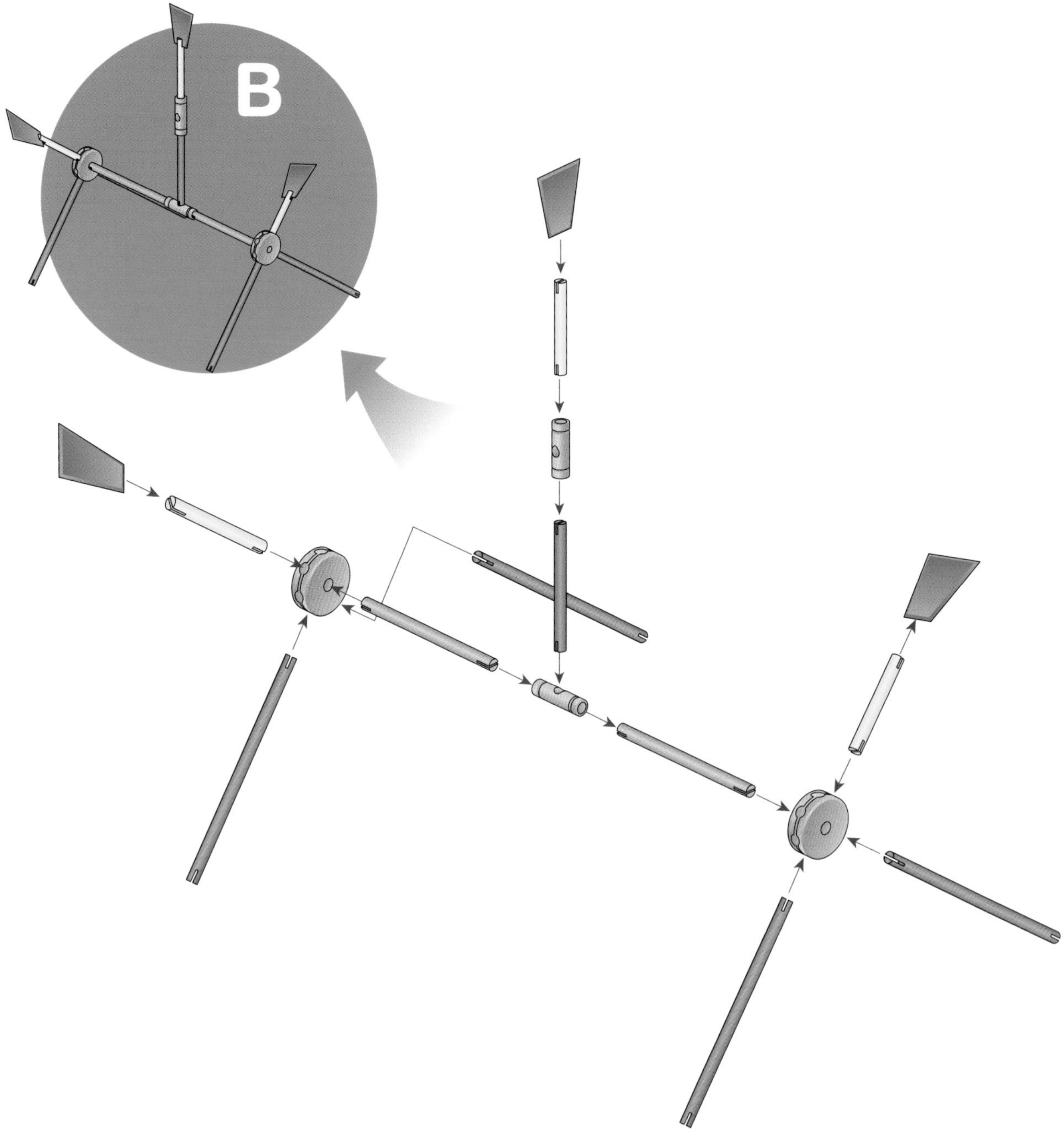
B

Duck

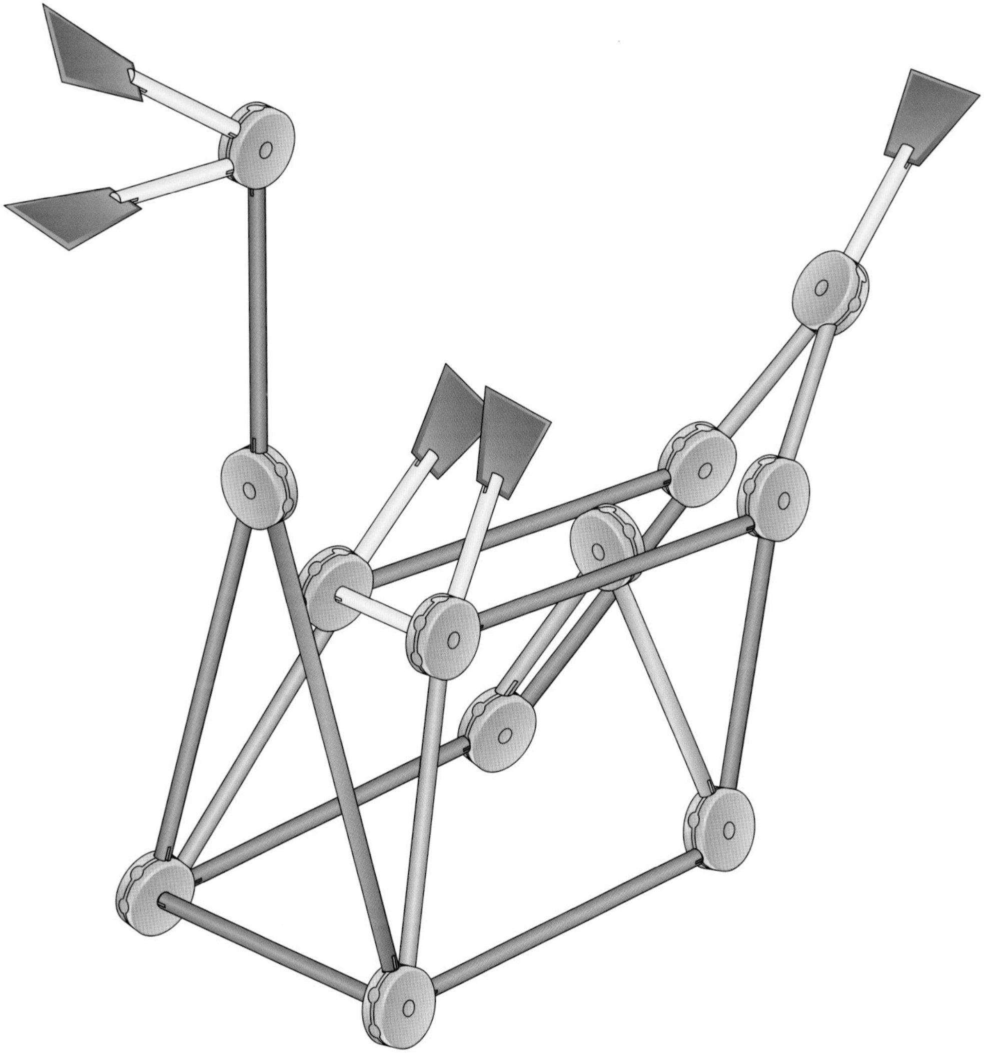

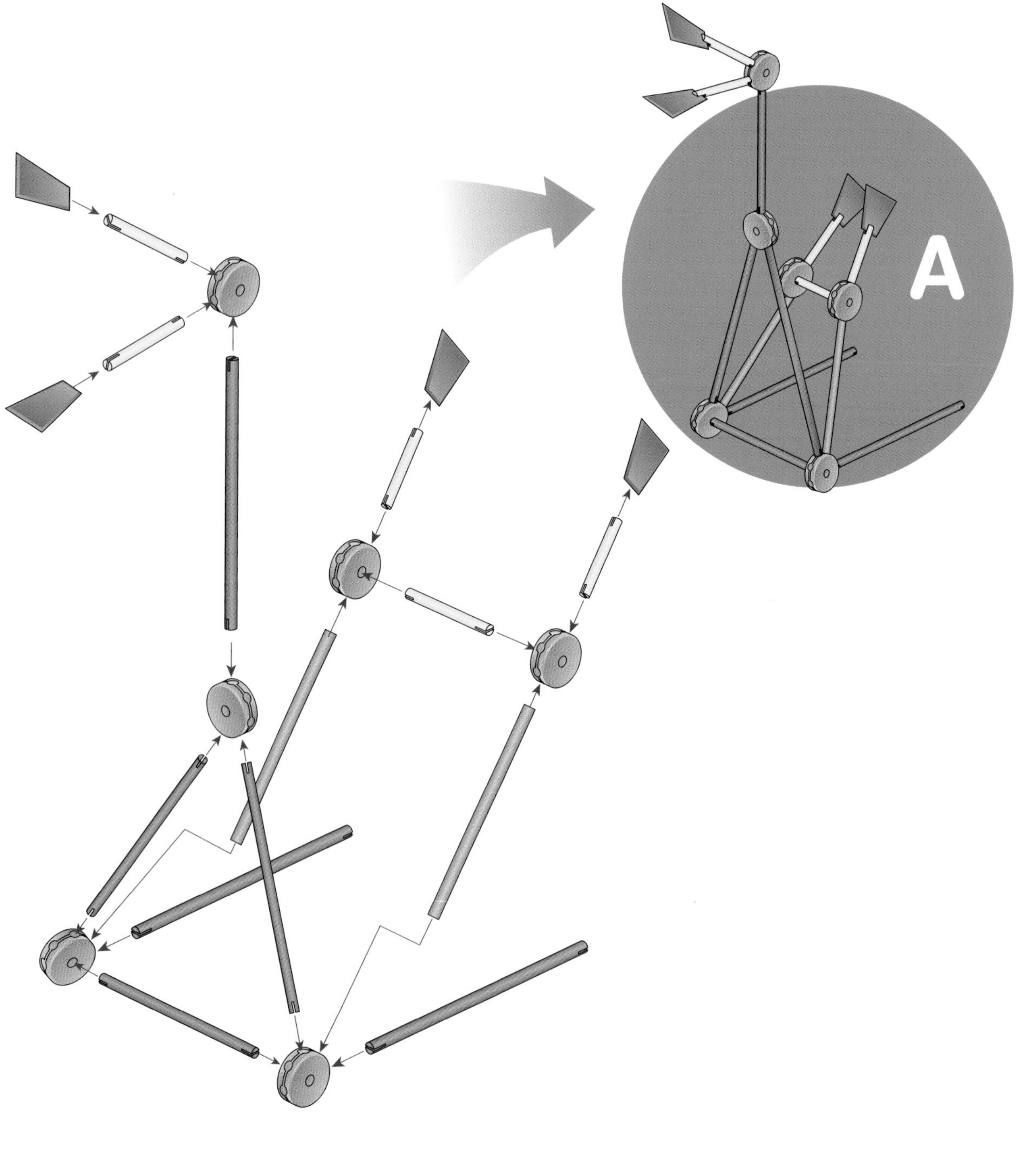
A

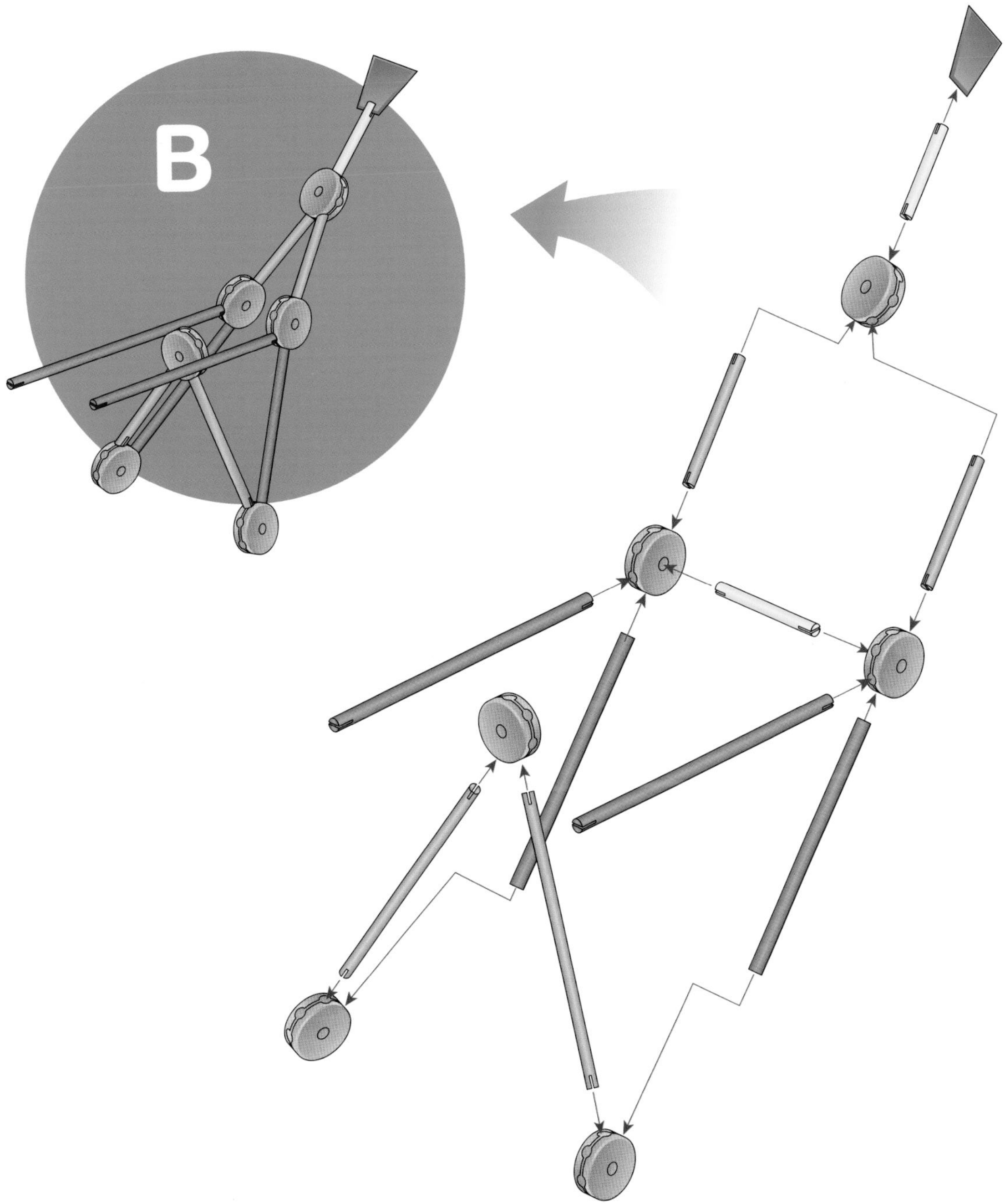
B

Bridge

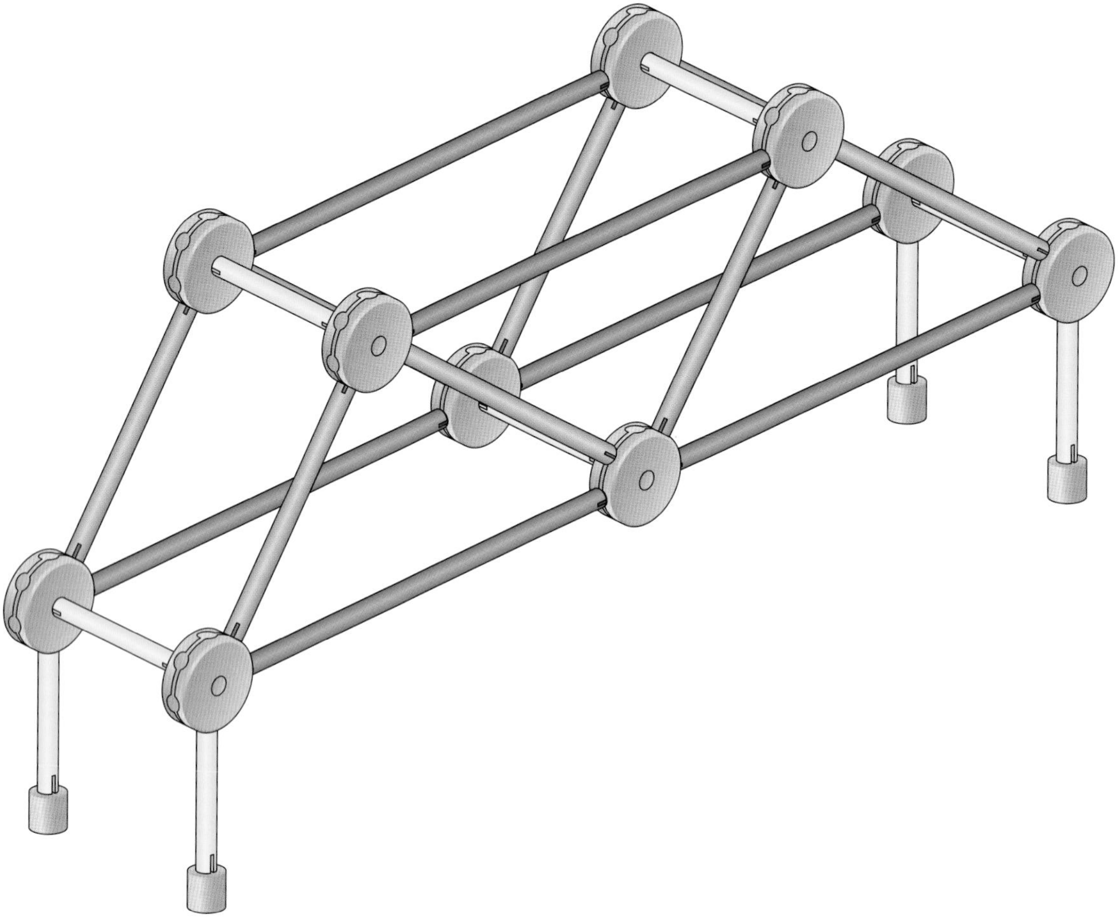

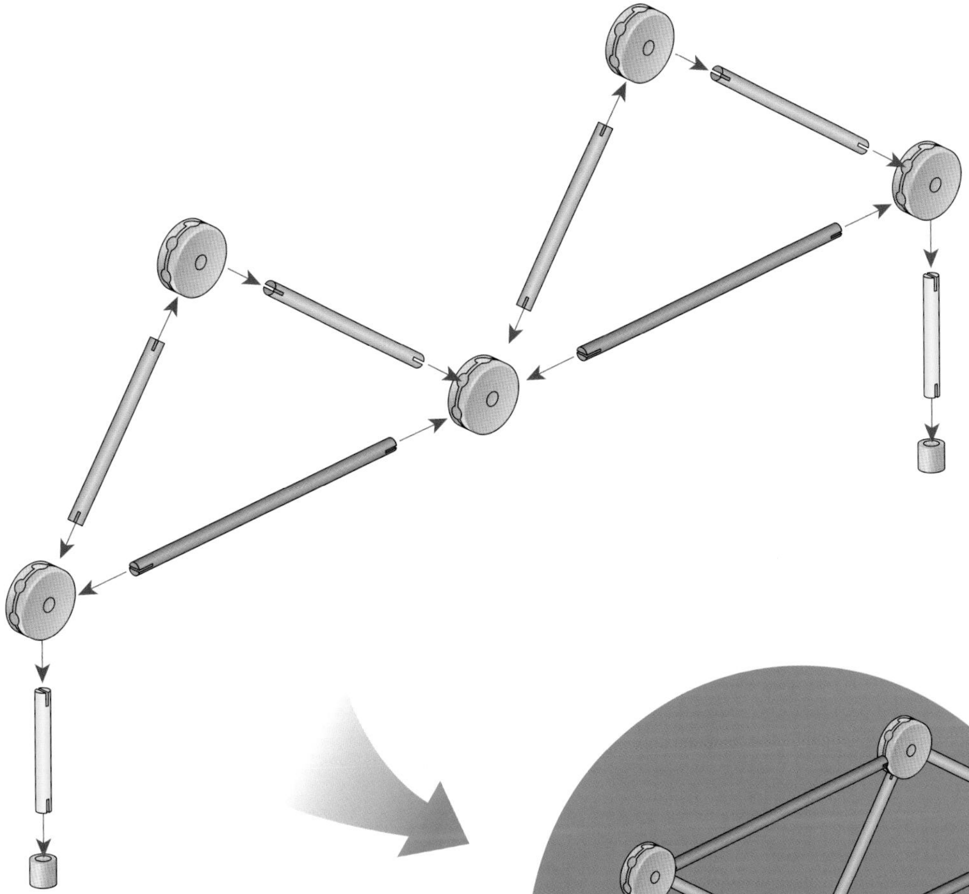

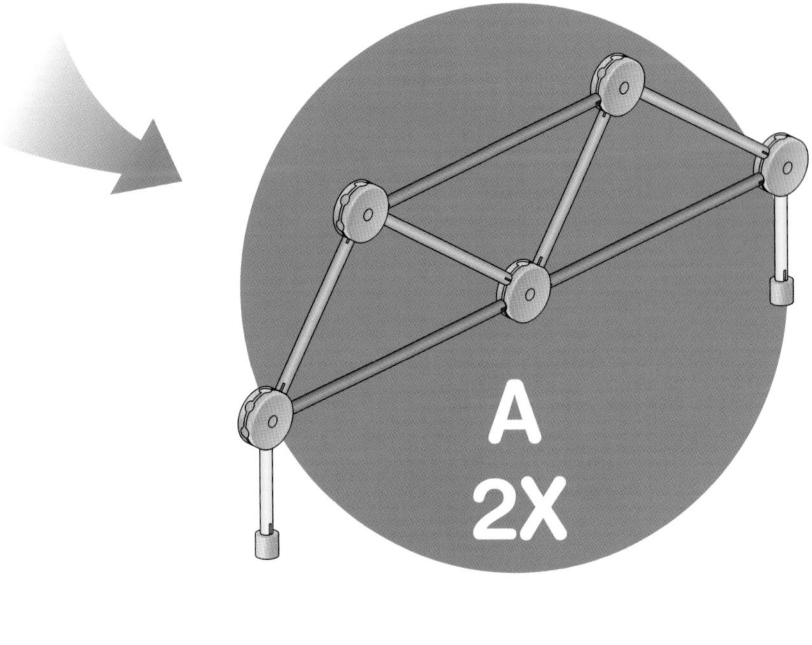
A
2X

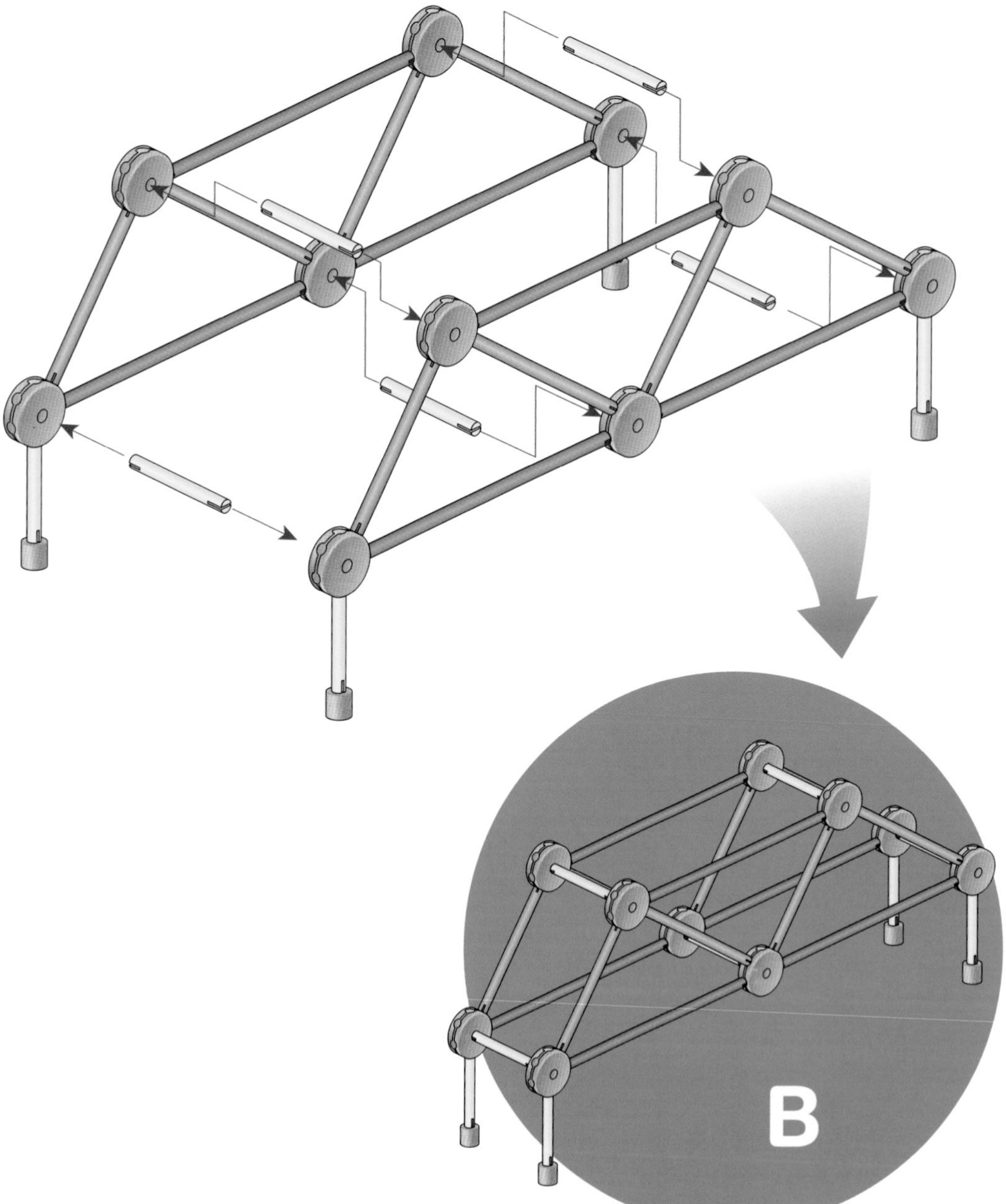
B

Tee-Pee

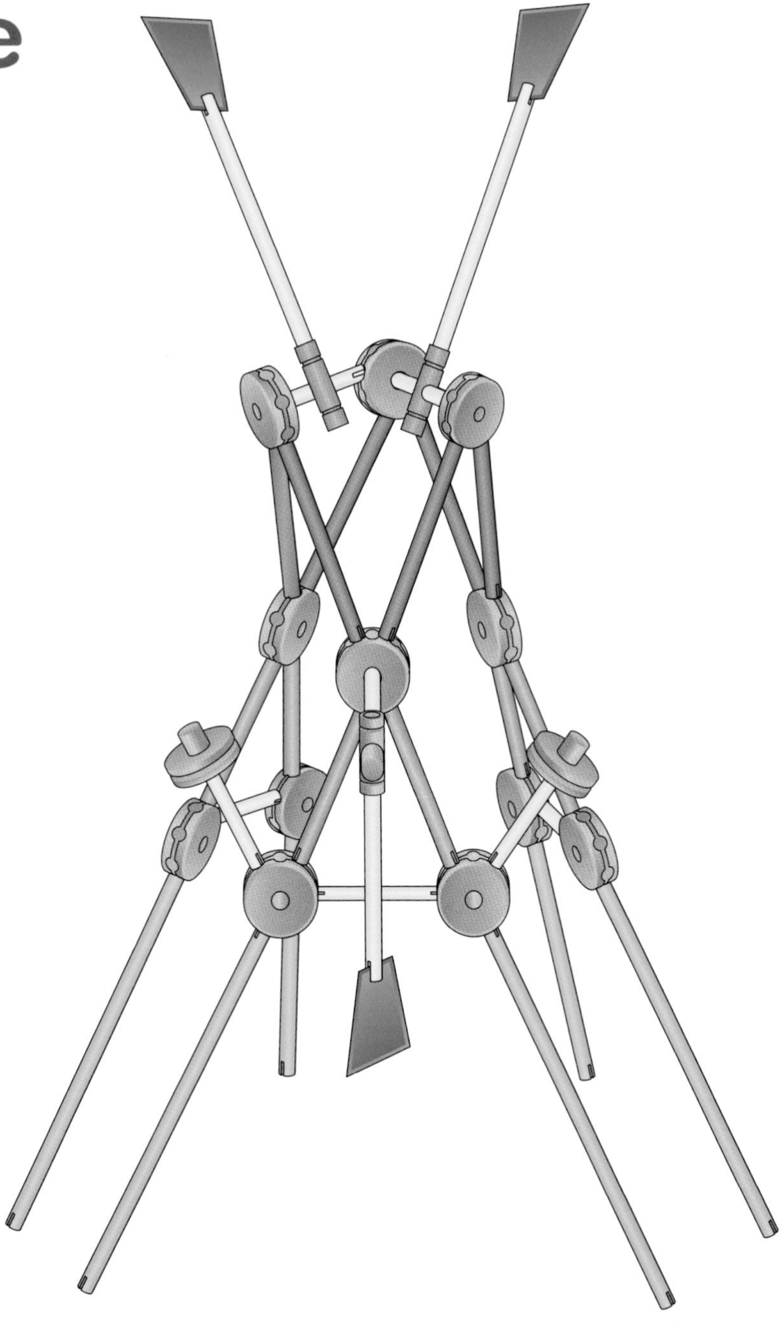

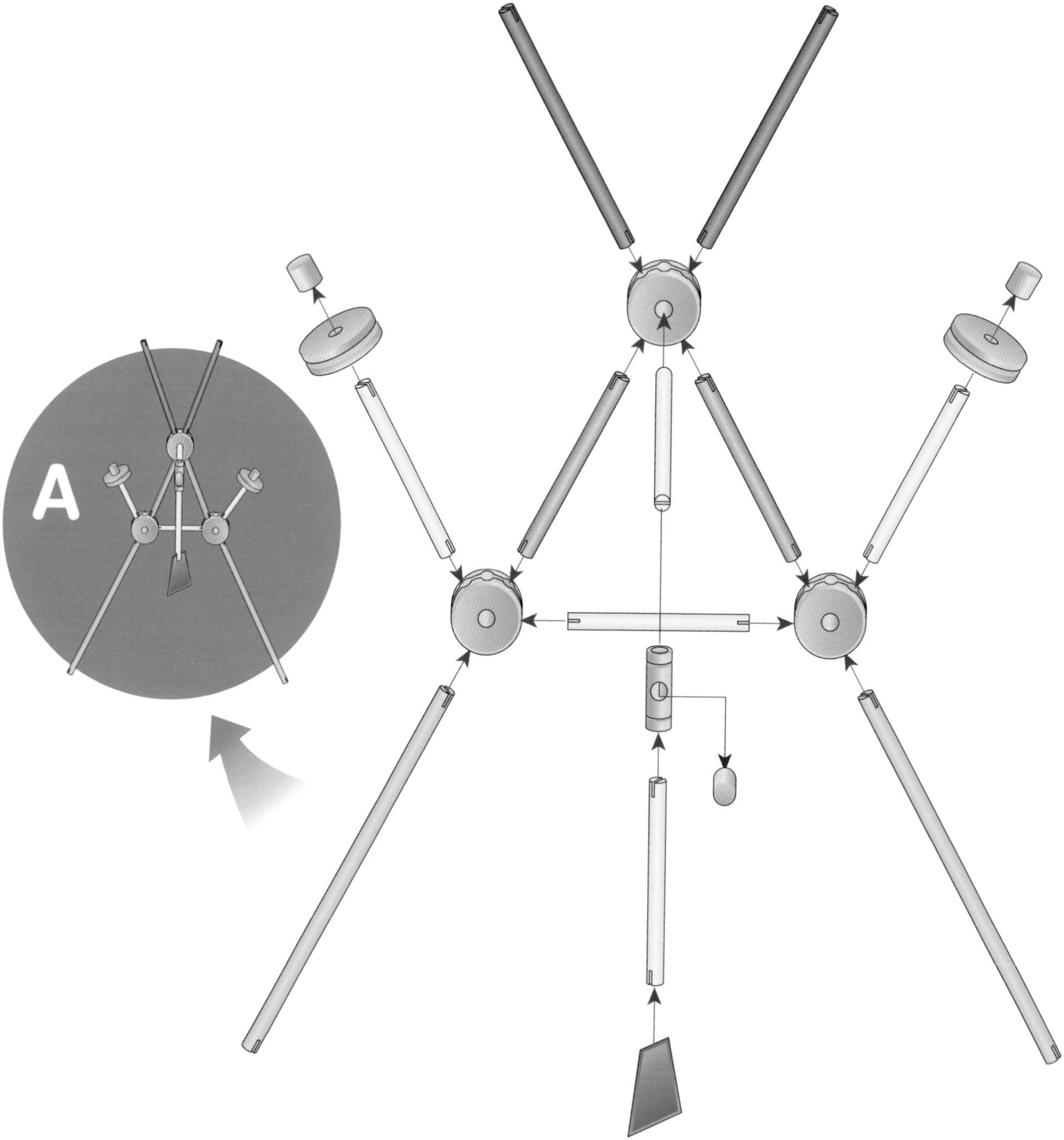
A

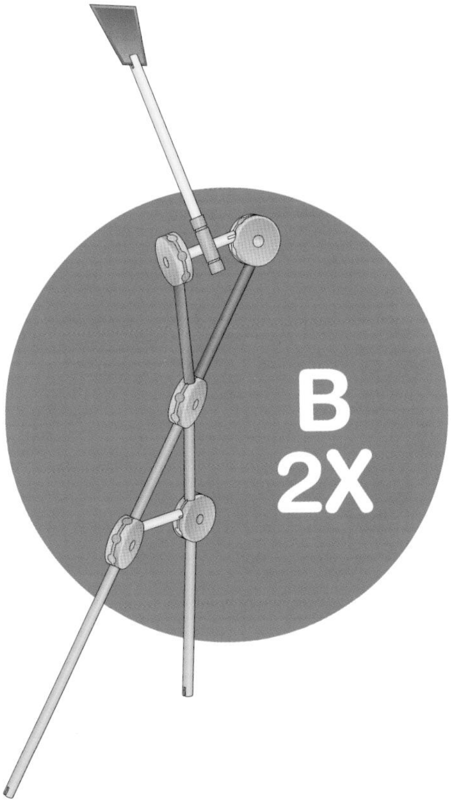
B
2X

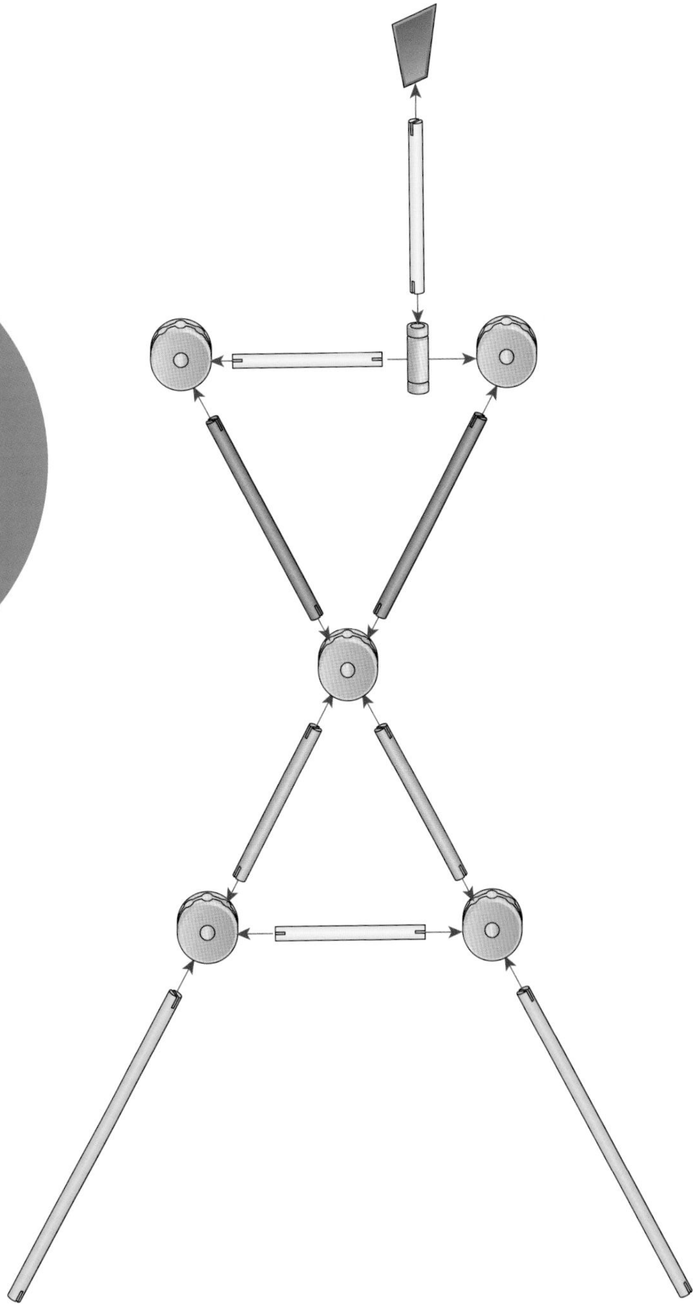

Chopper

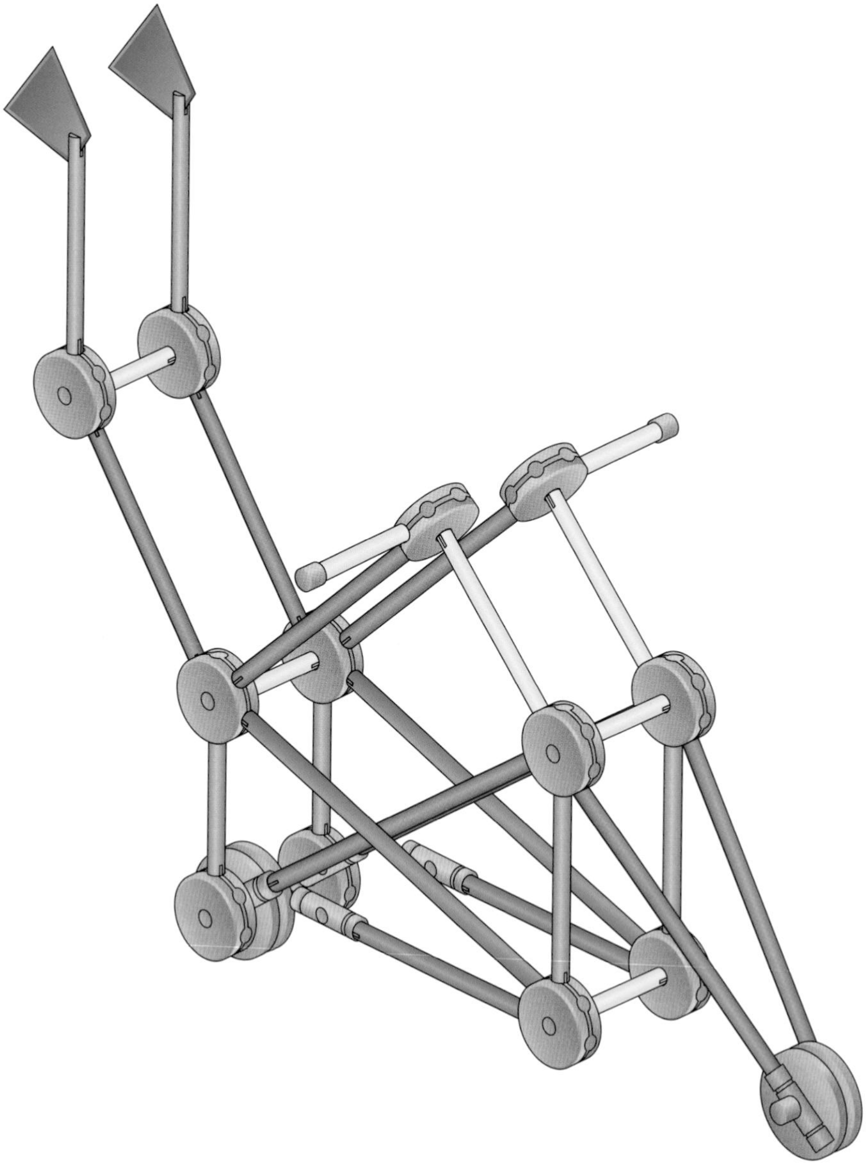

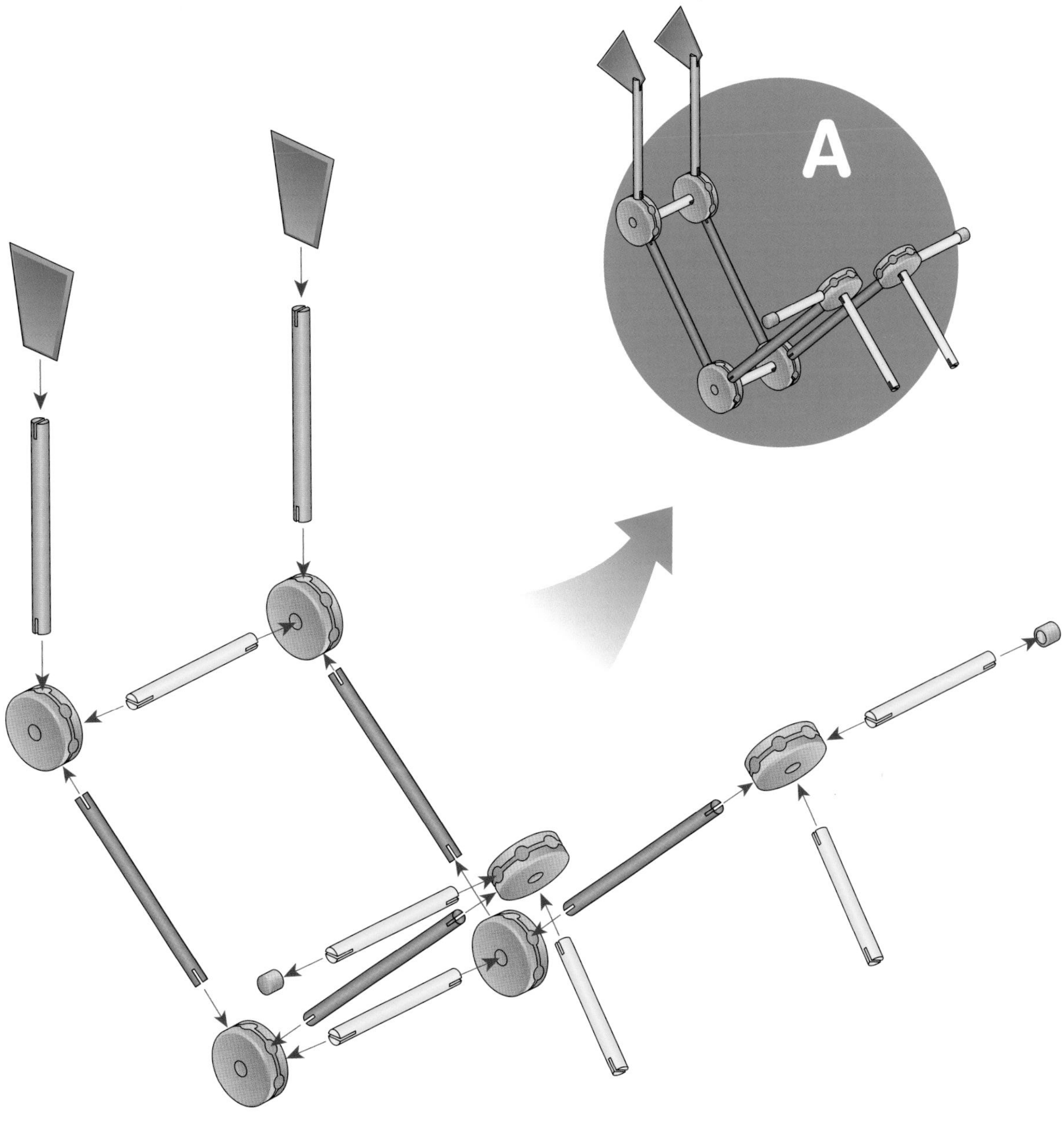
A

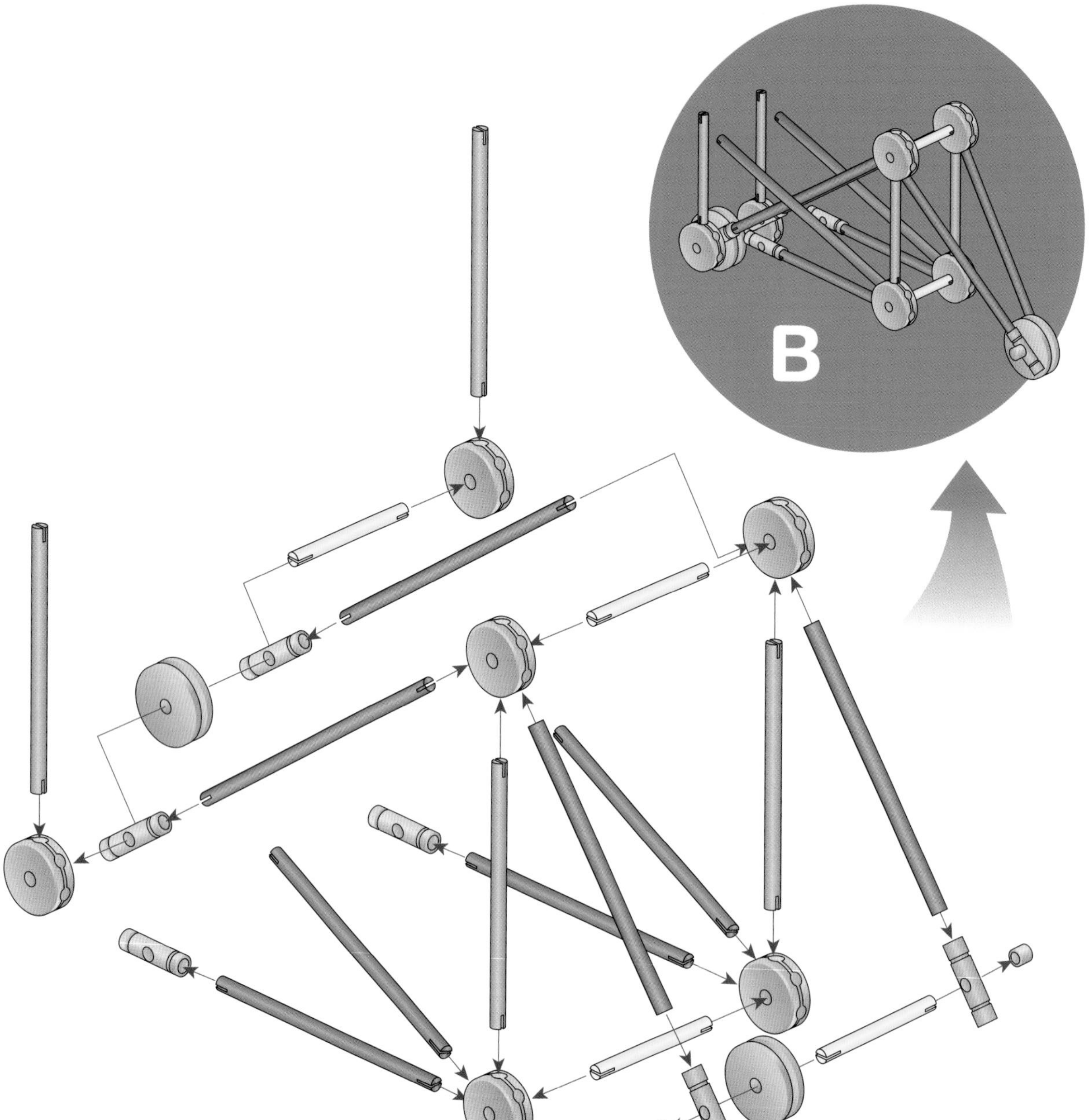
B

Dinosaur

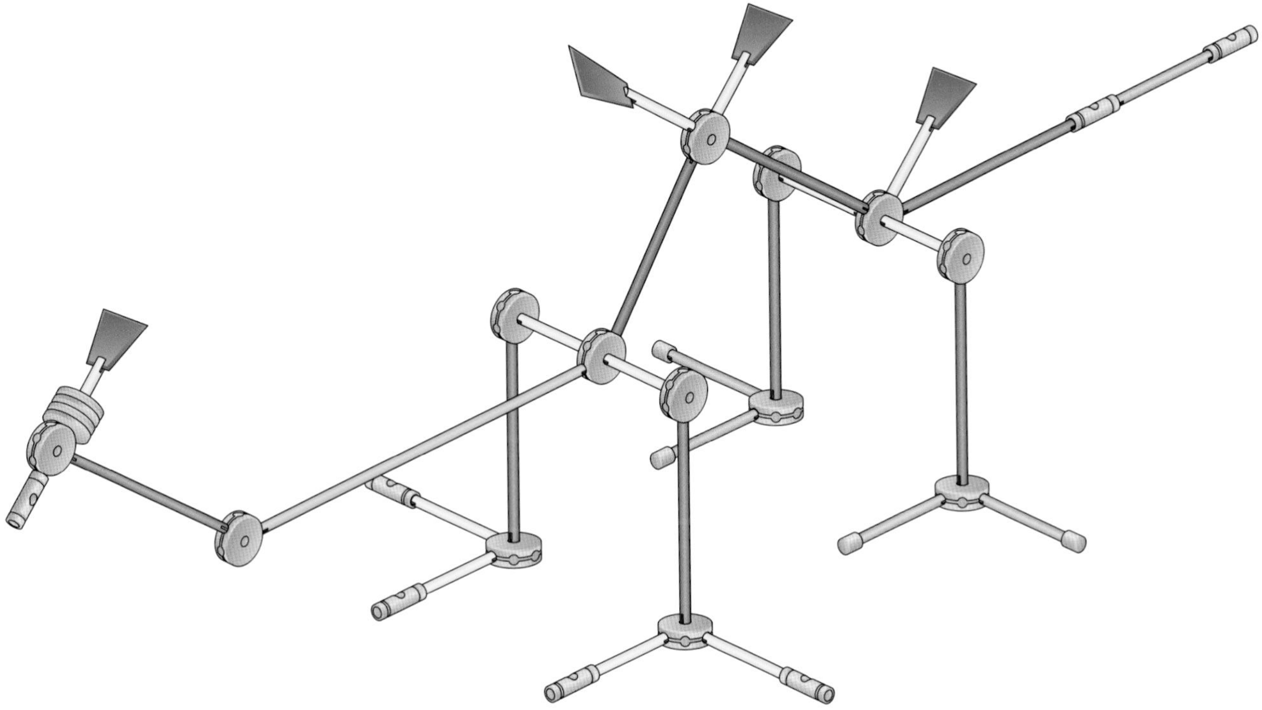

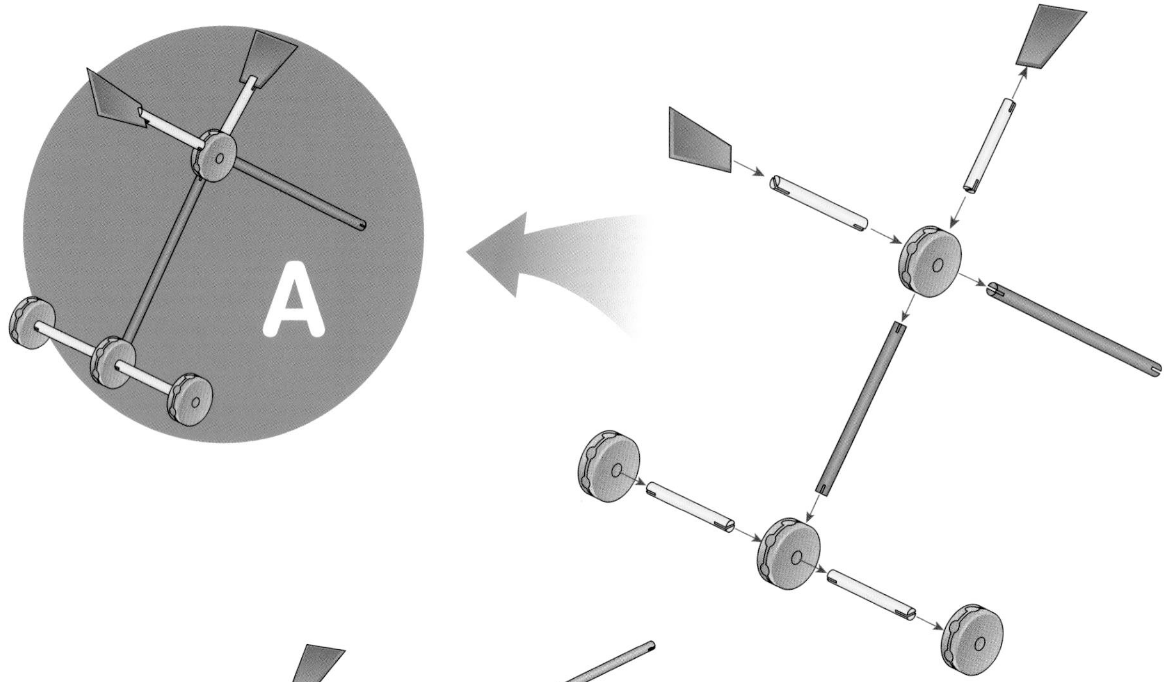
A

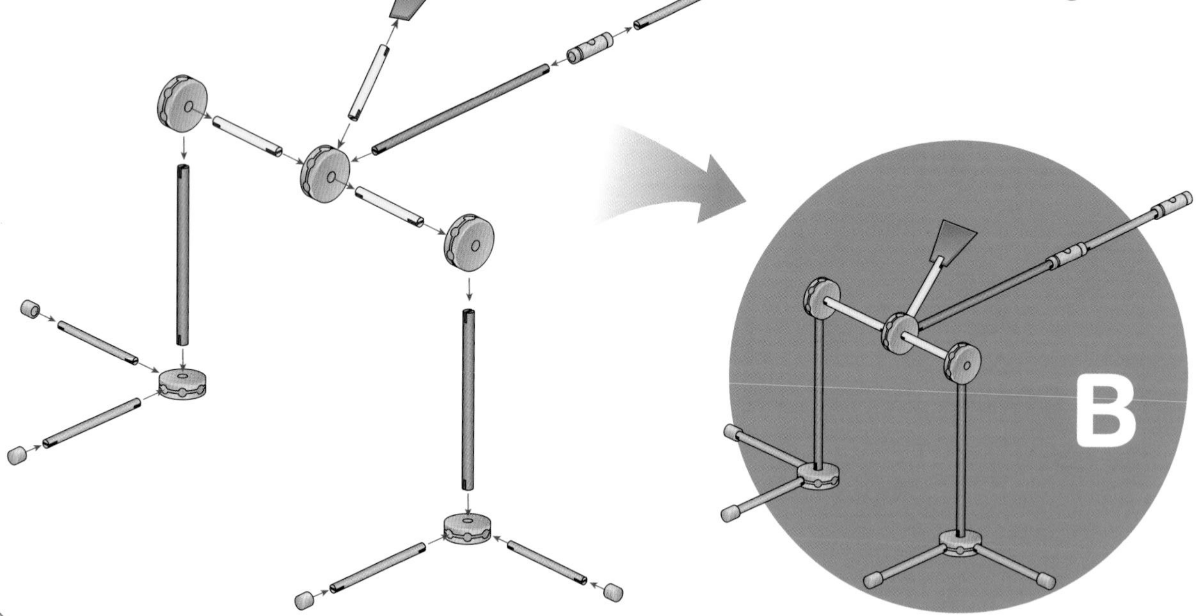
B

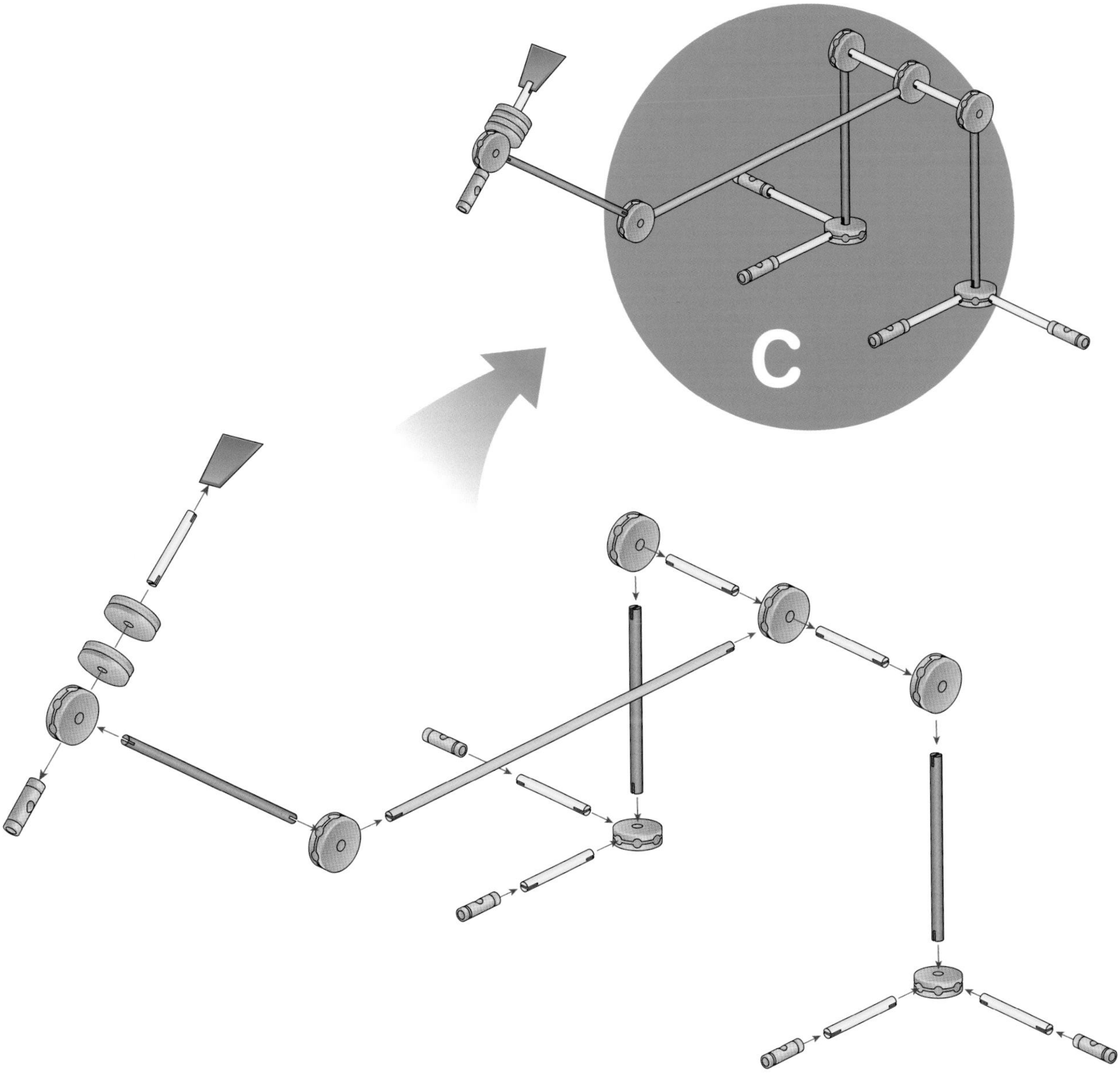
C

Dragster

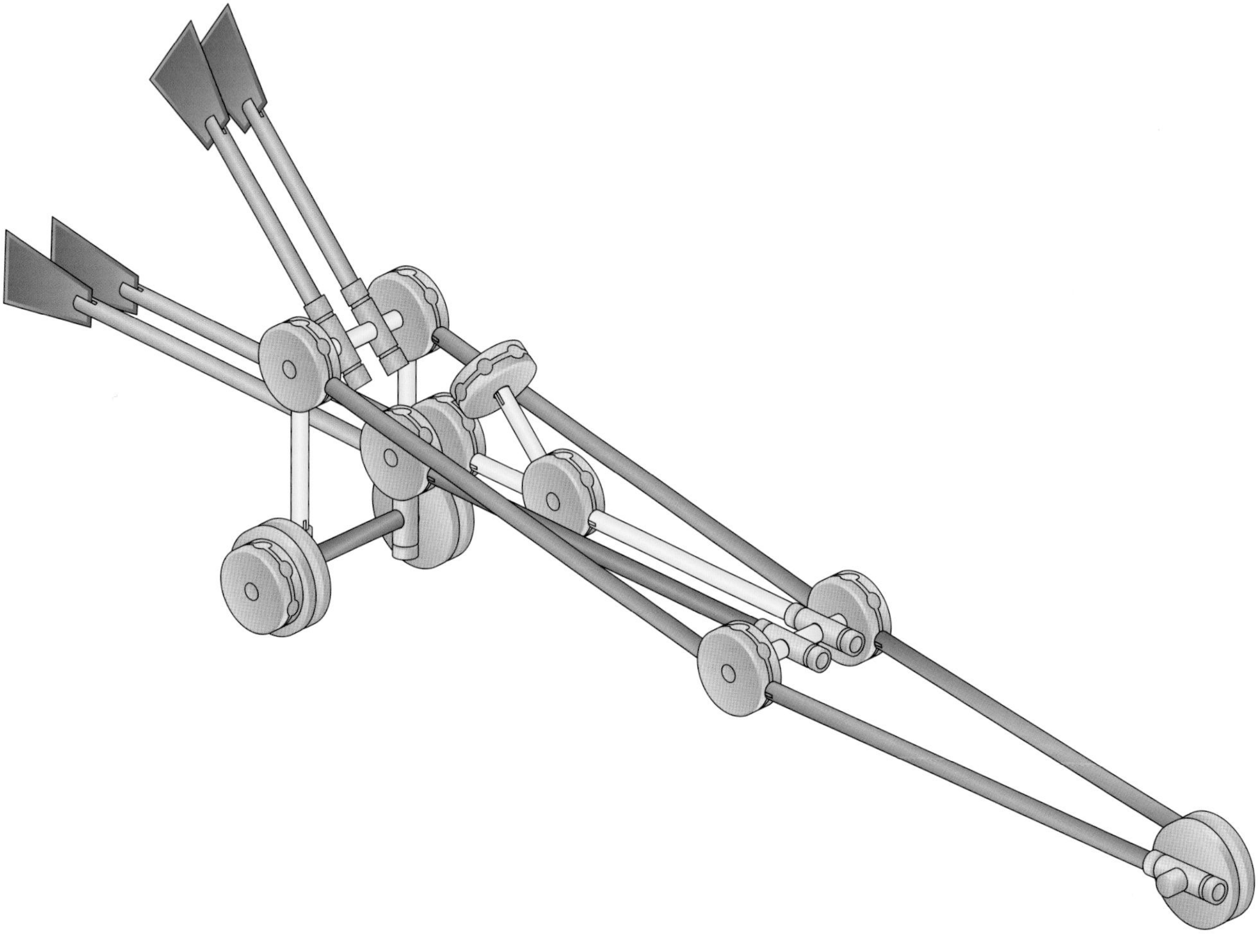

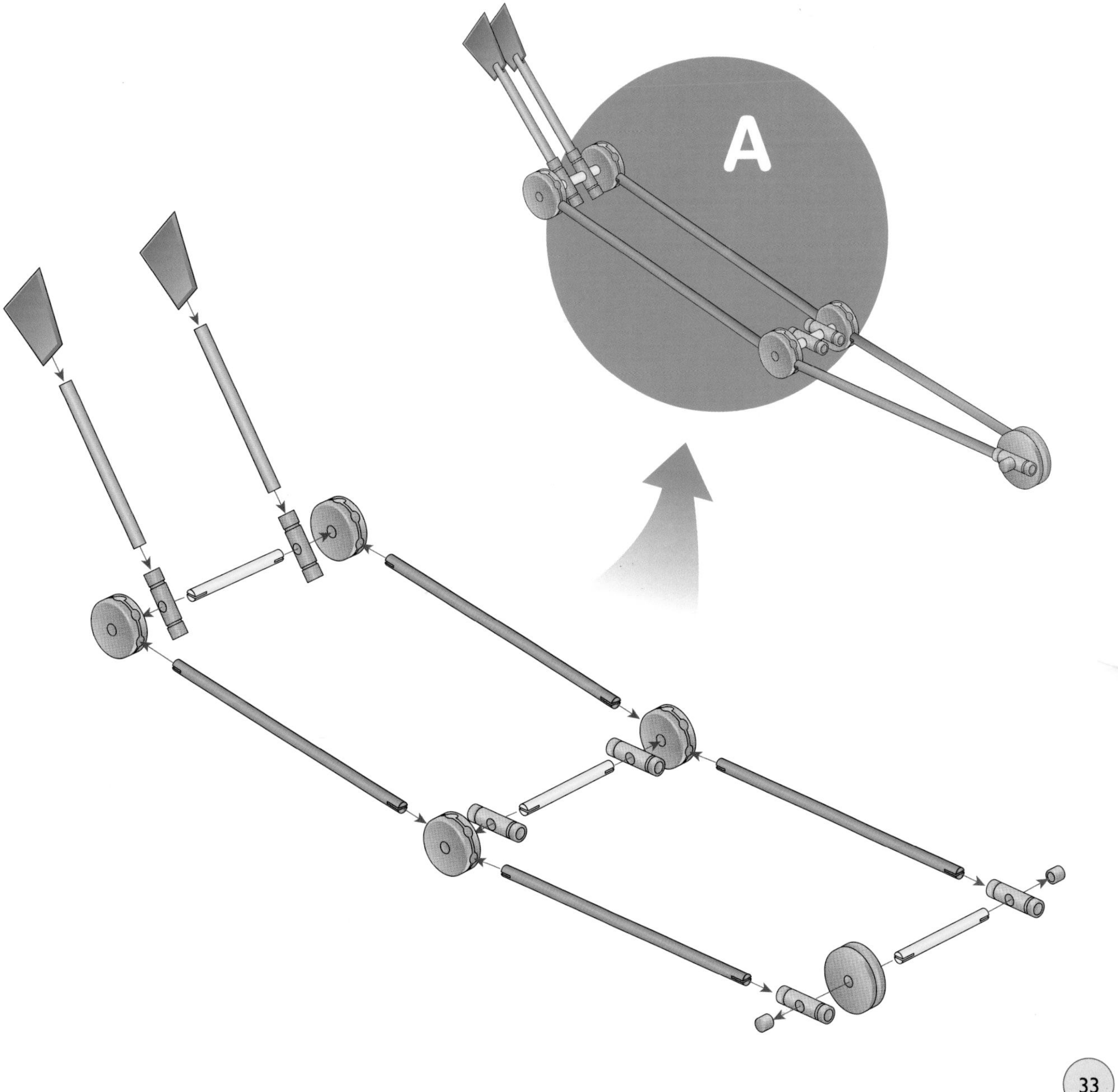
A

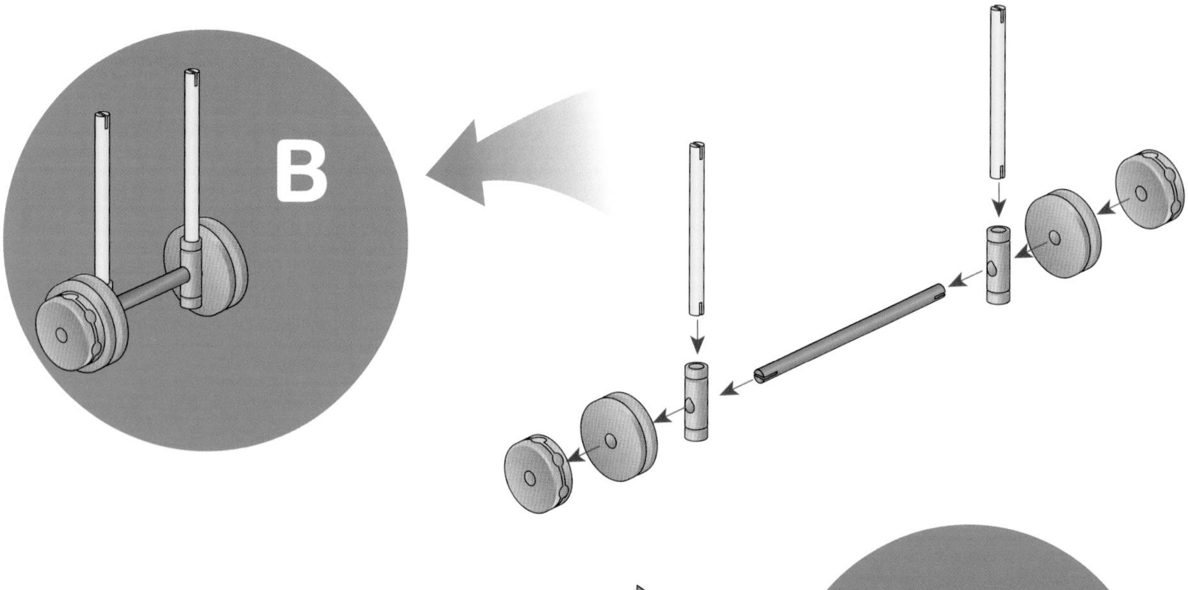
B

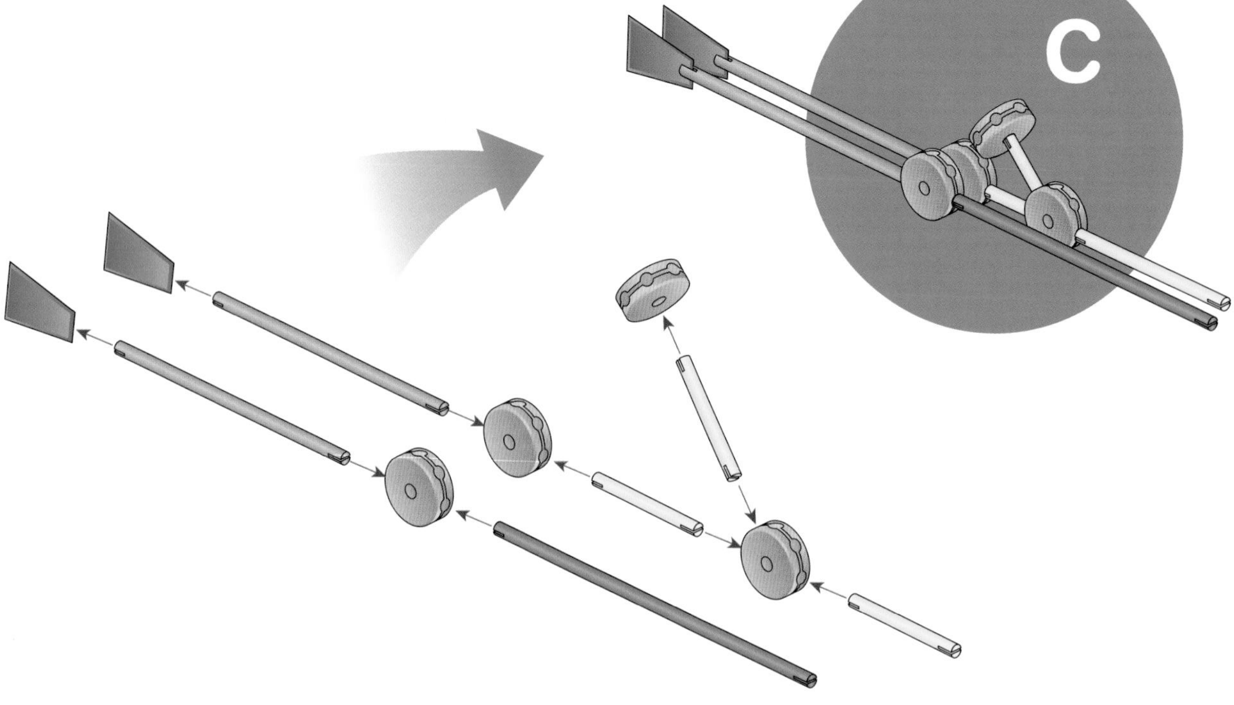
C

Clock

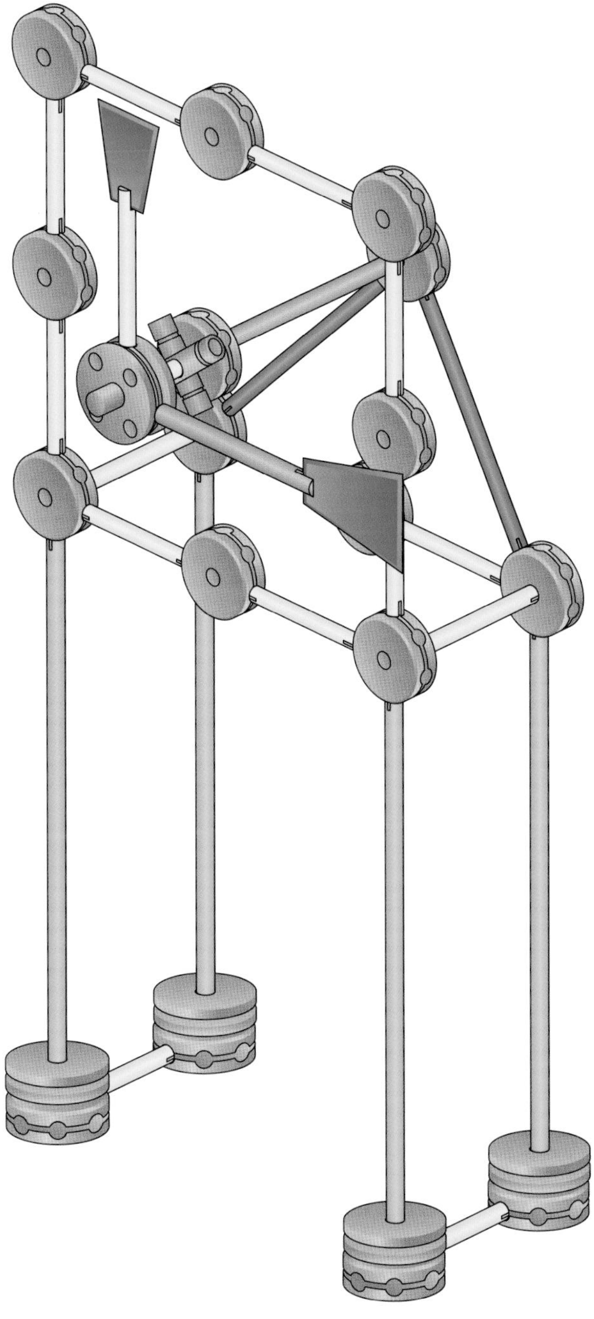

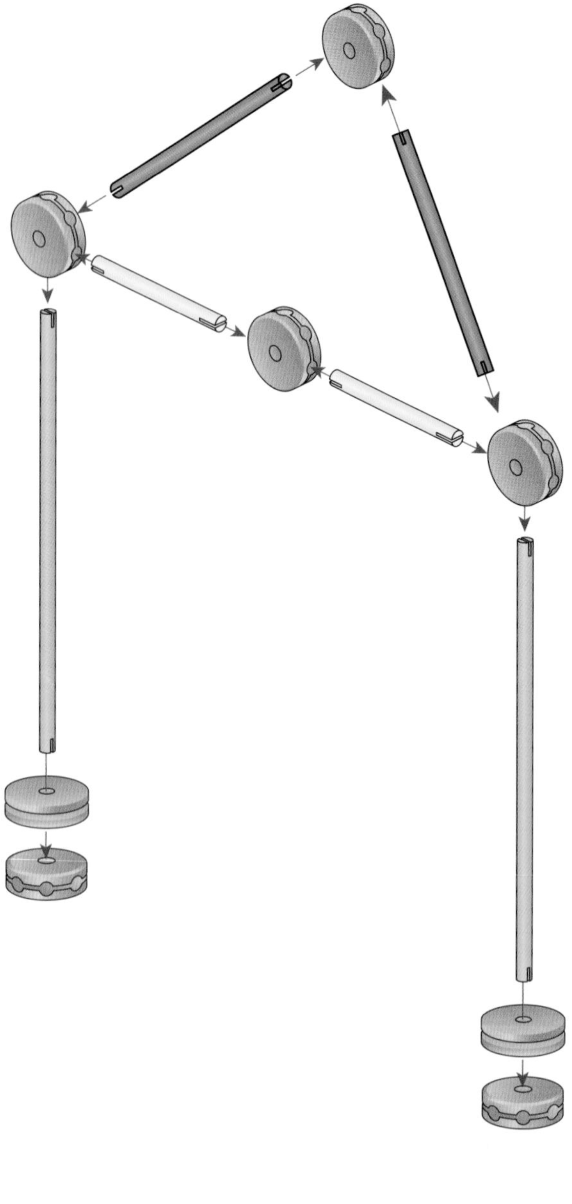

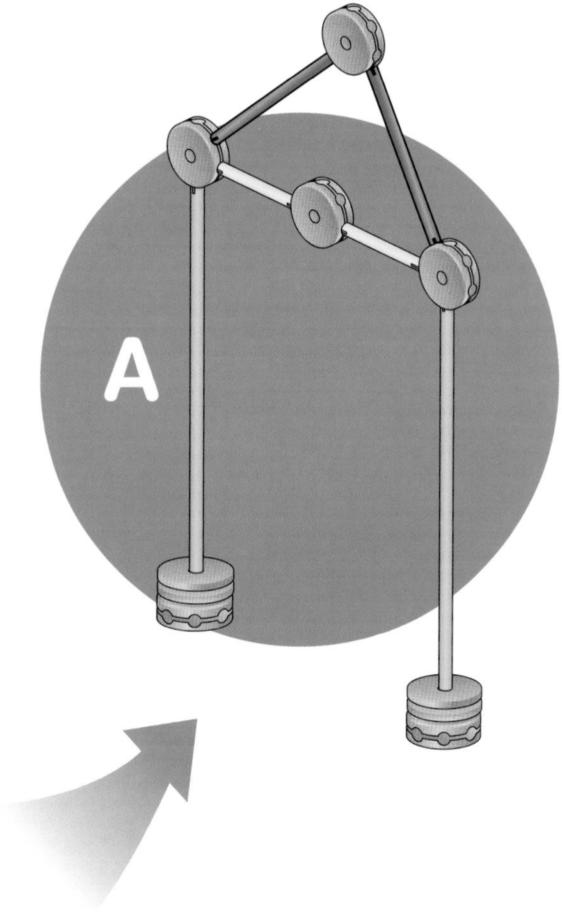
A

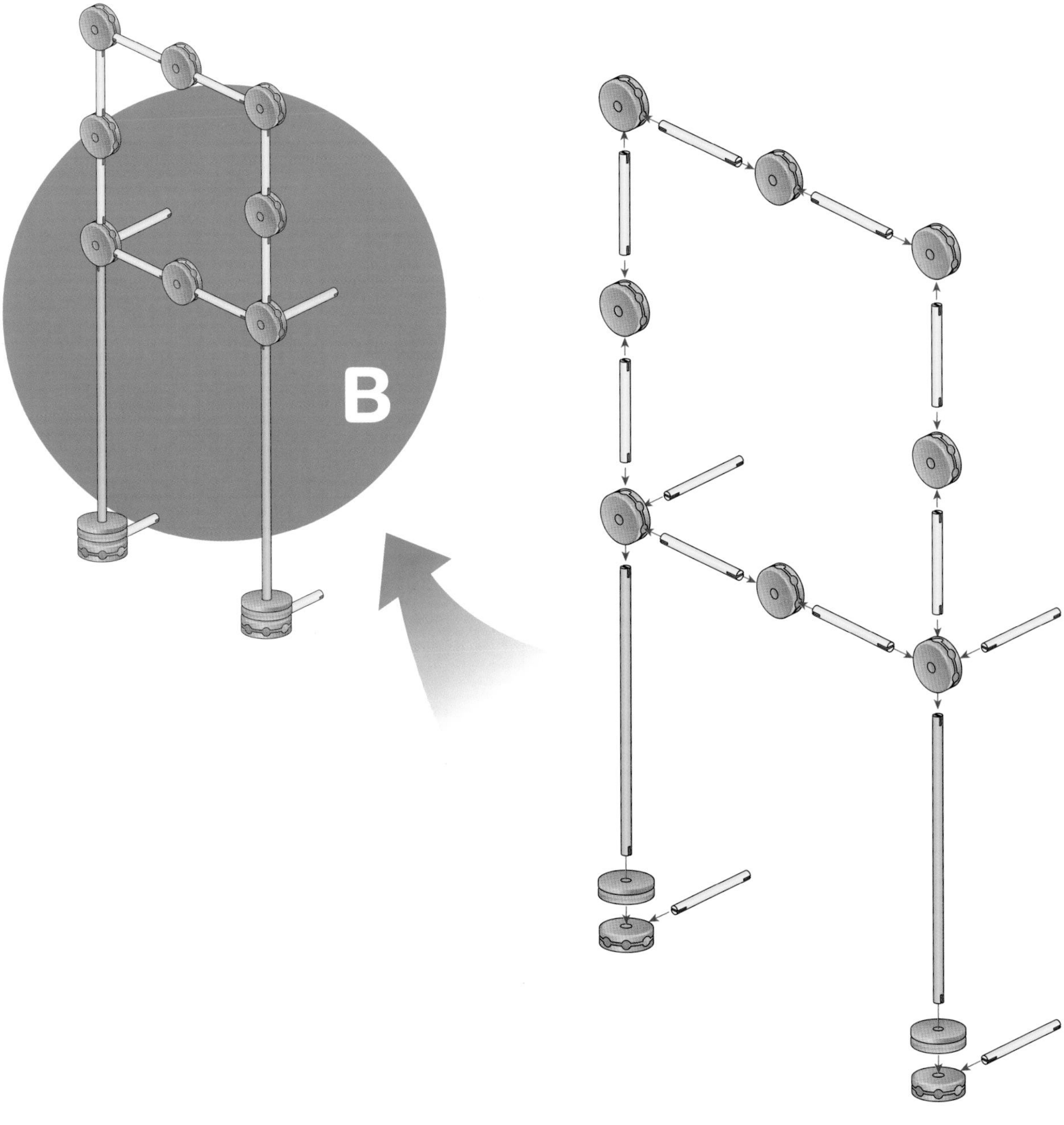
B

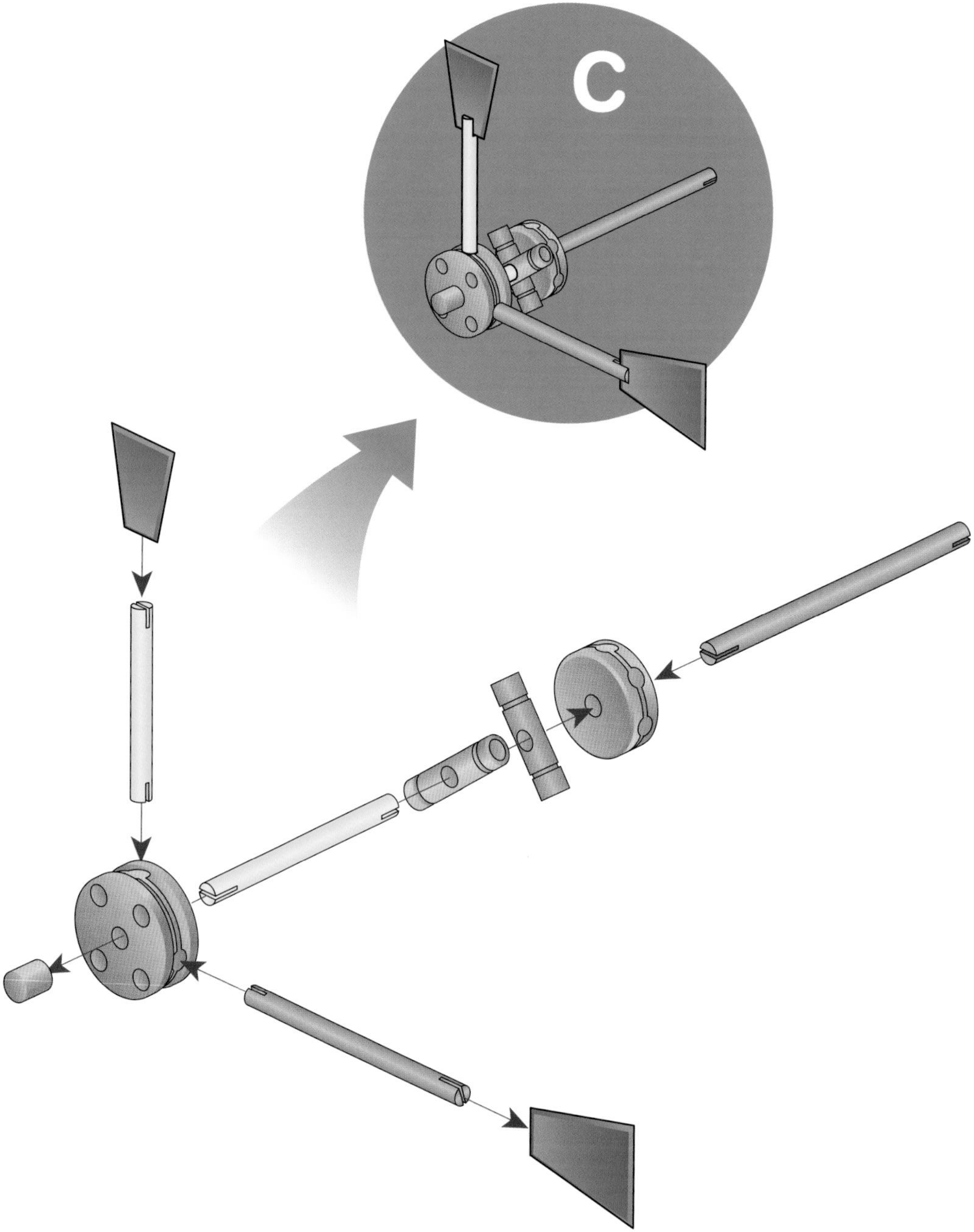
C

Hammock

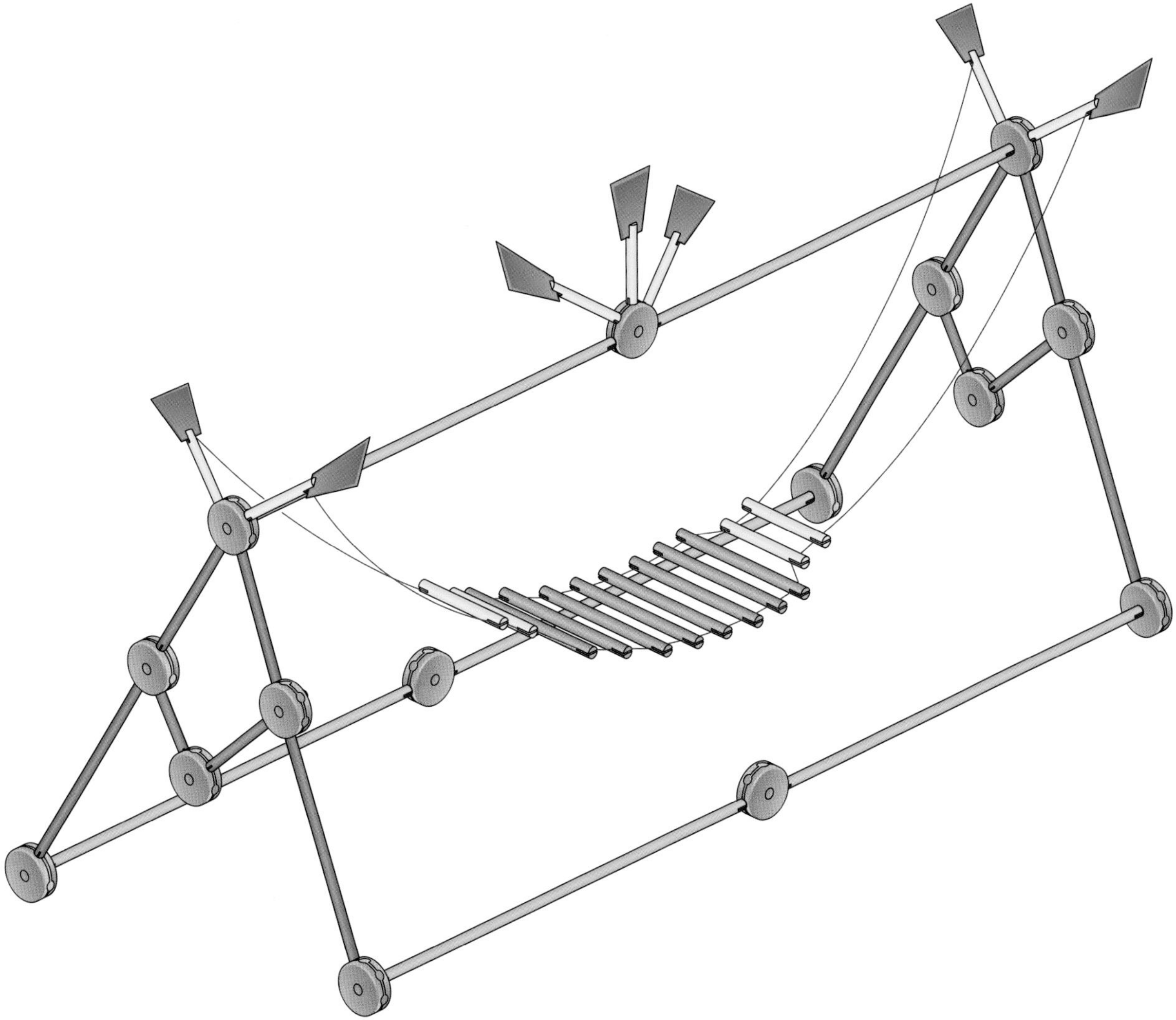

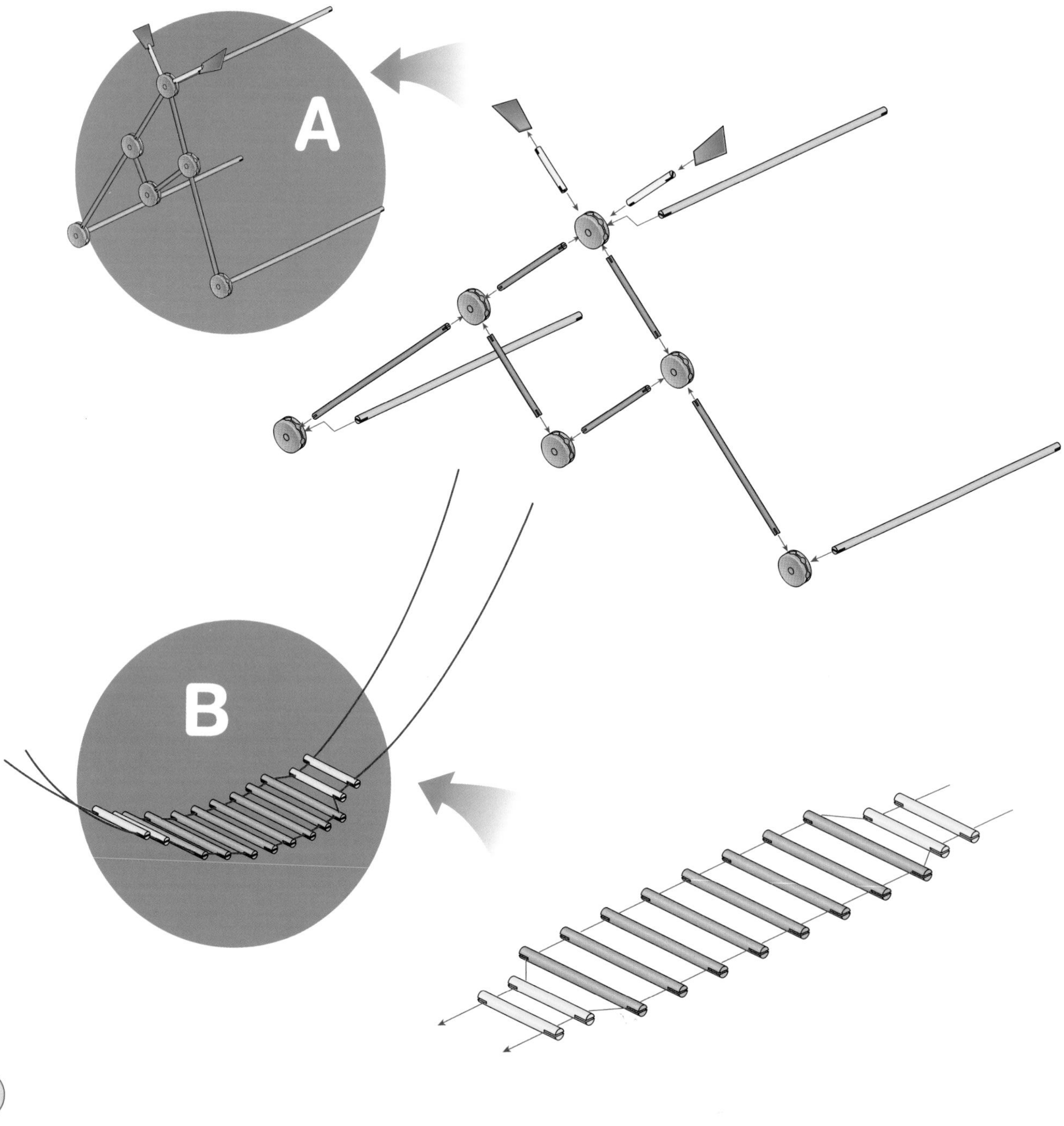
A
B

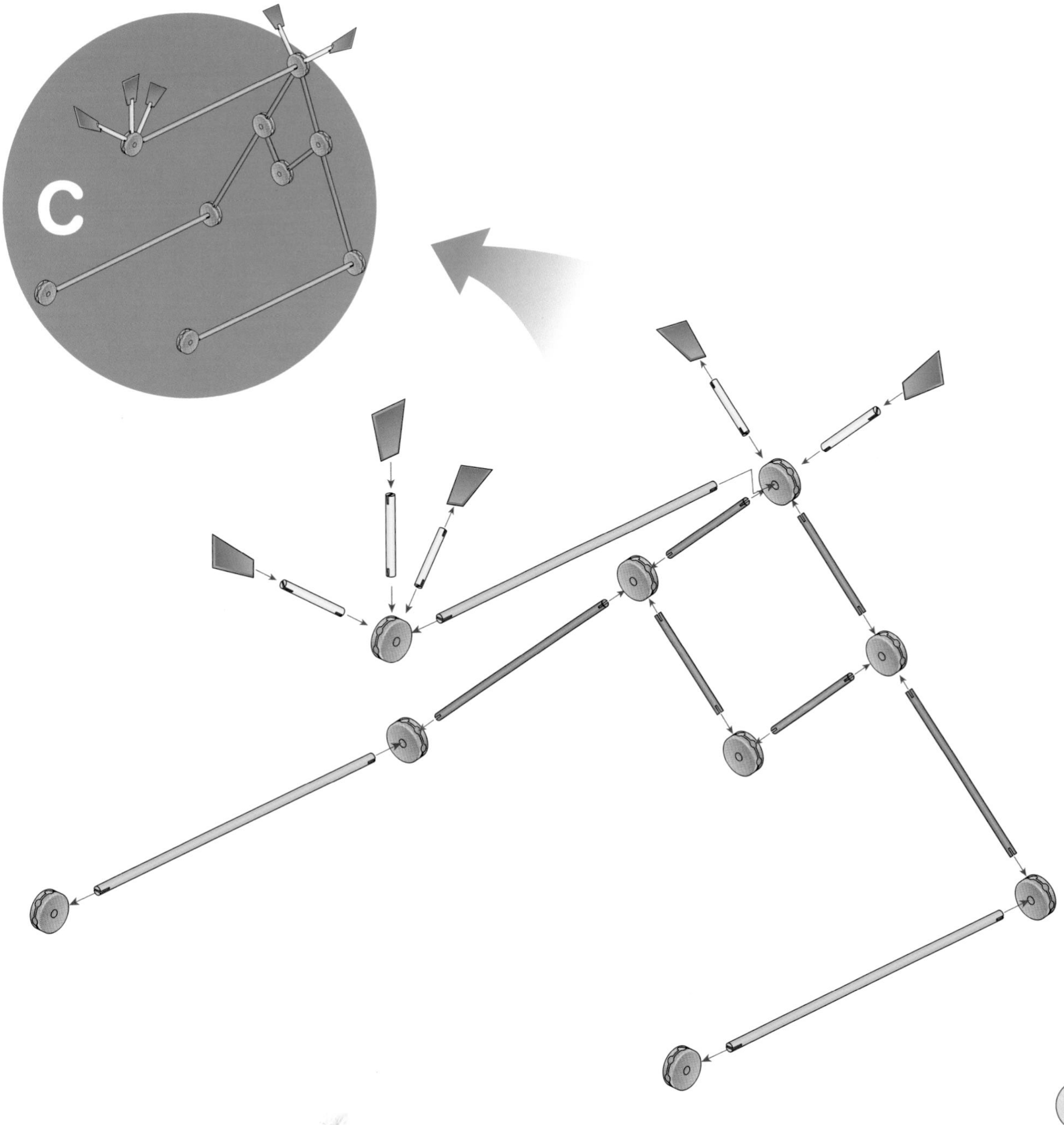
C

Barn

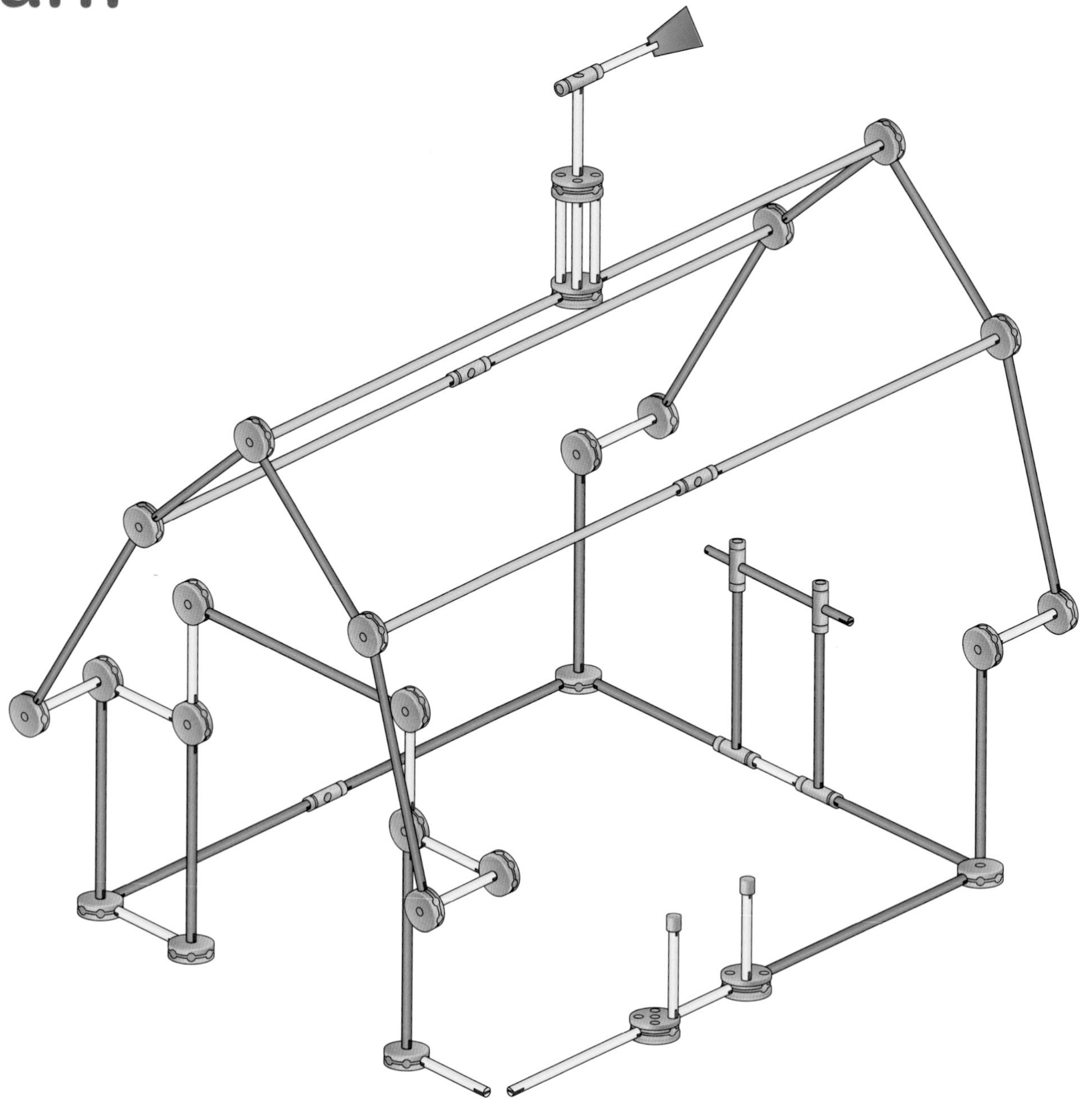

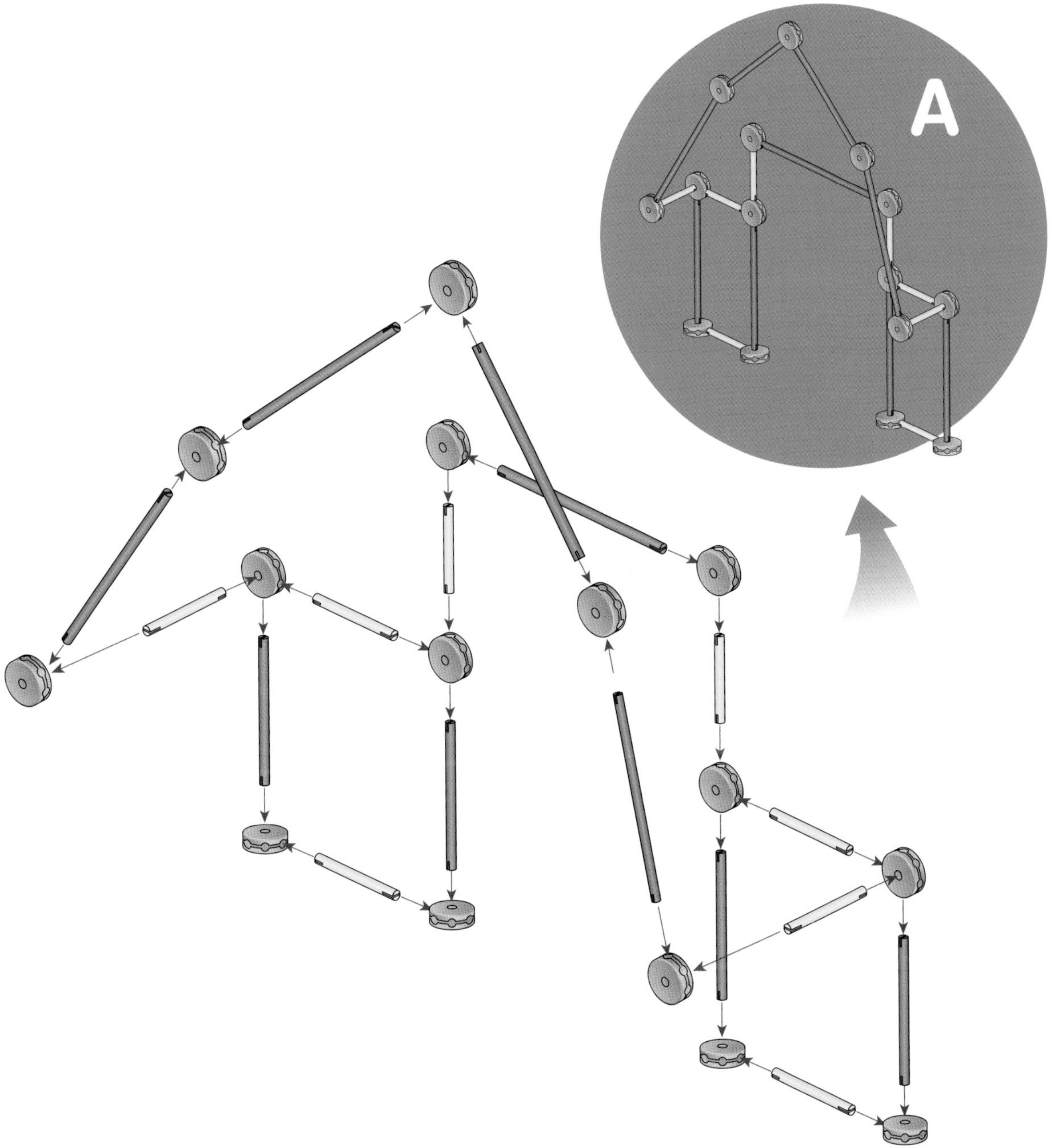
A

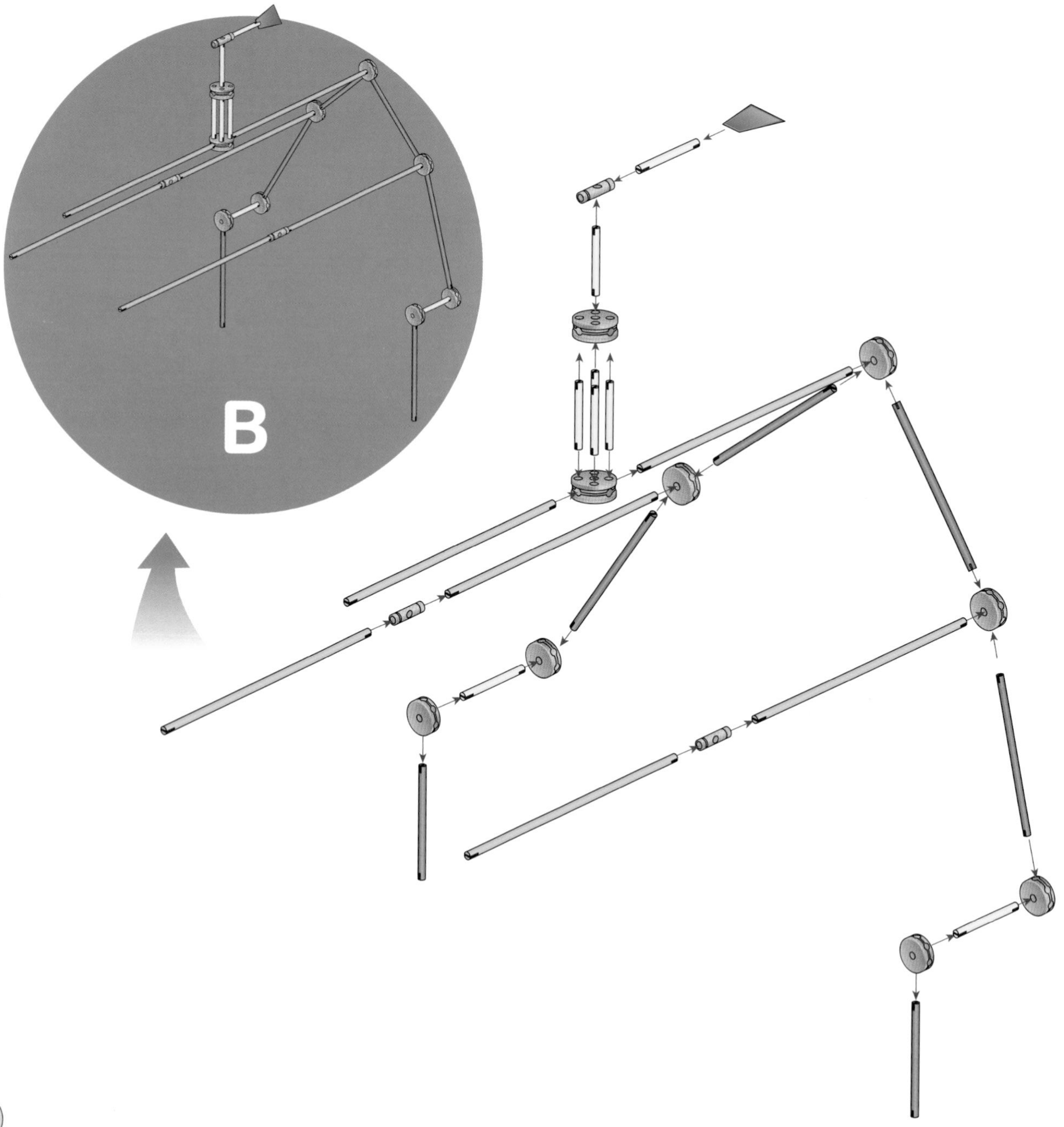
B

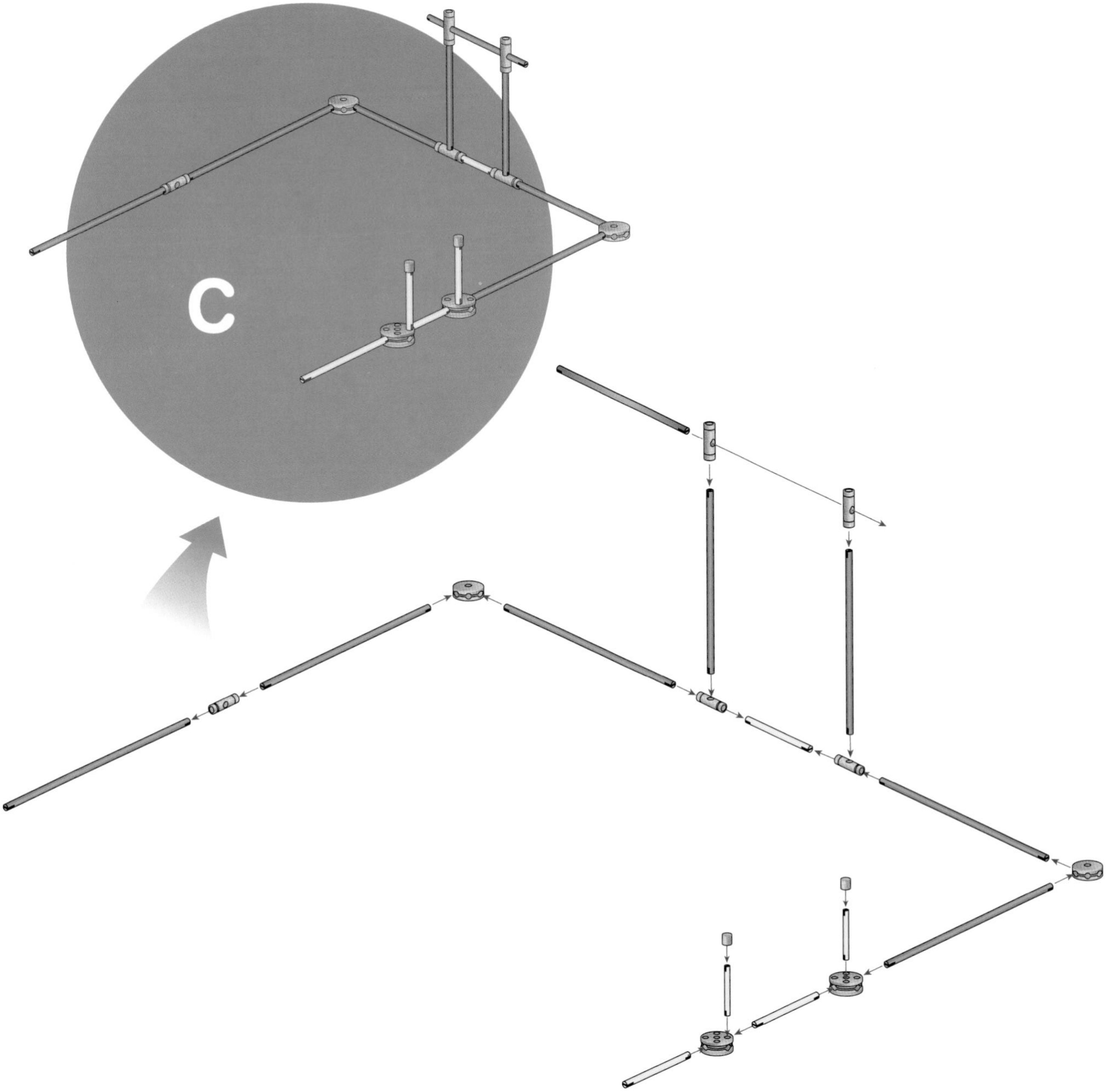
C

Rocket Ship

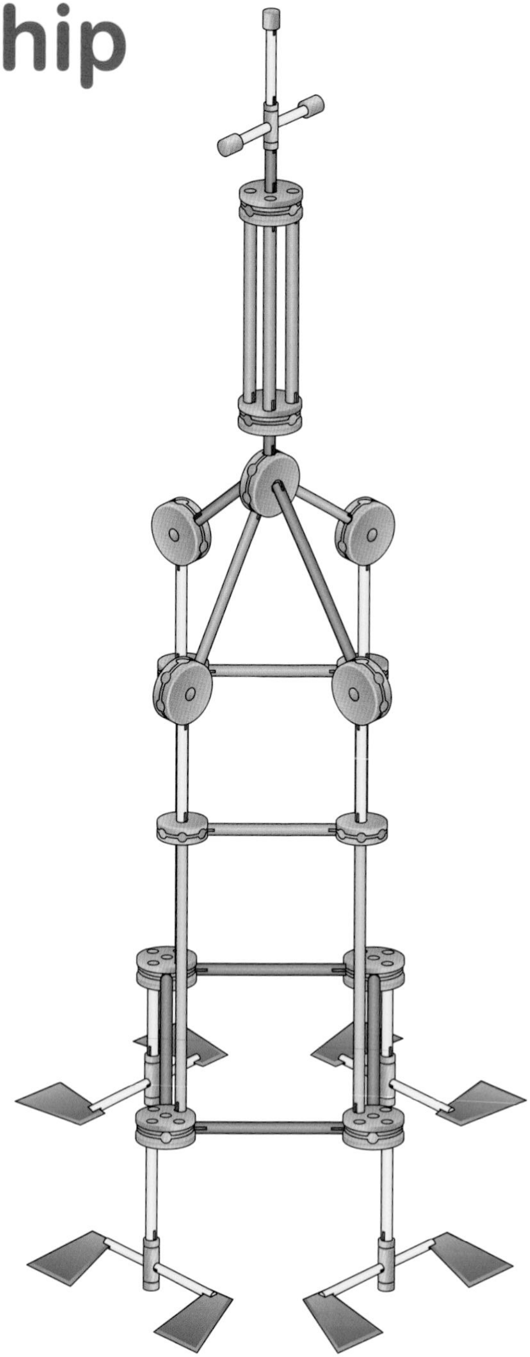

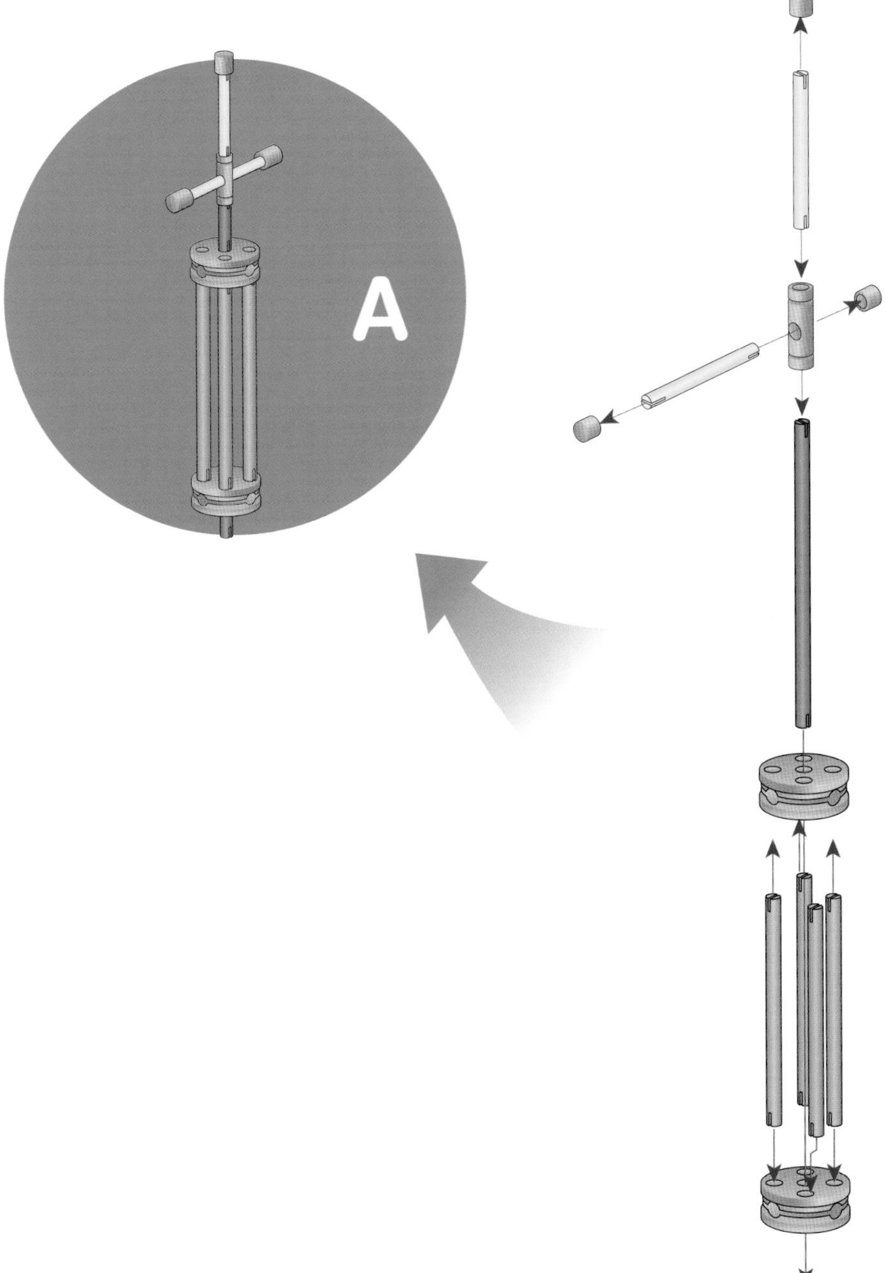
A

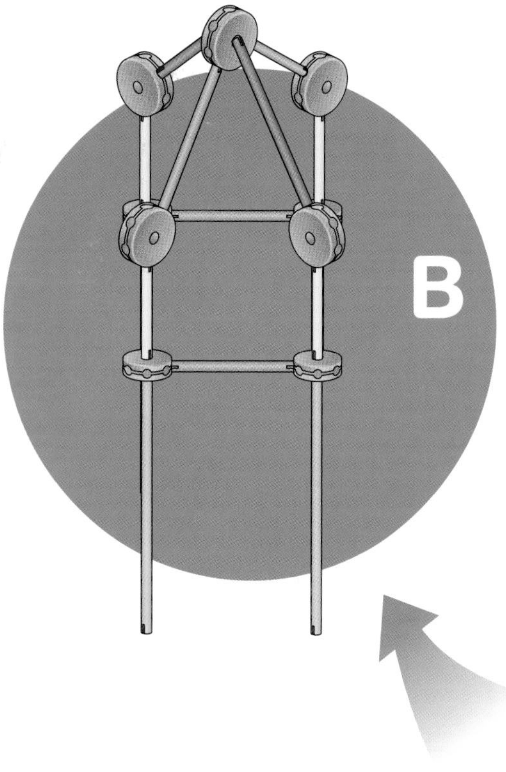
B

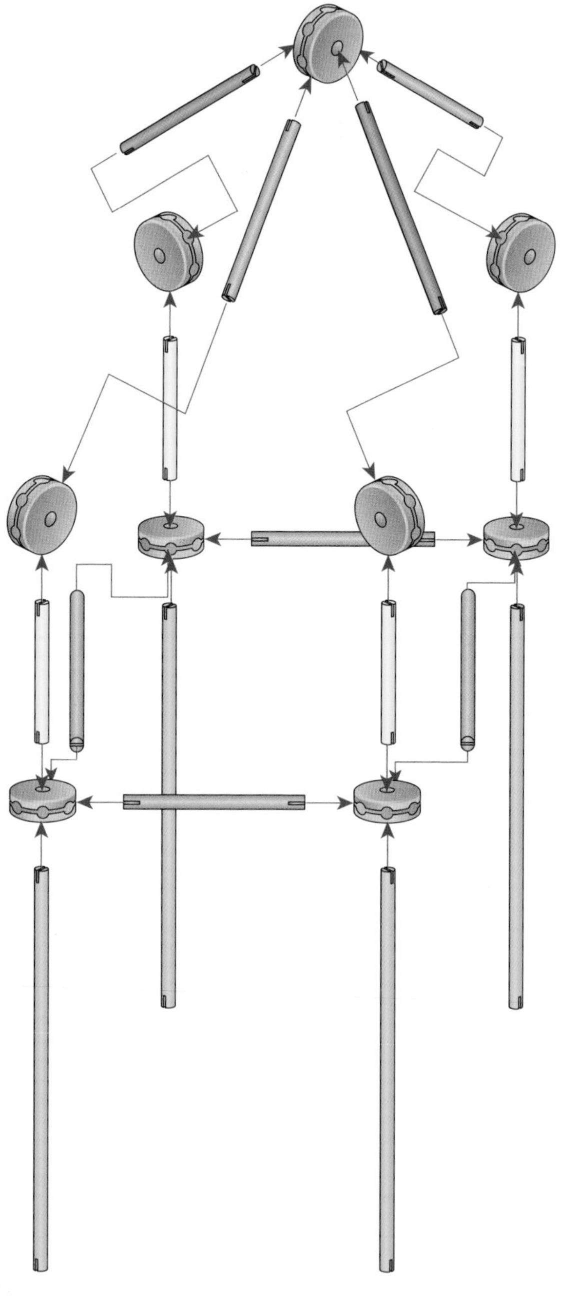

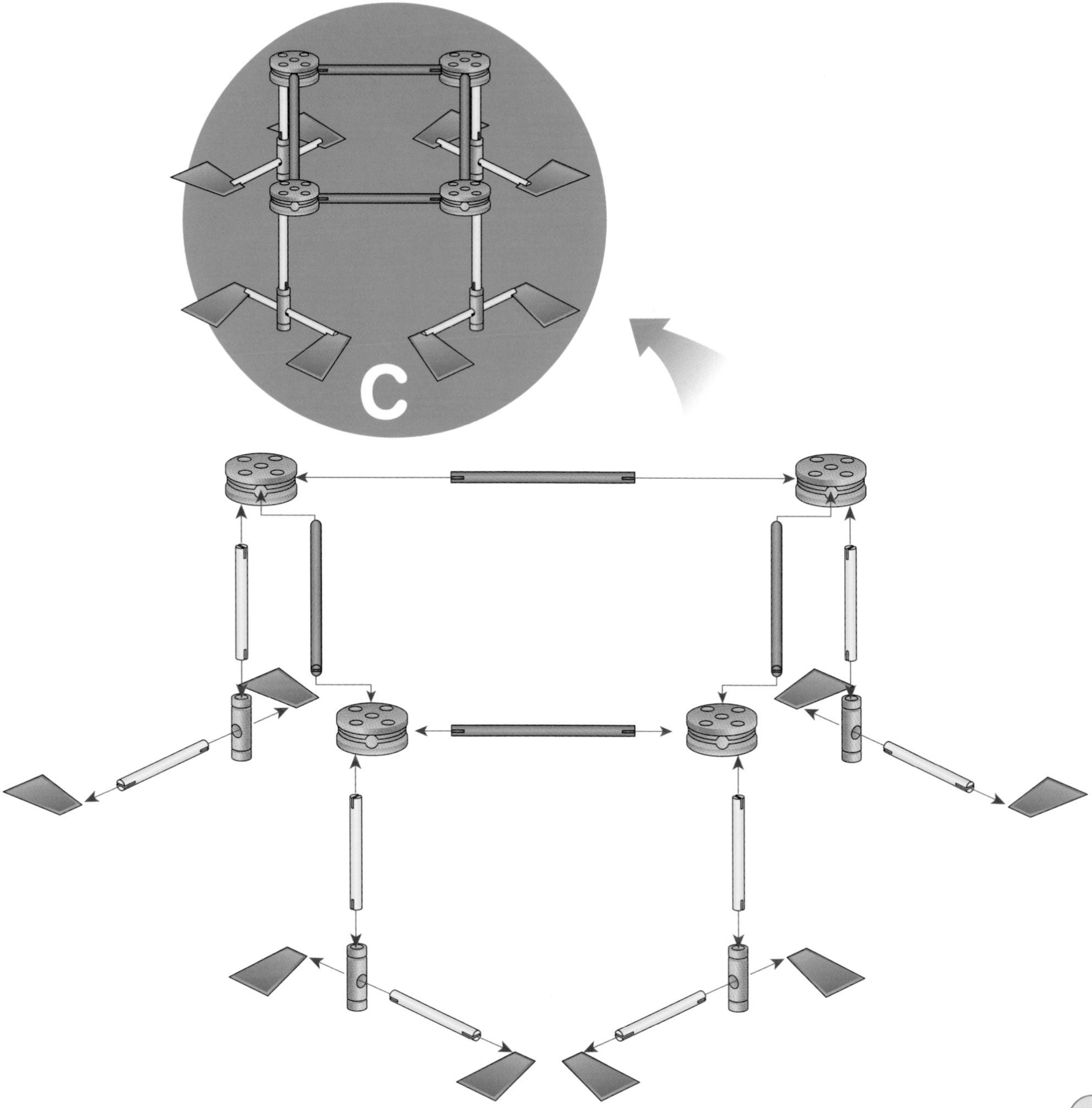
C

Stealth Plane

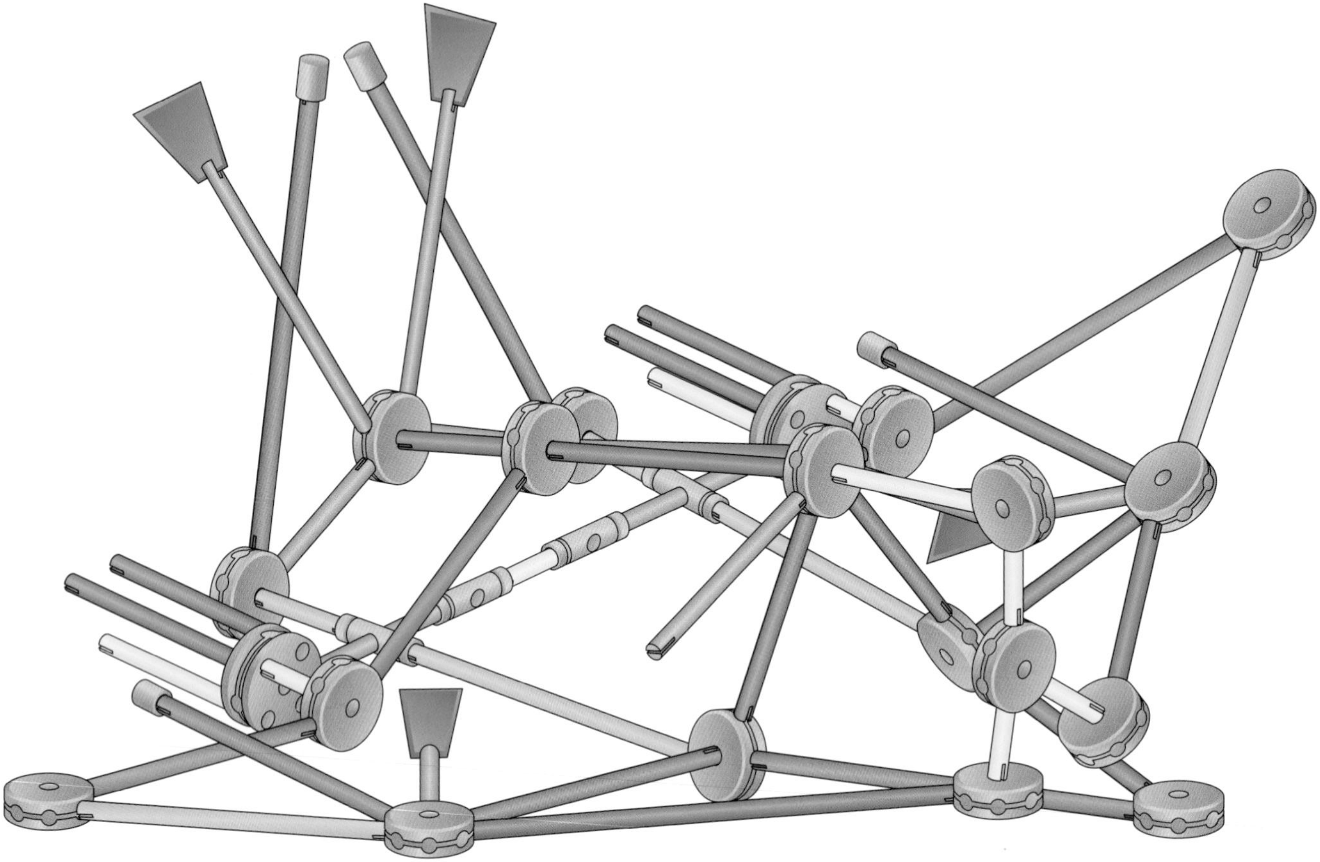

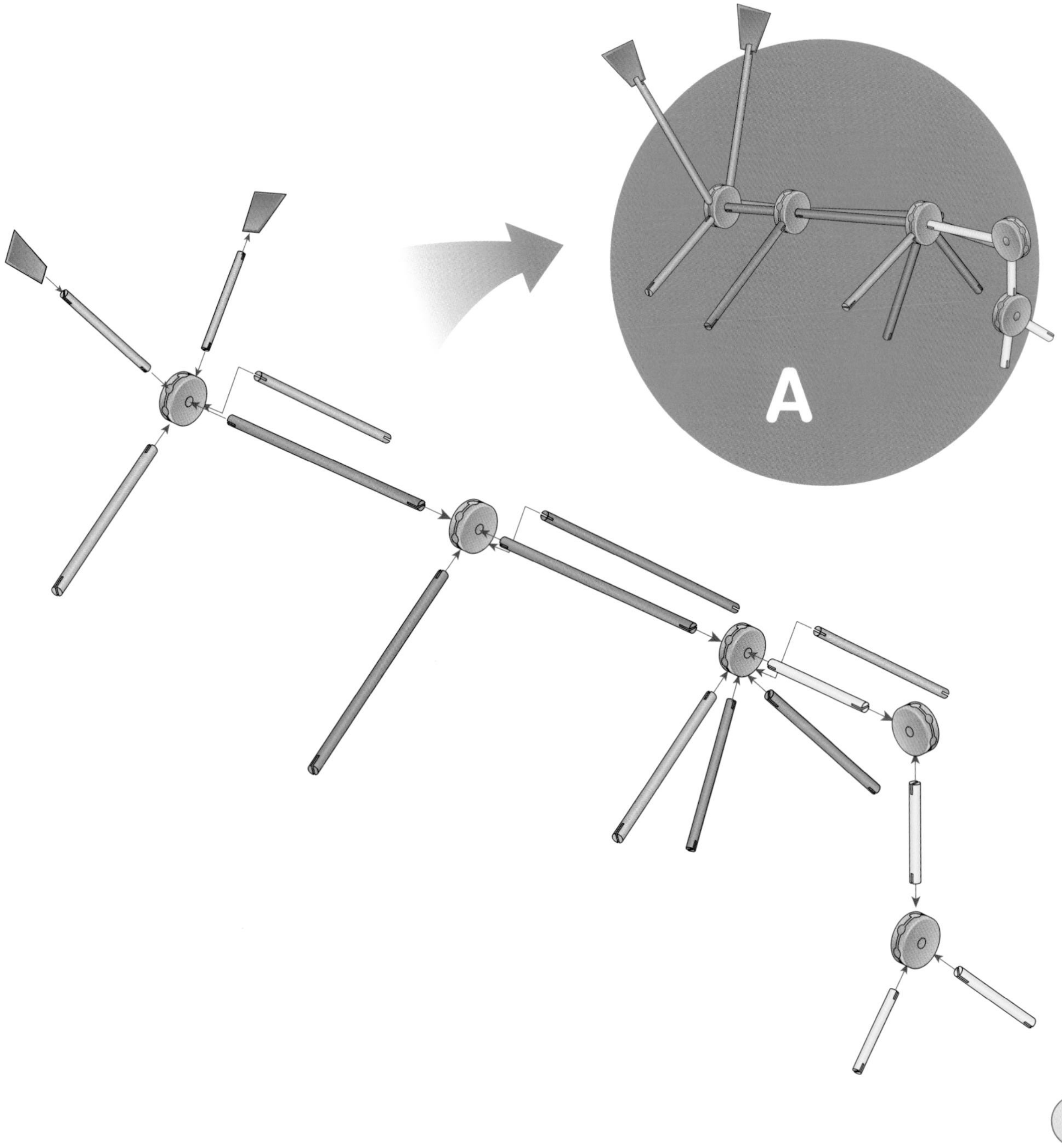
A

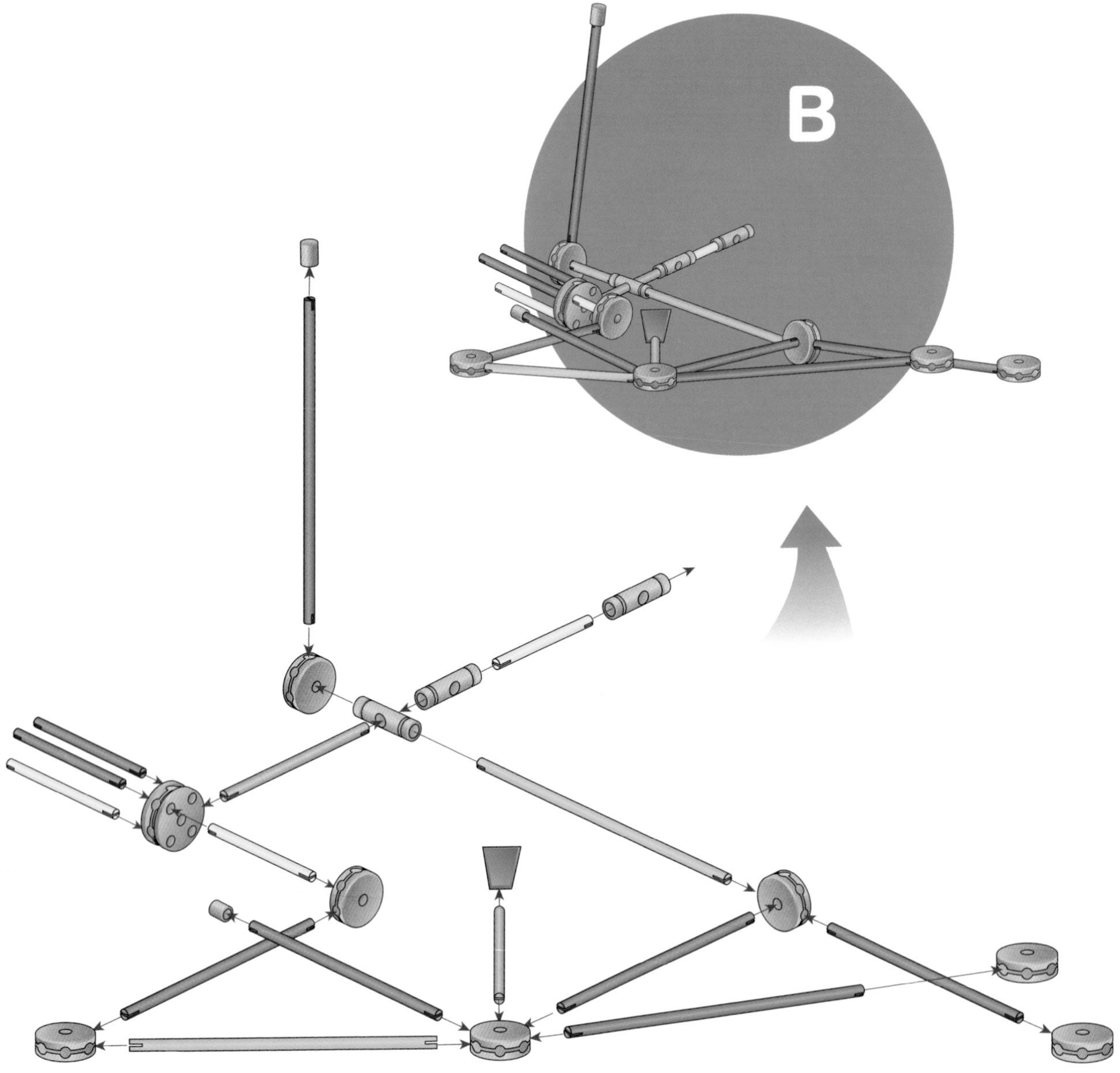
B

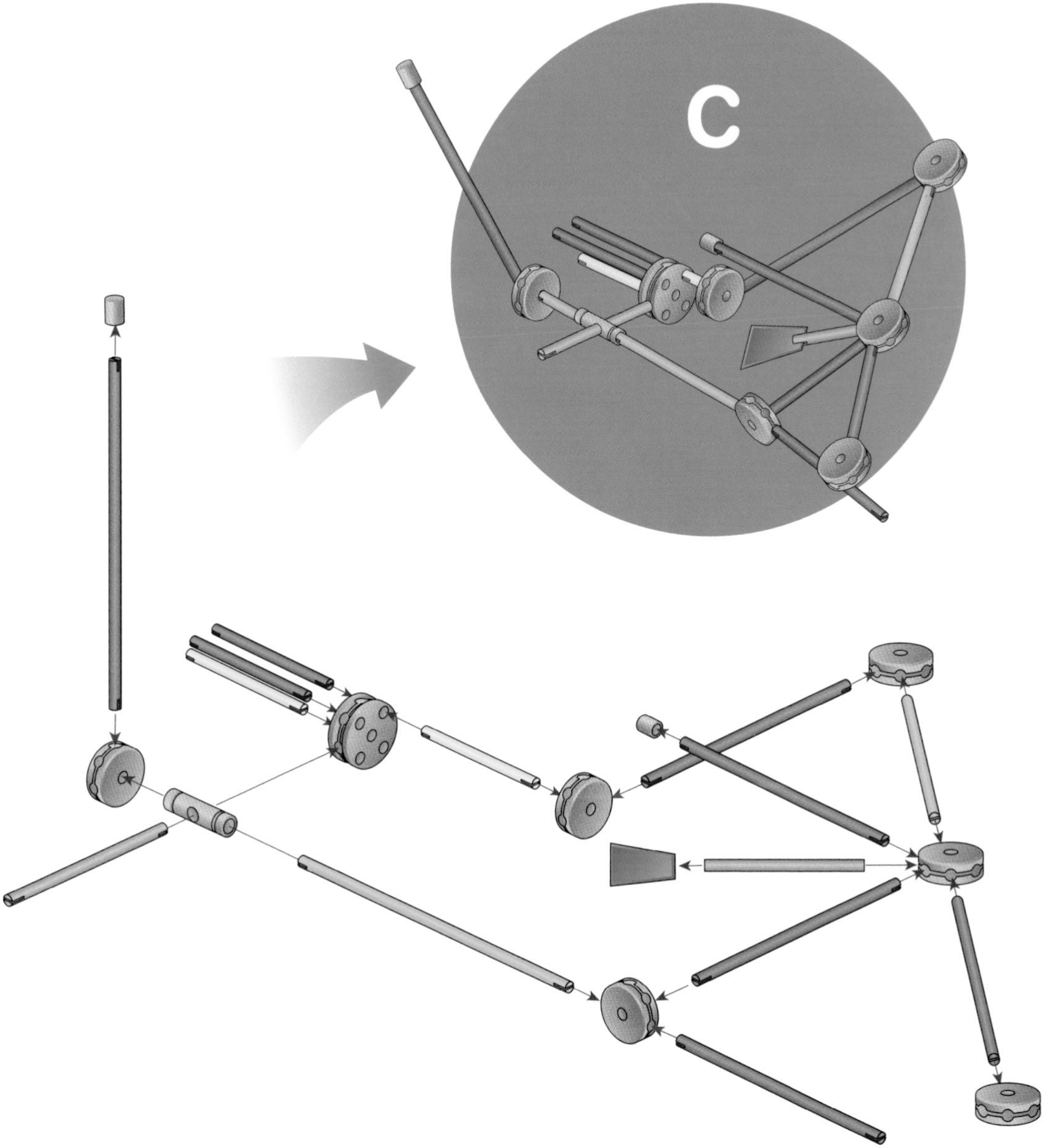
C

Skyscraper

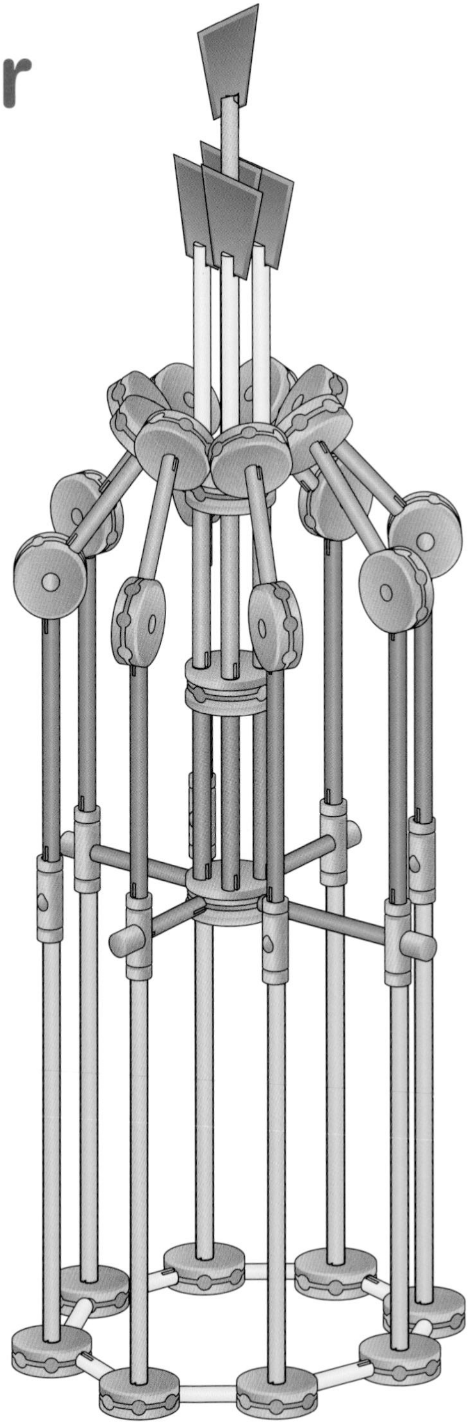

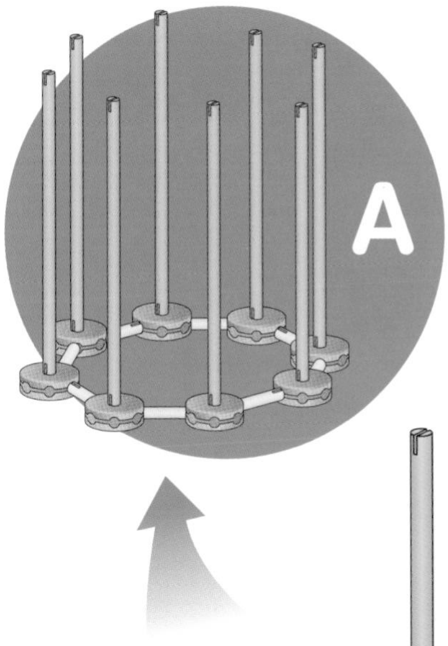
A

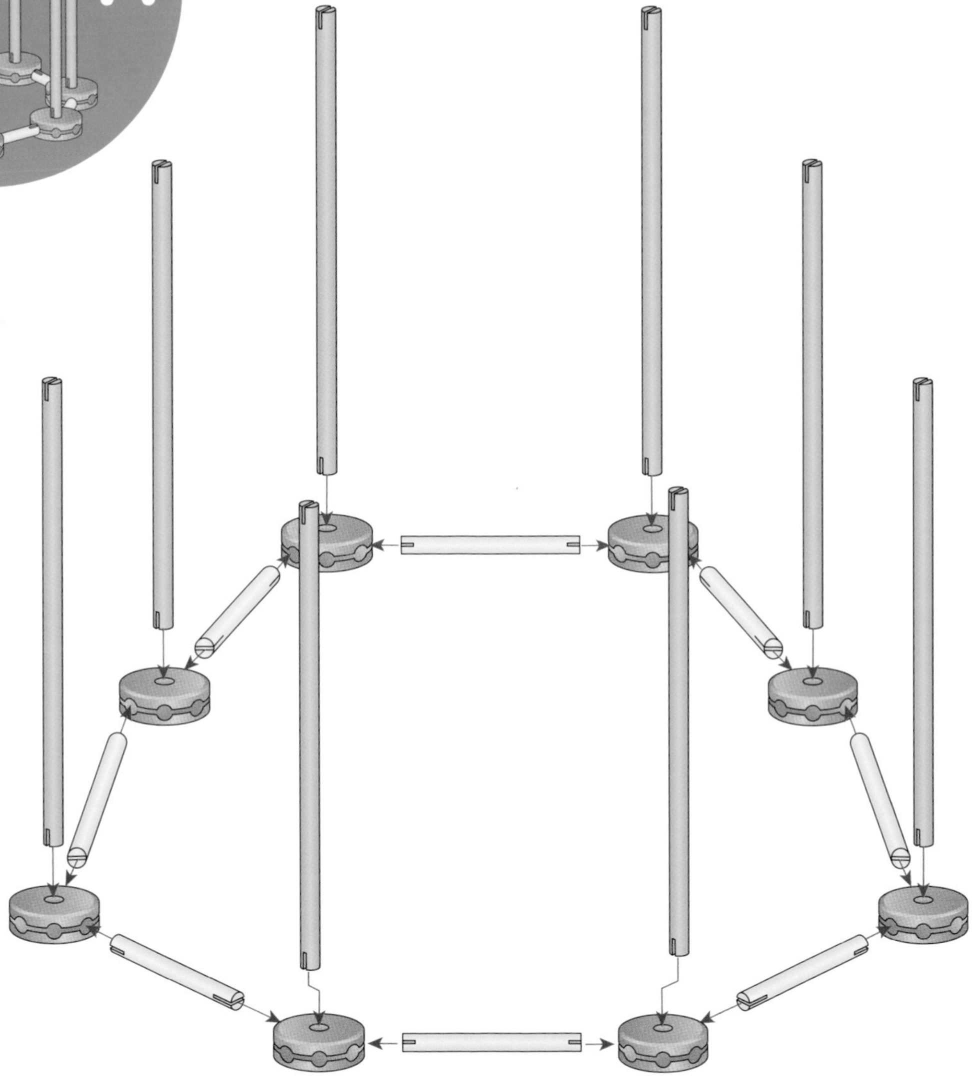

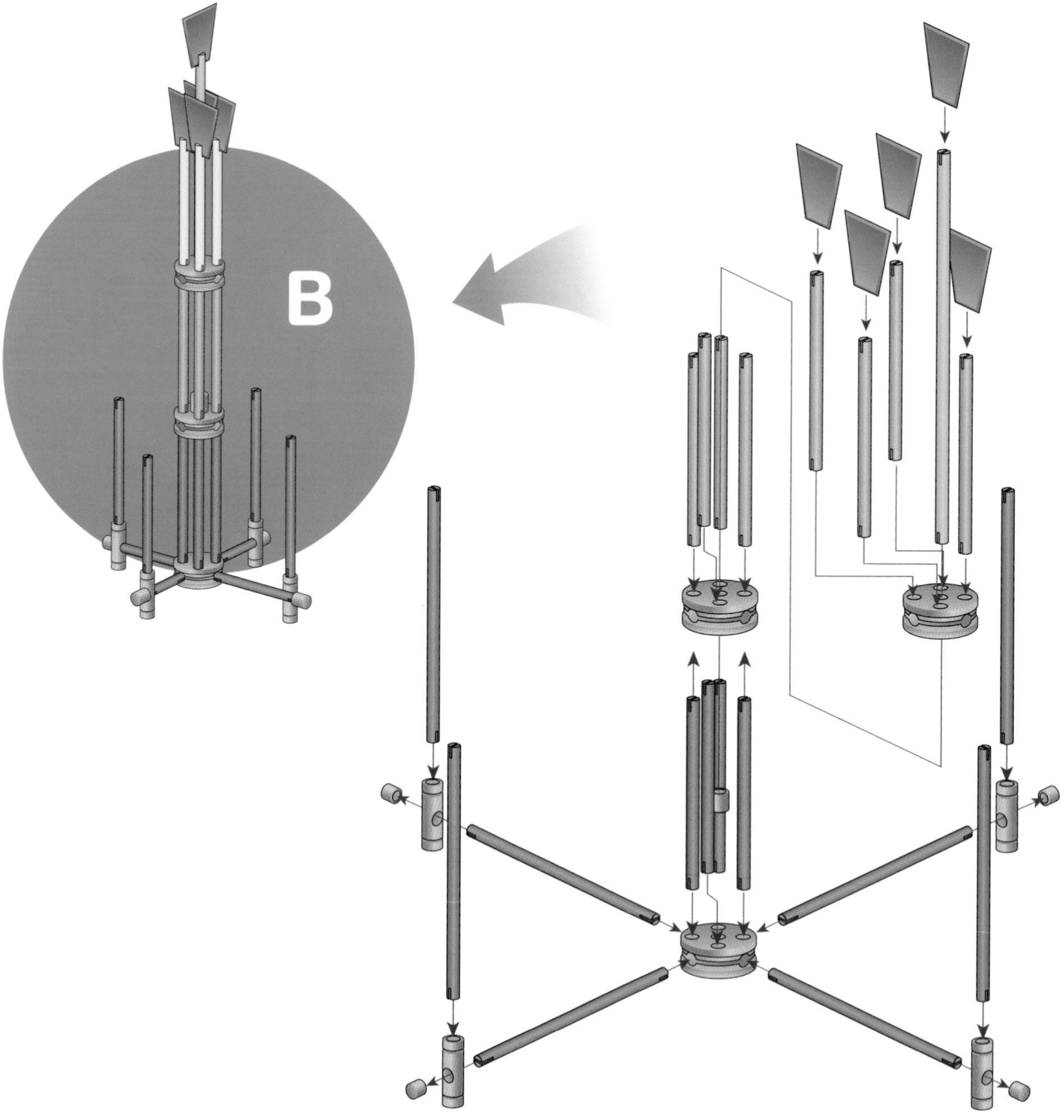
B

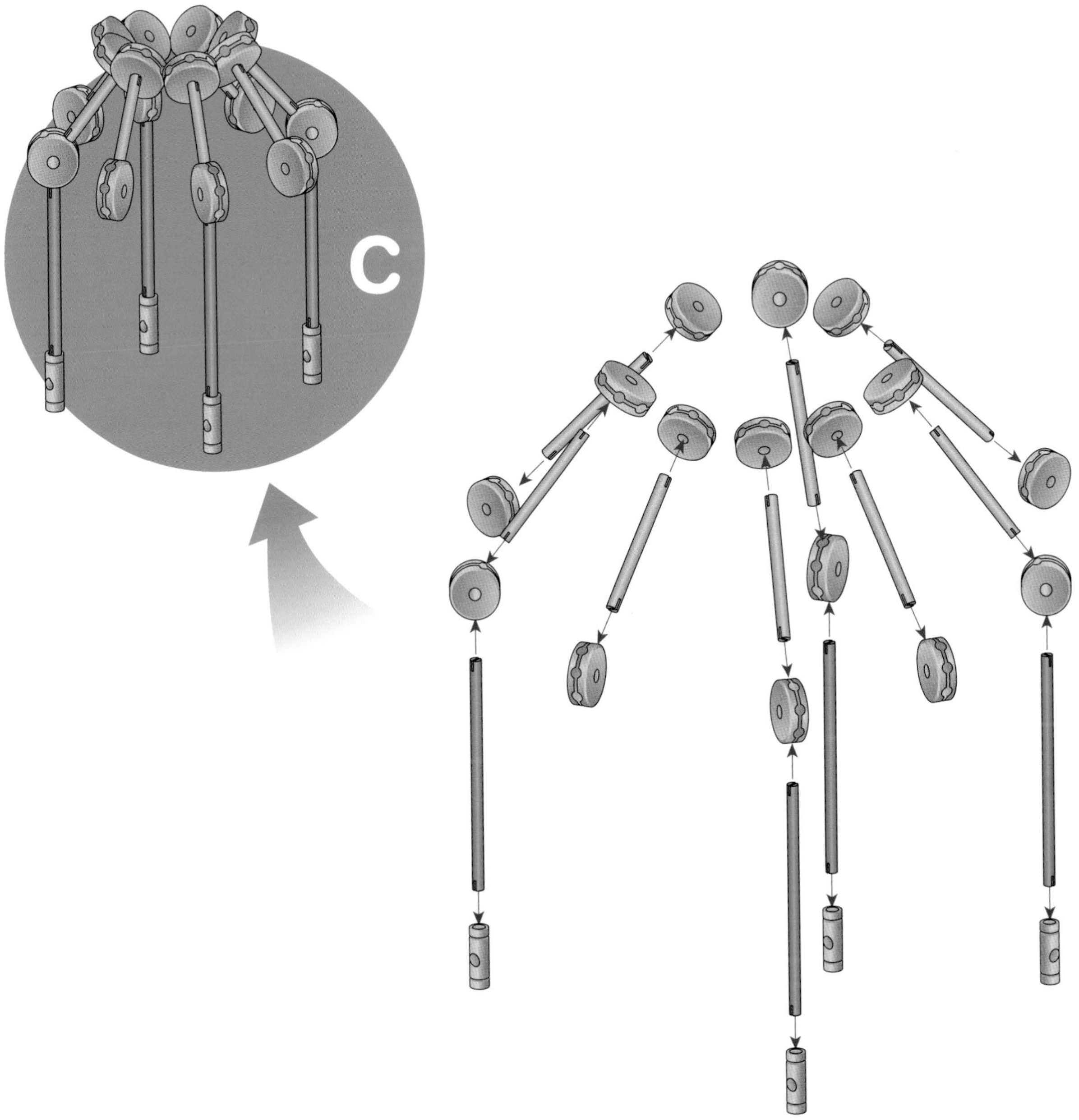
C

Tank

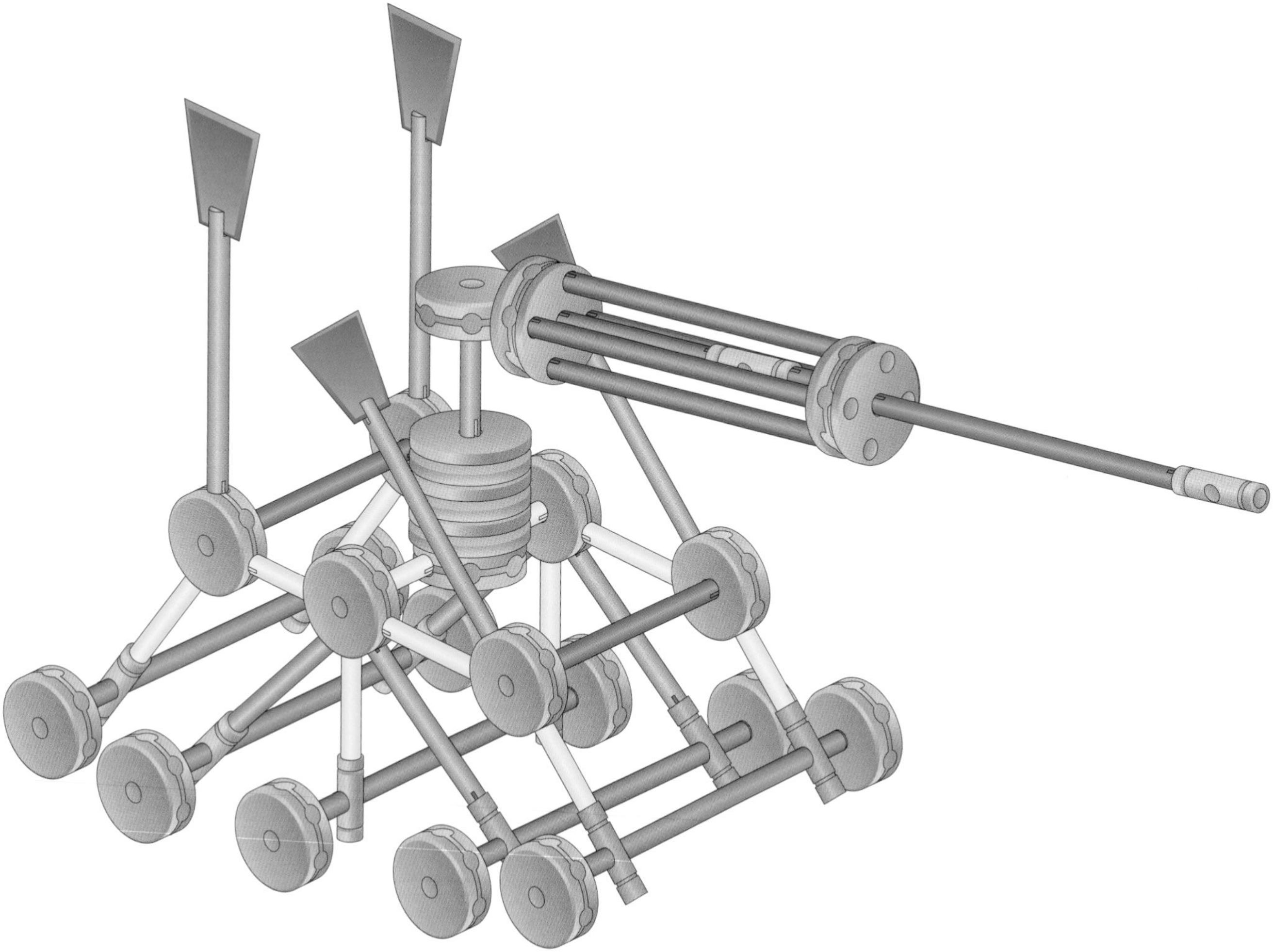

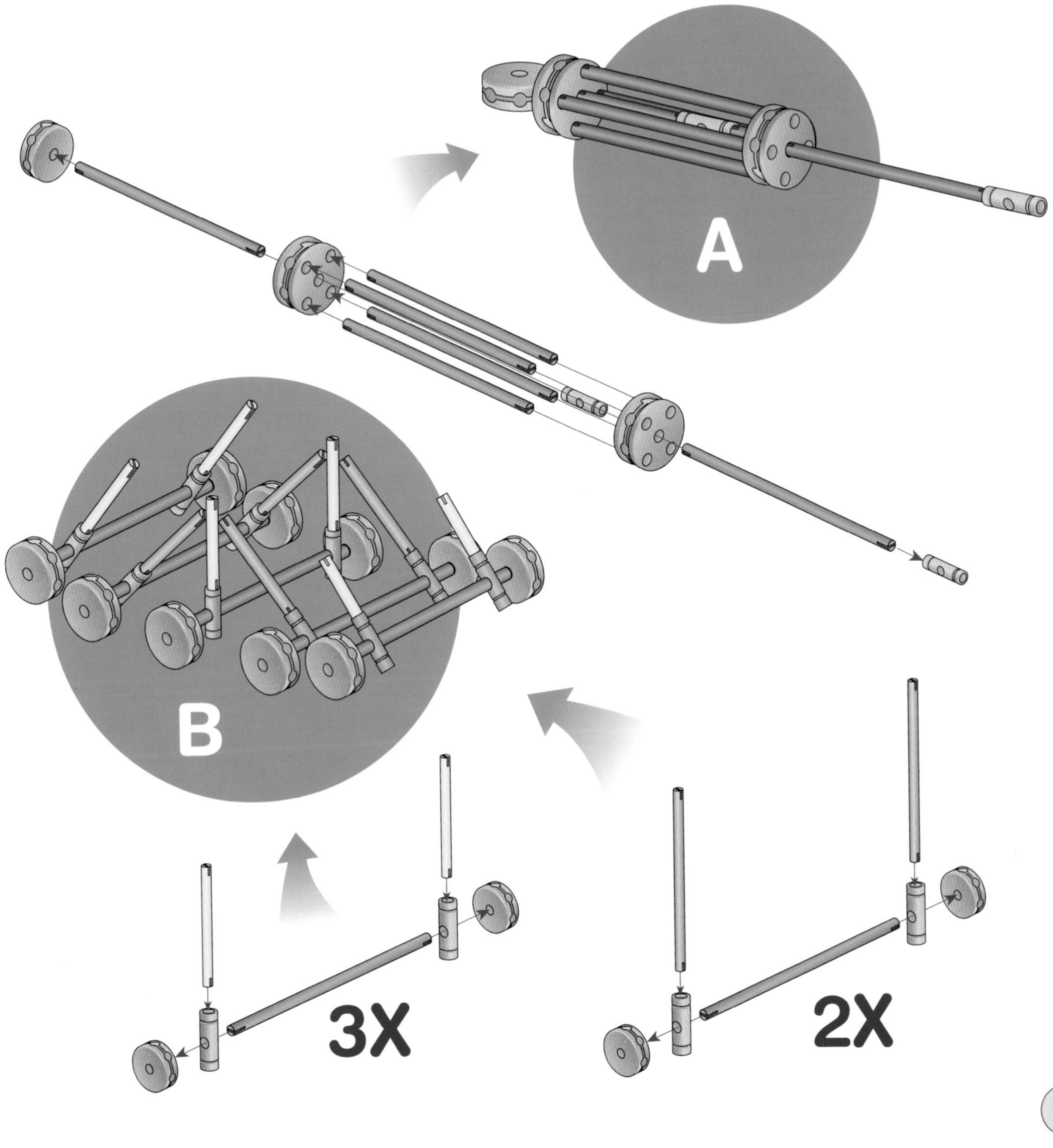
A
B
3X
2X

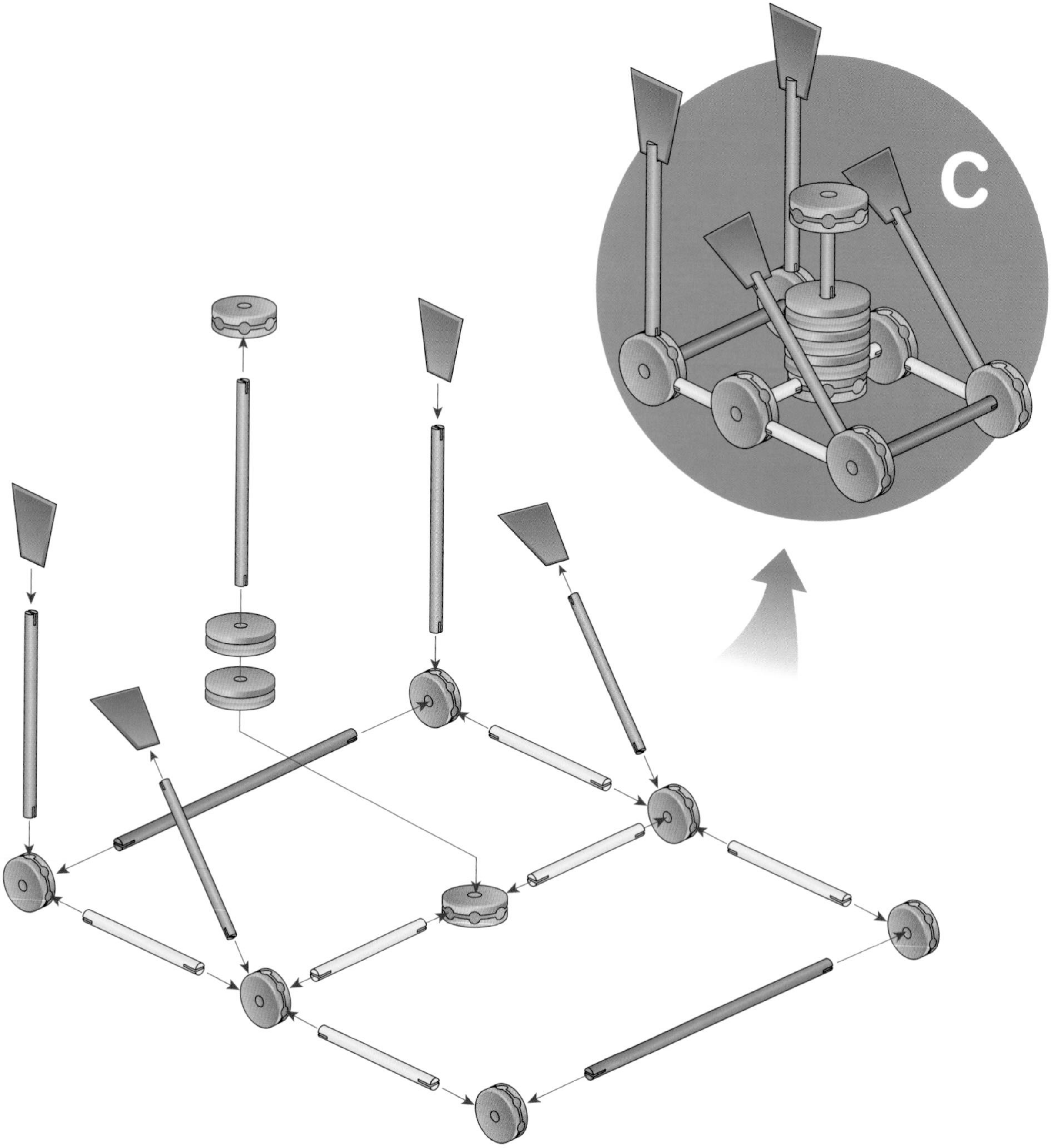
C

Super Tanker

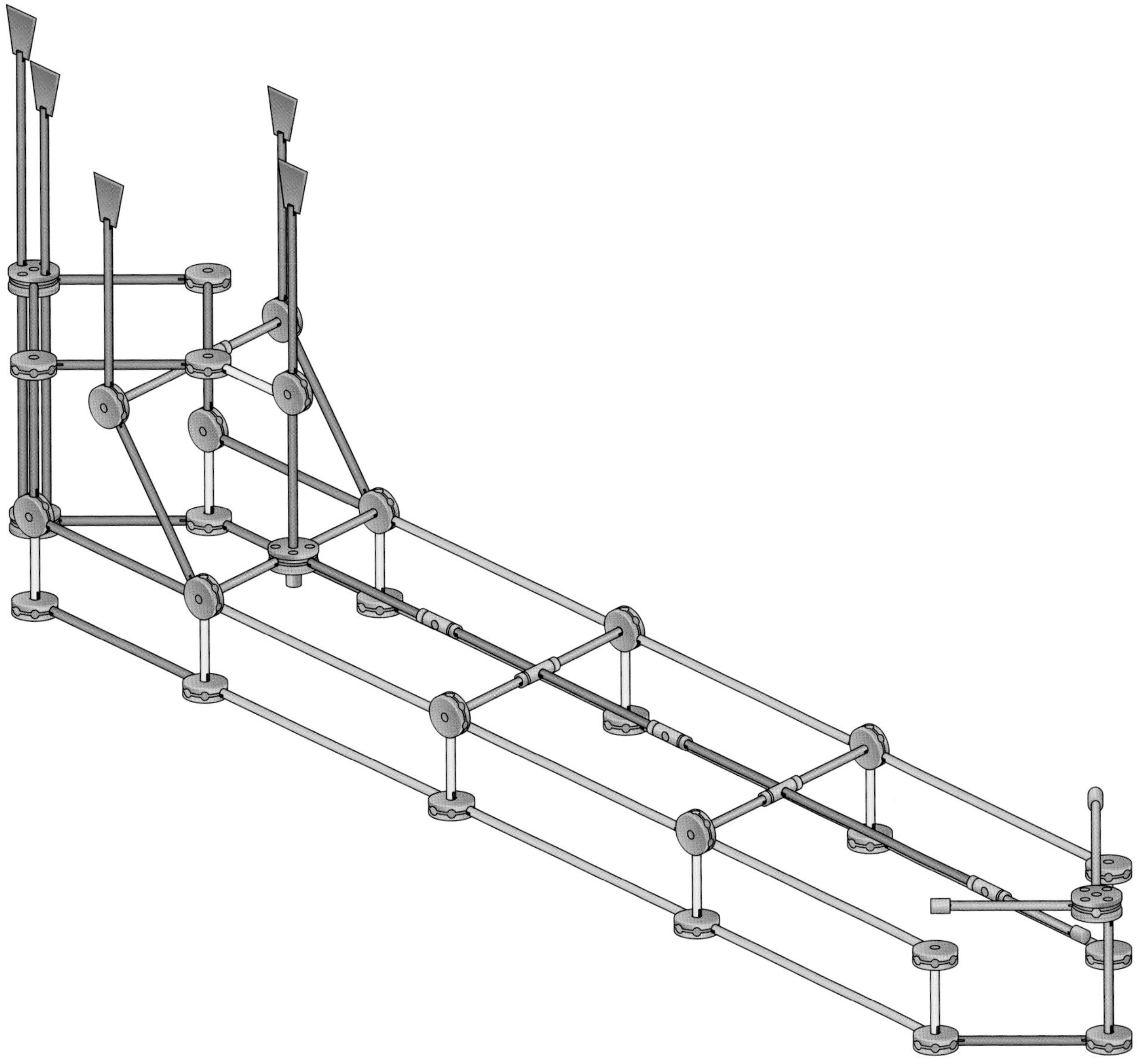

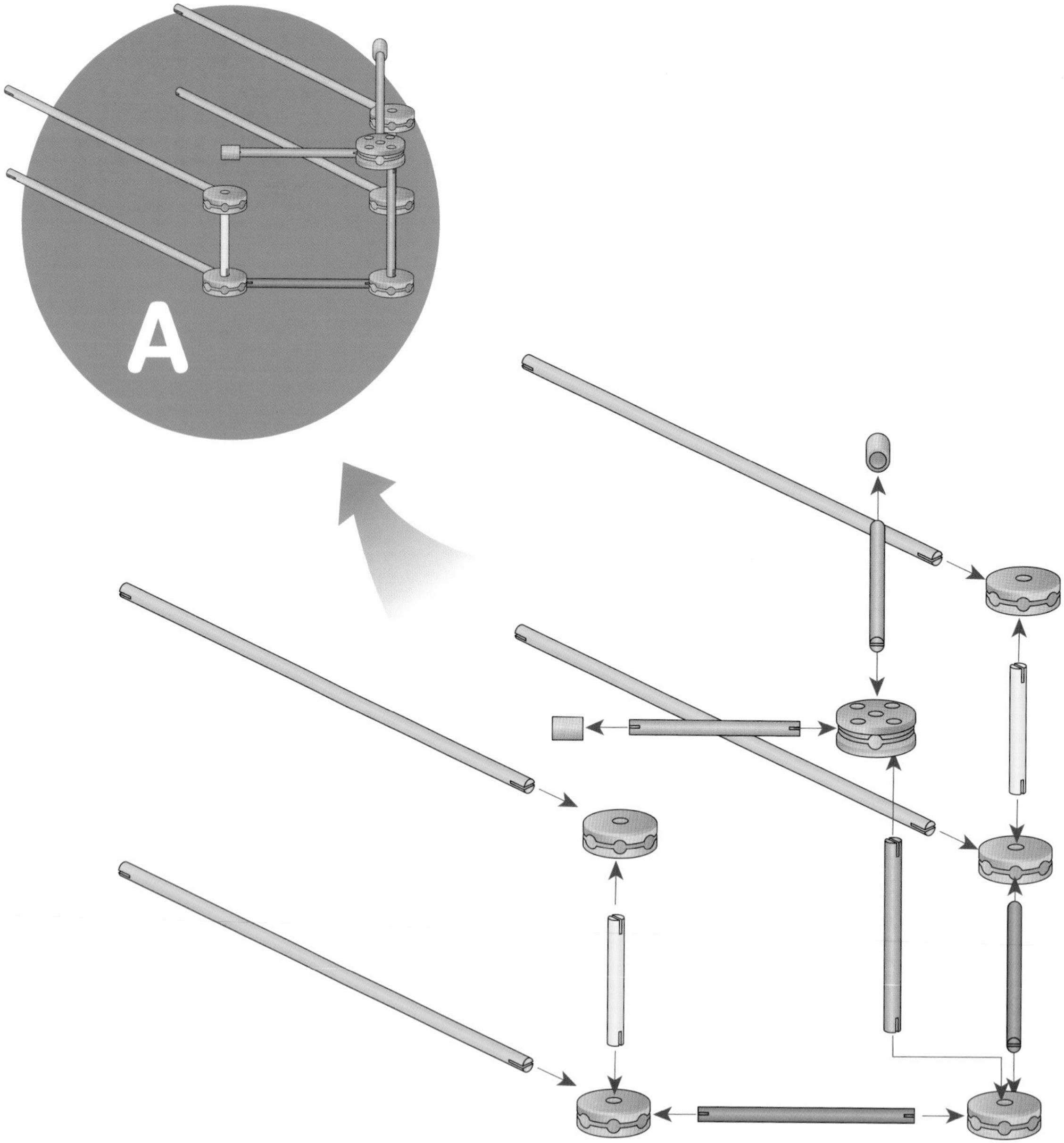
A

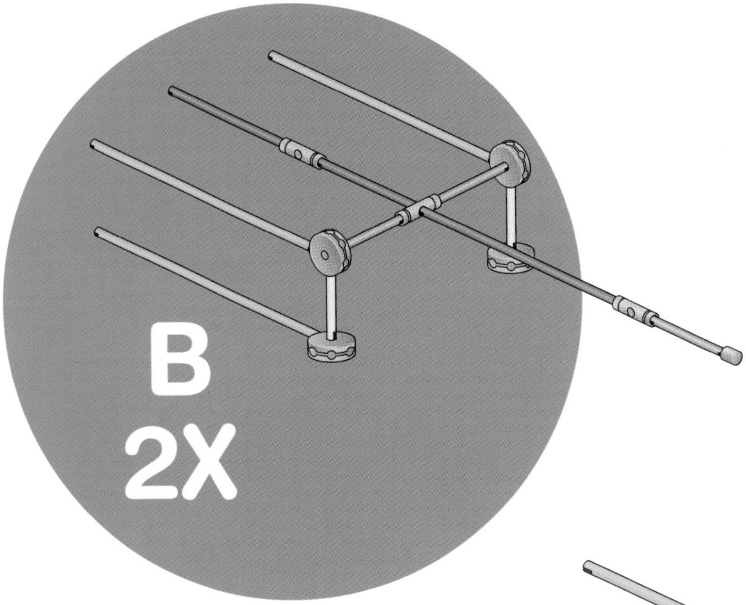
B
2X

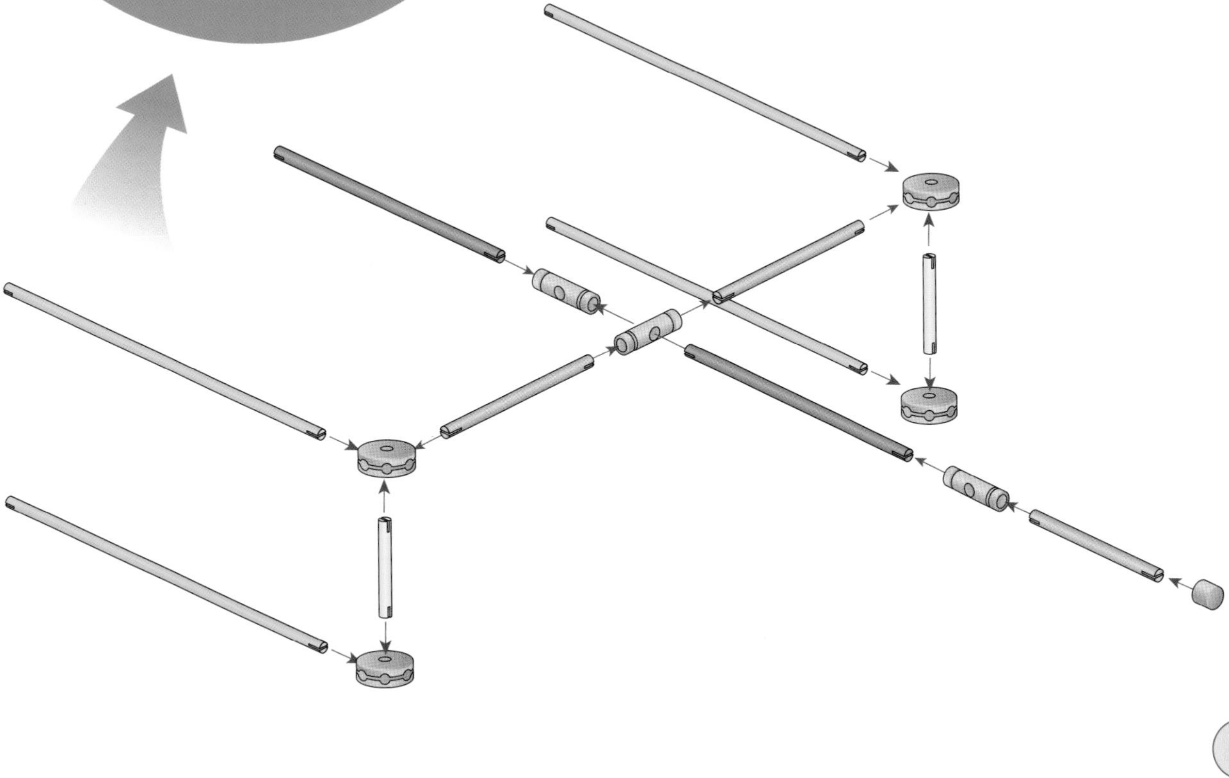

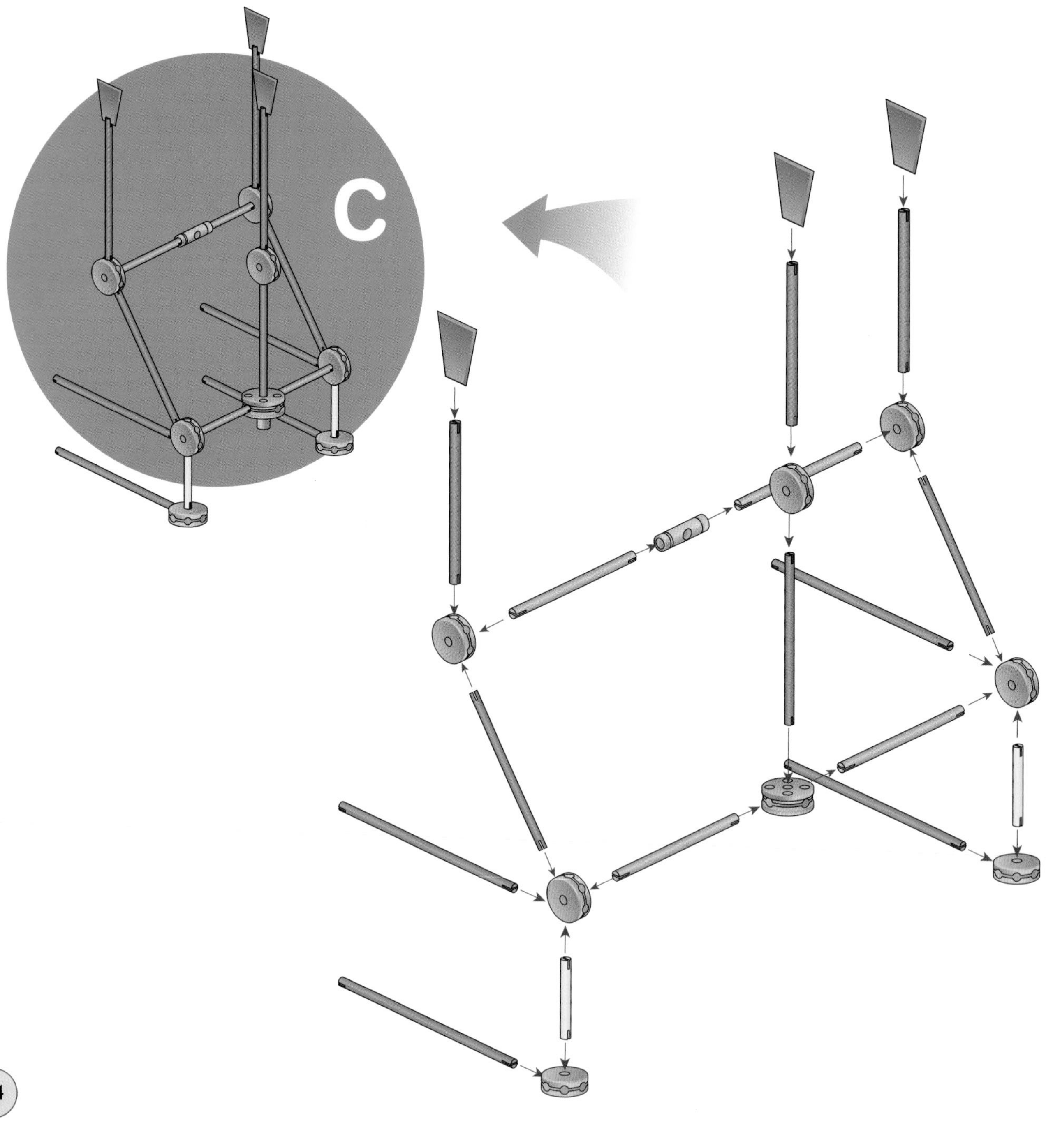
C

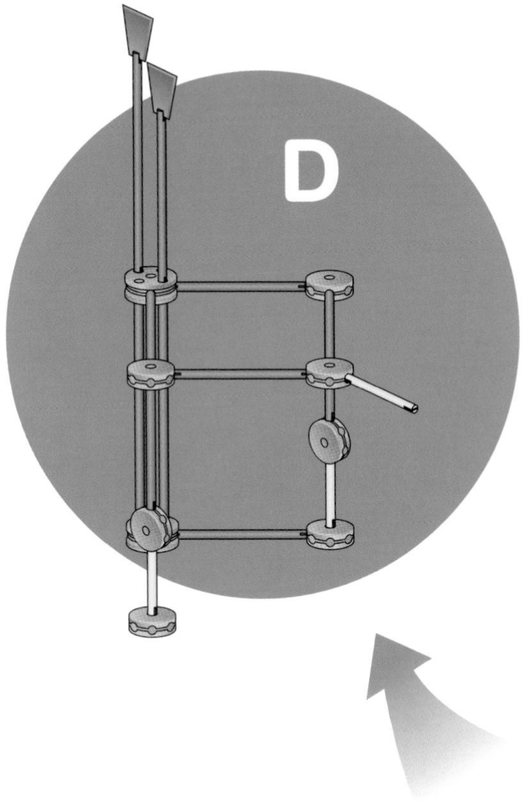
D

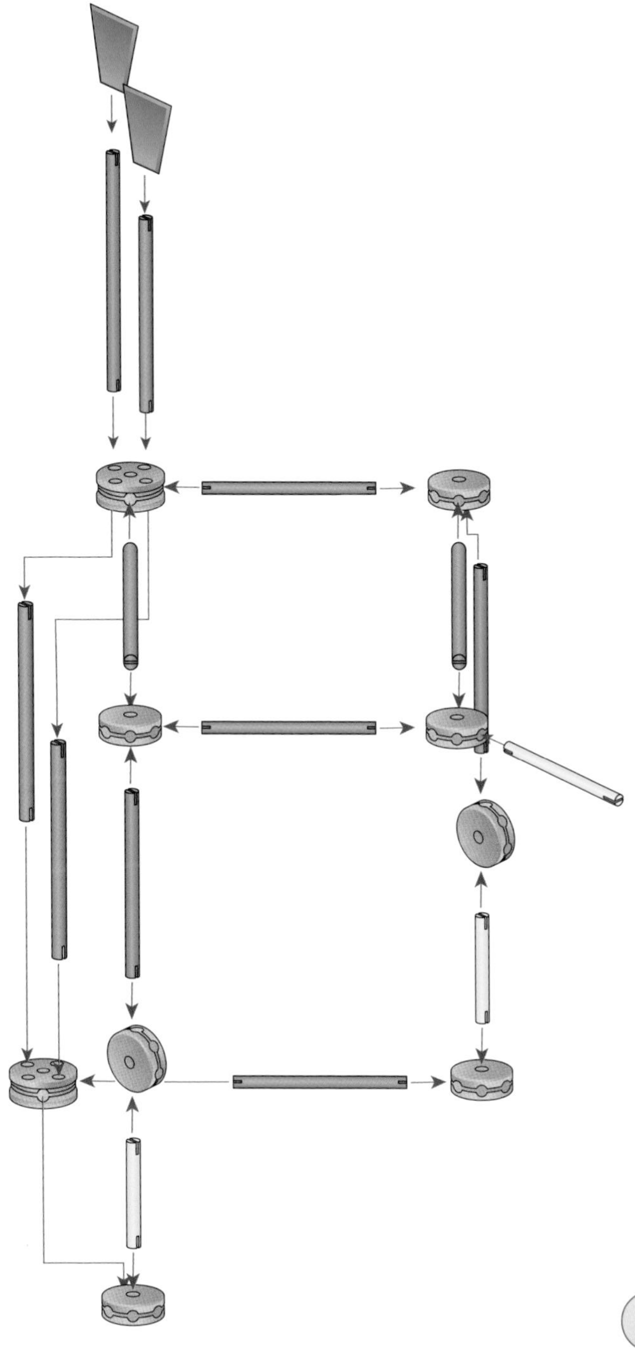

Helicopter

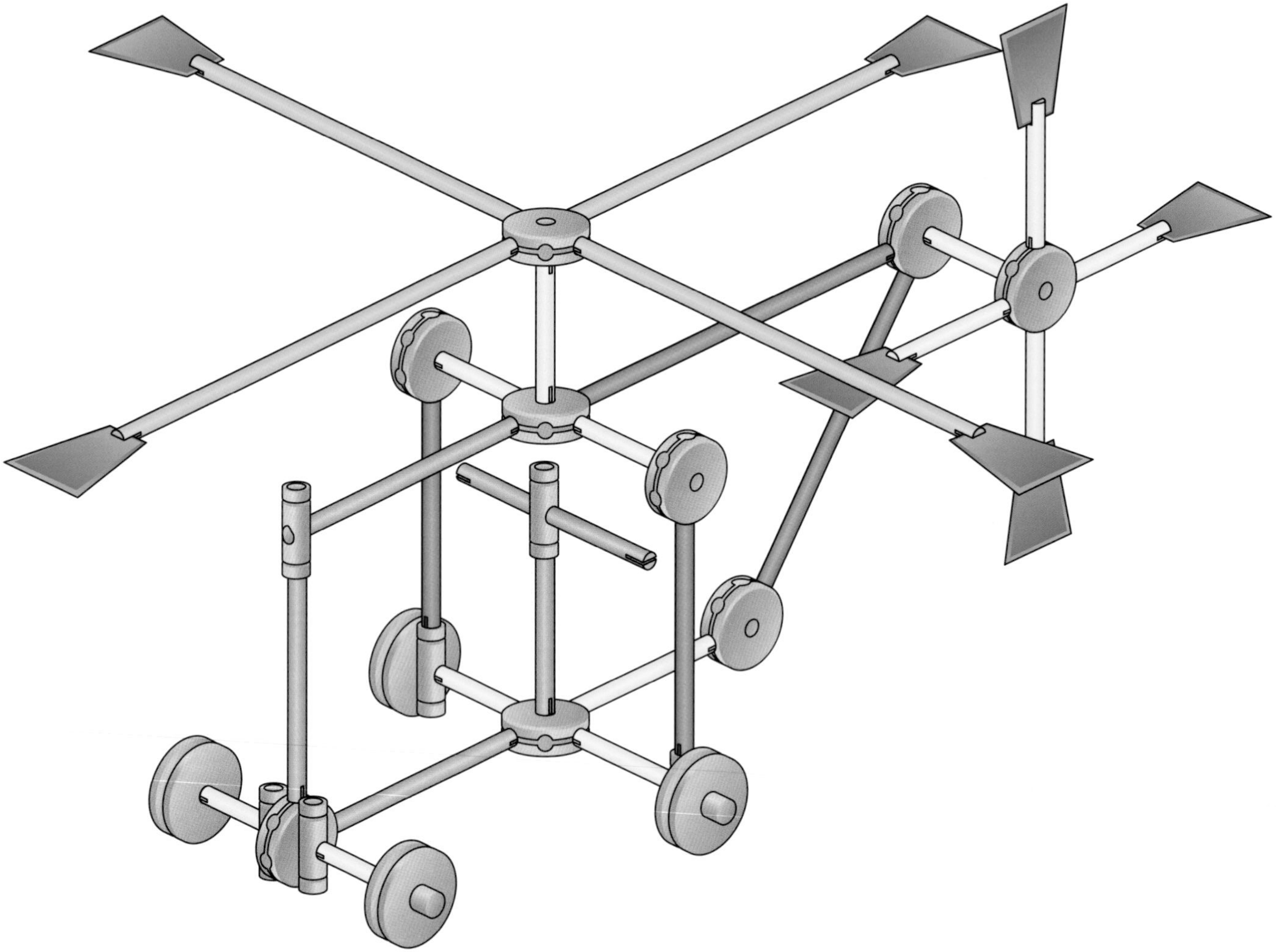

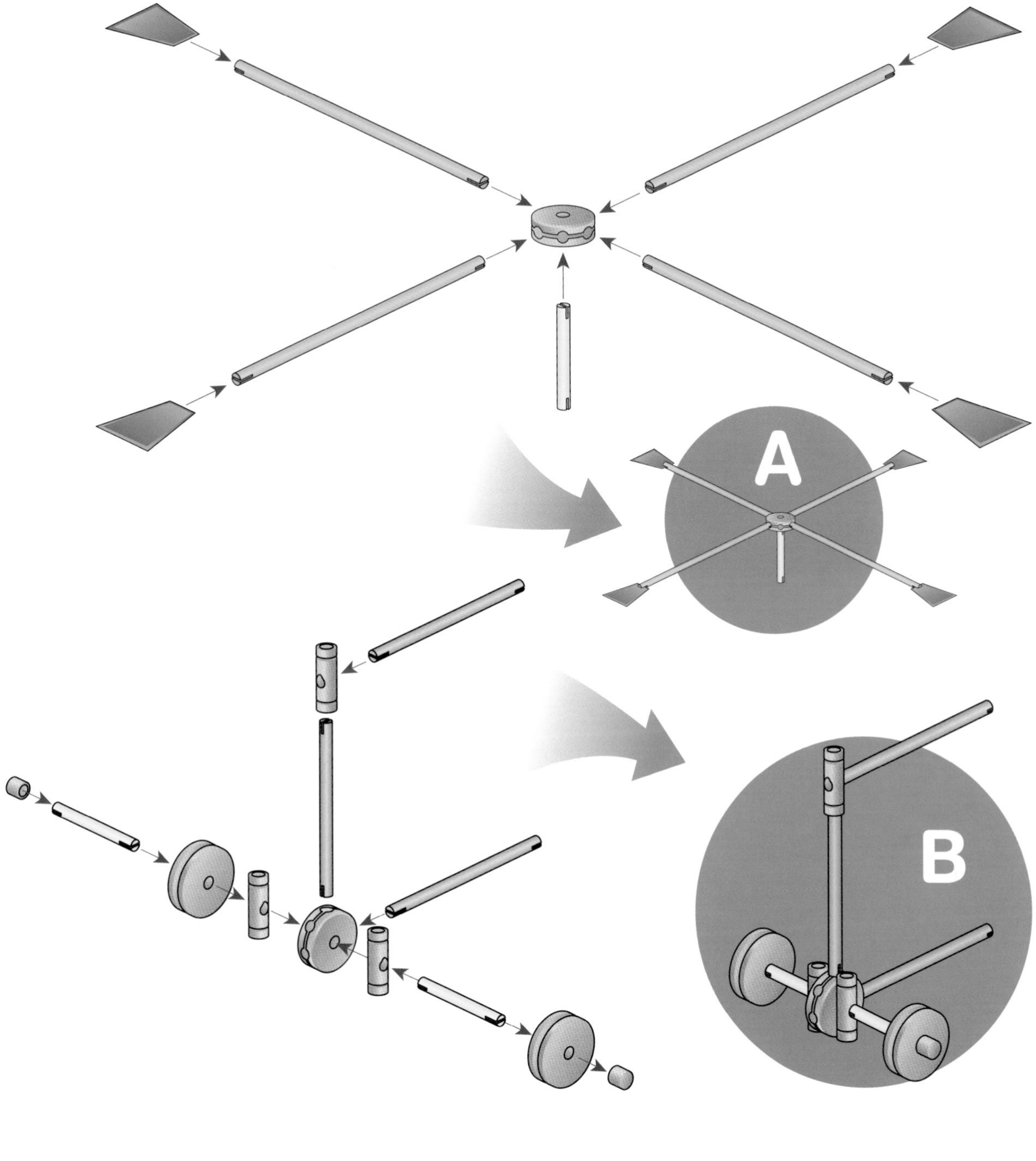
A
B

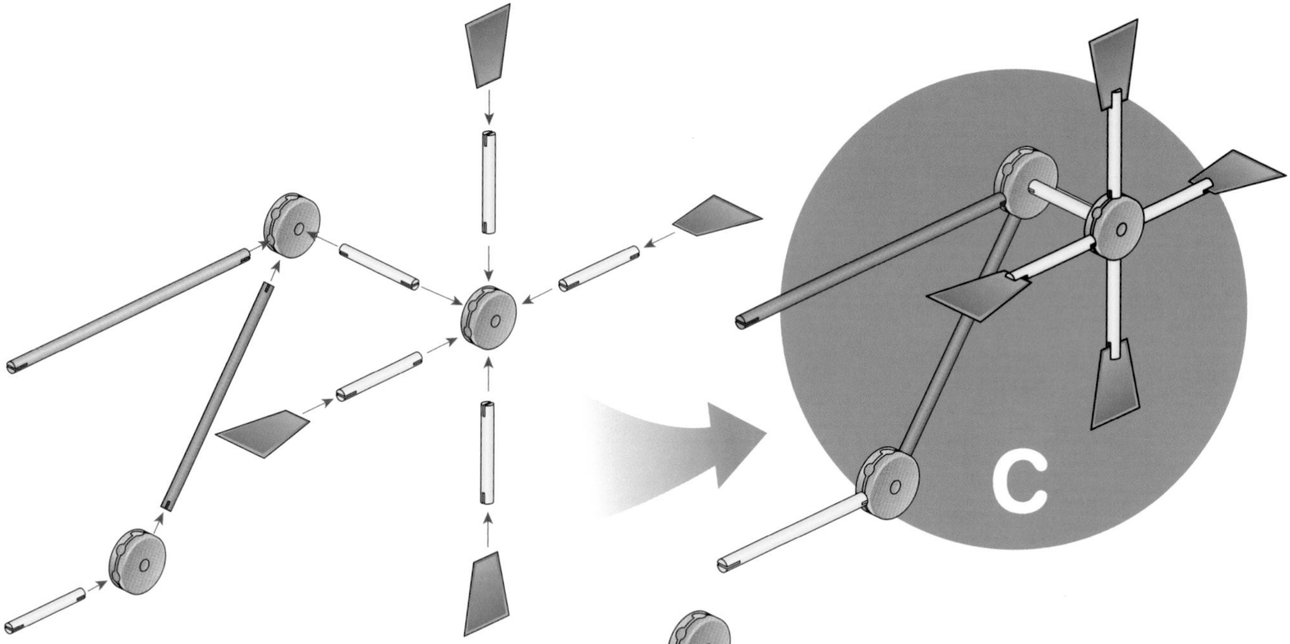
C

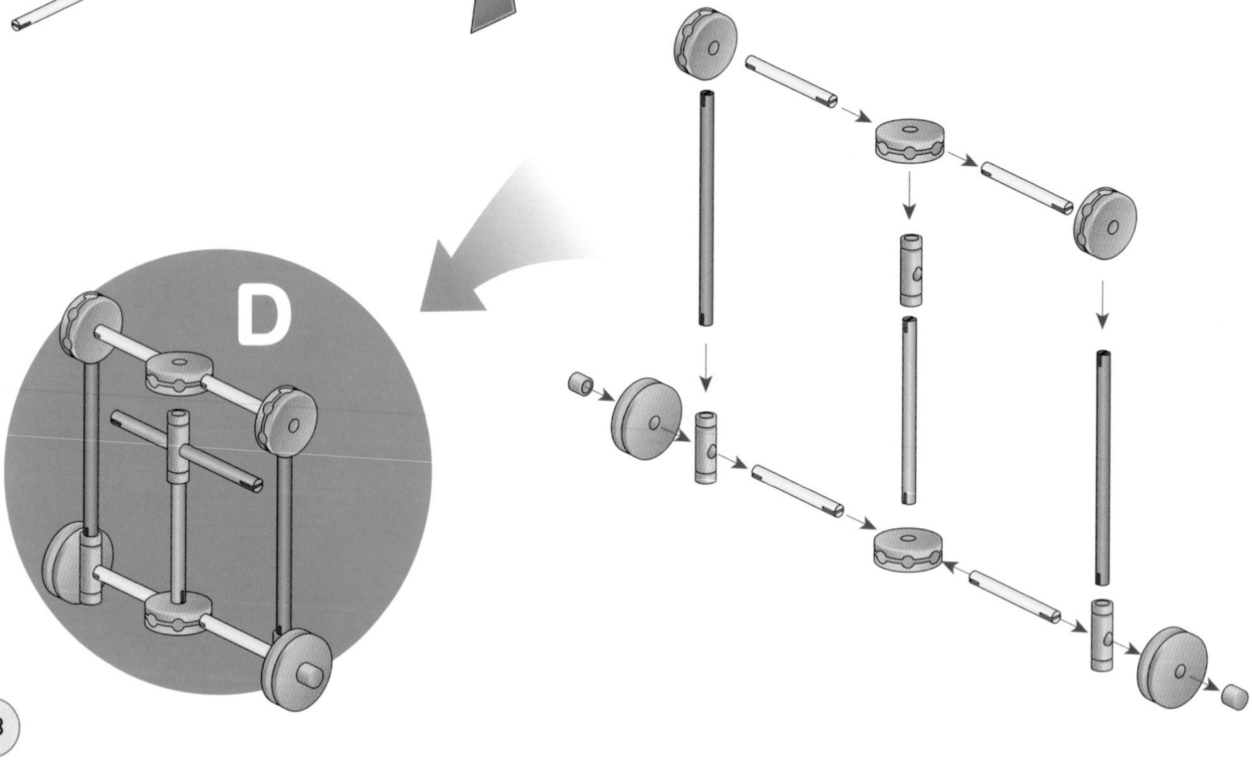
D

Windmill

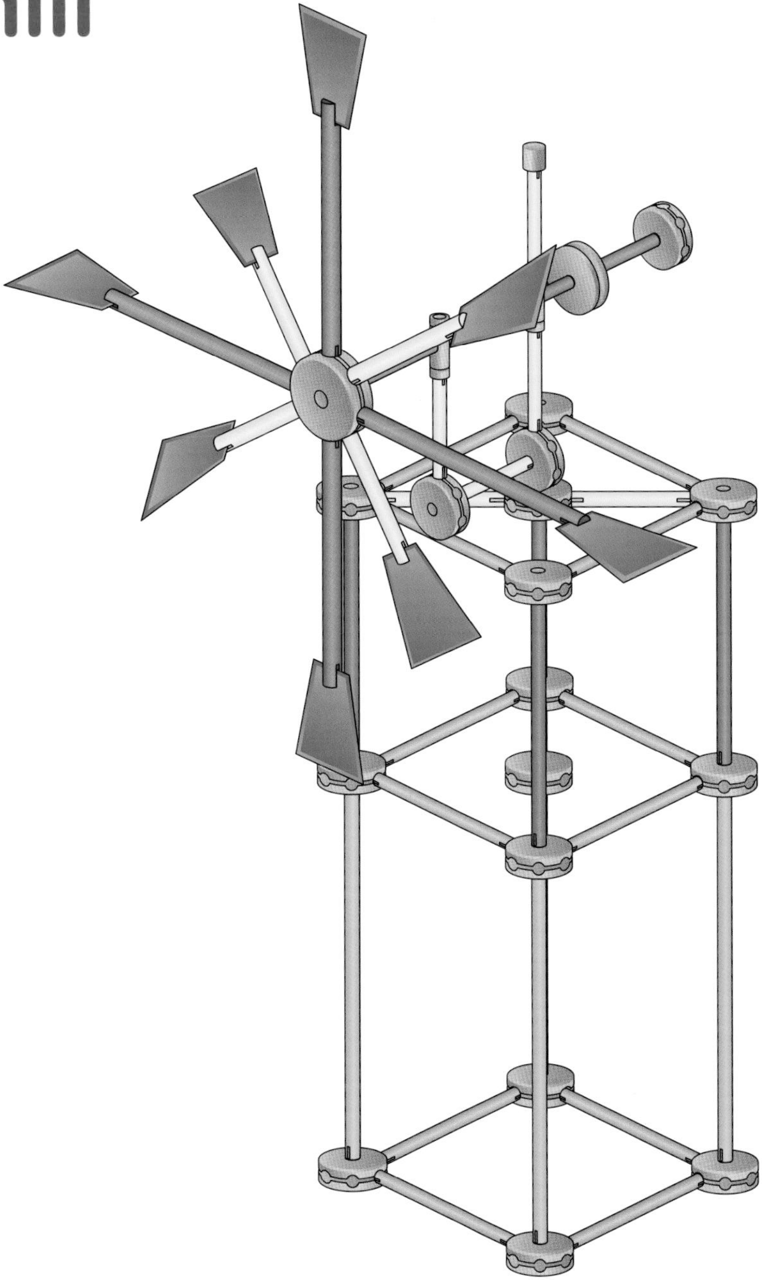

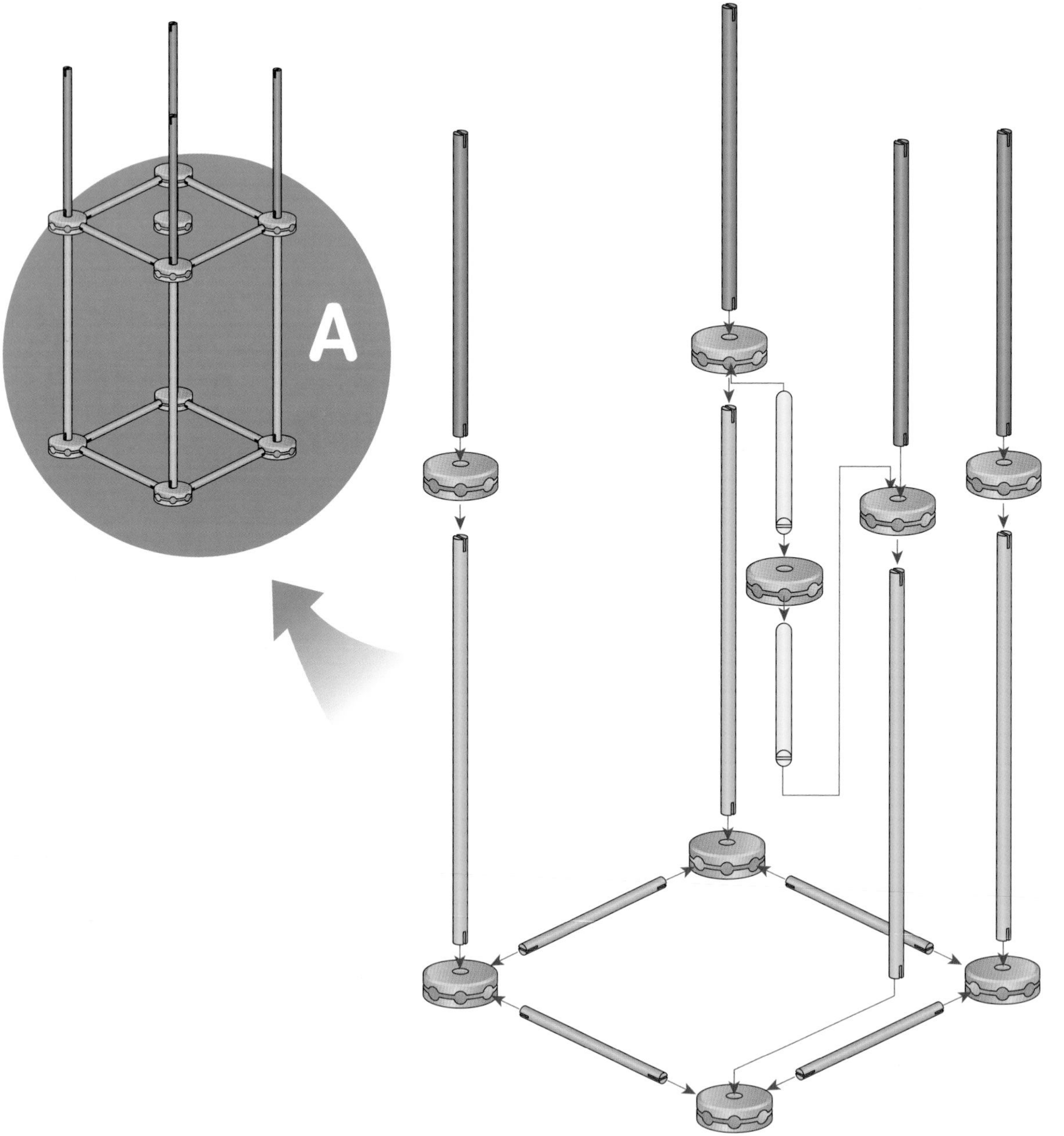
A

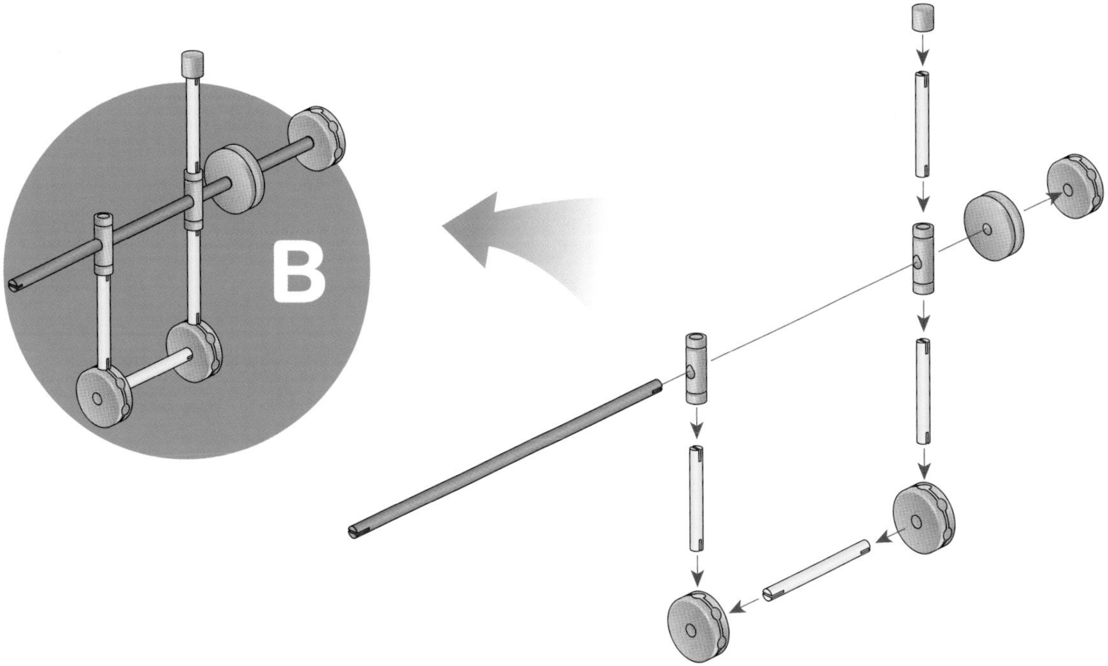
B

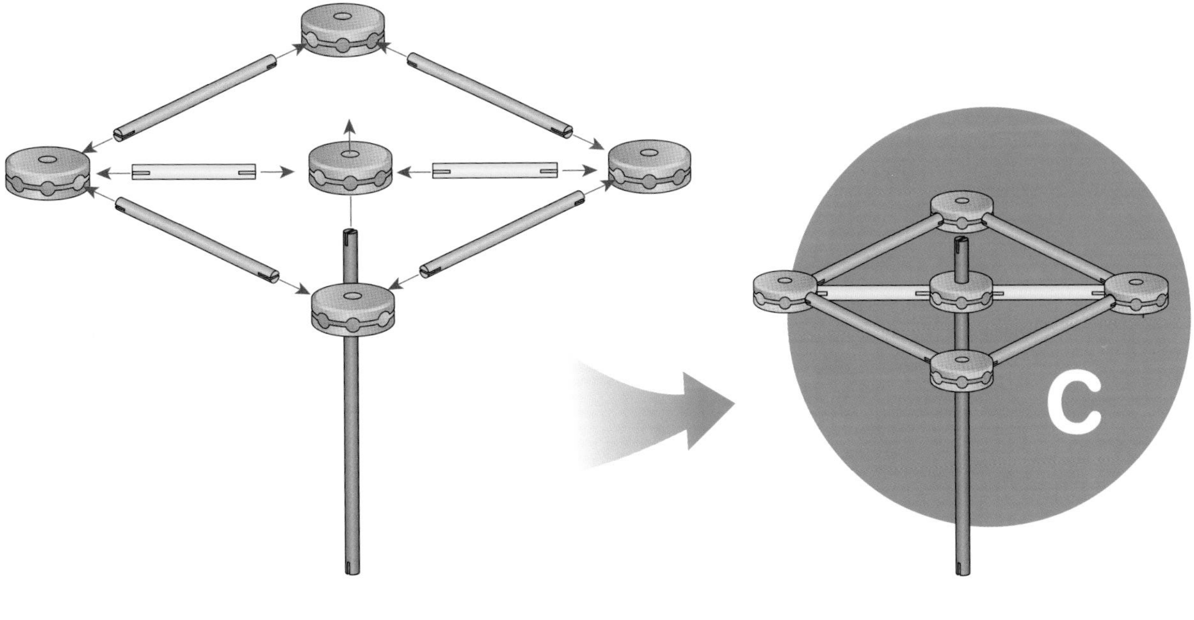
C

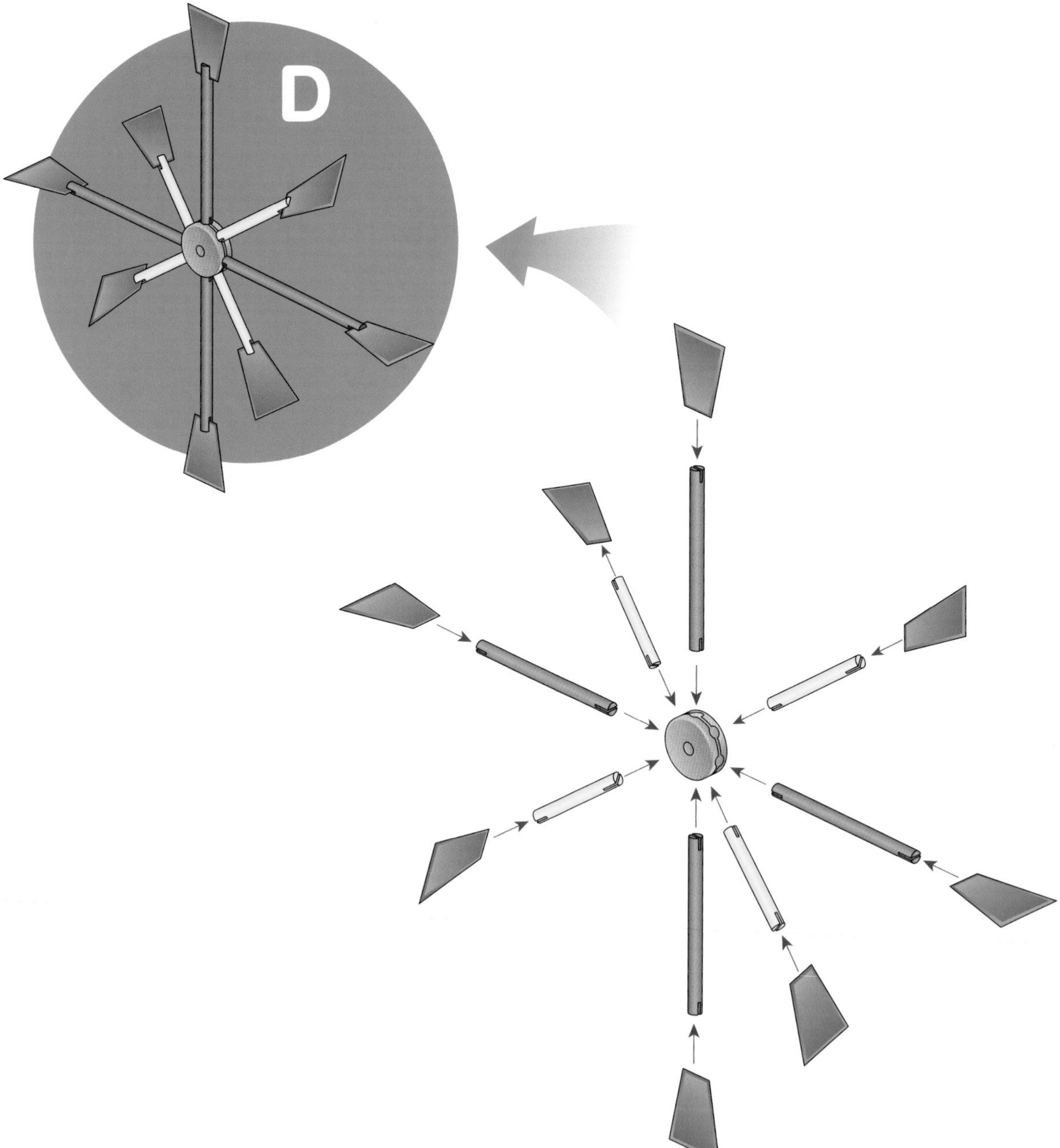
D

Car and Trailer

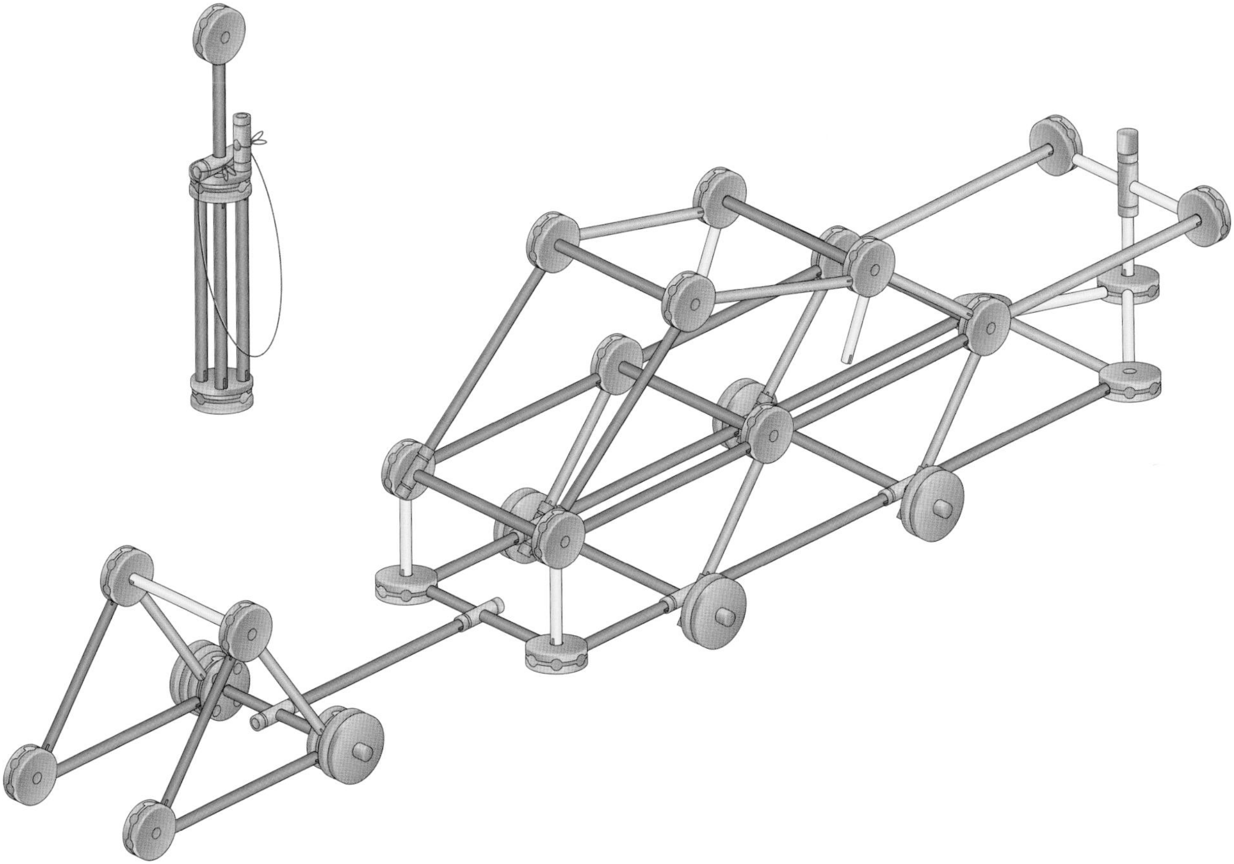

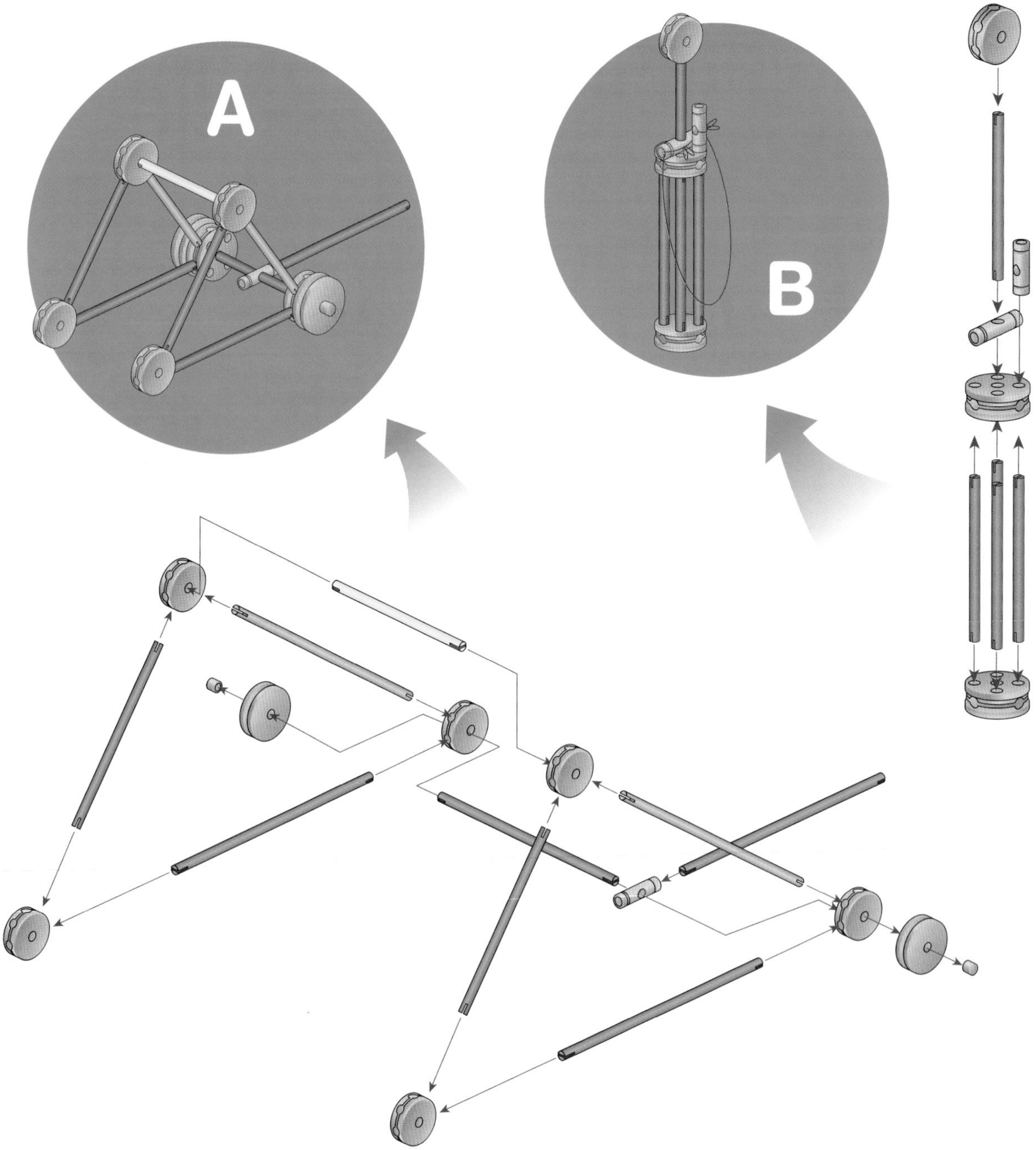
A
B

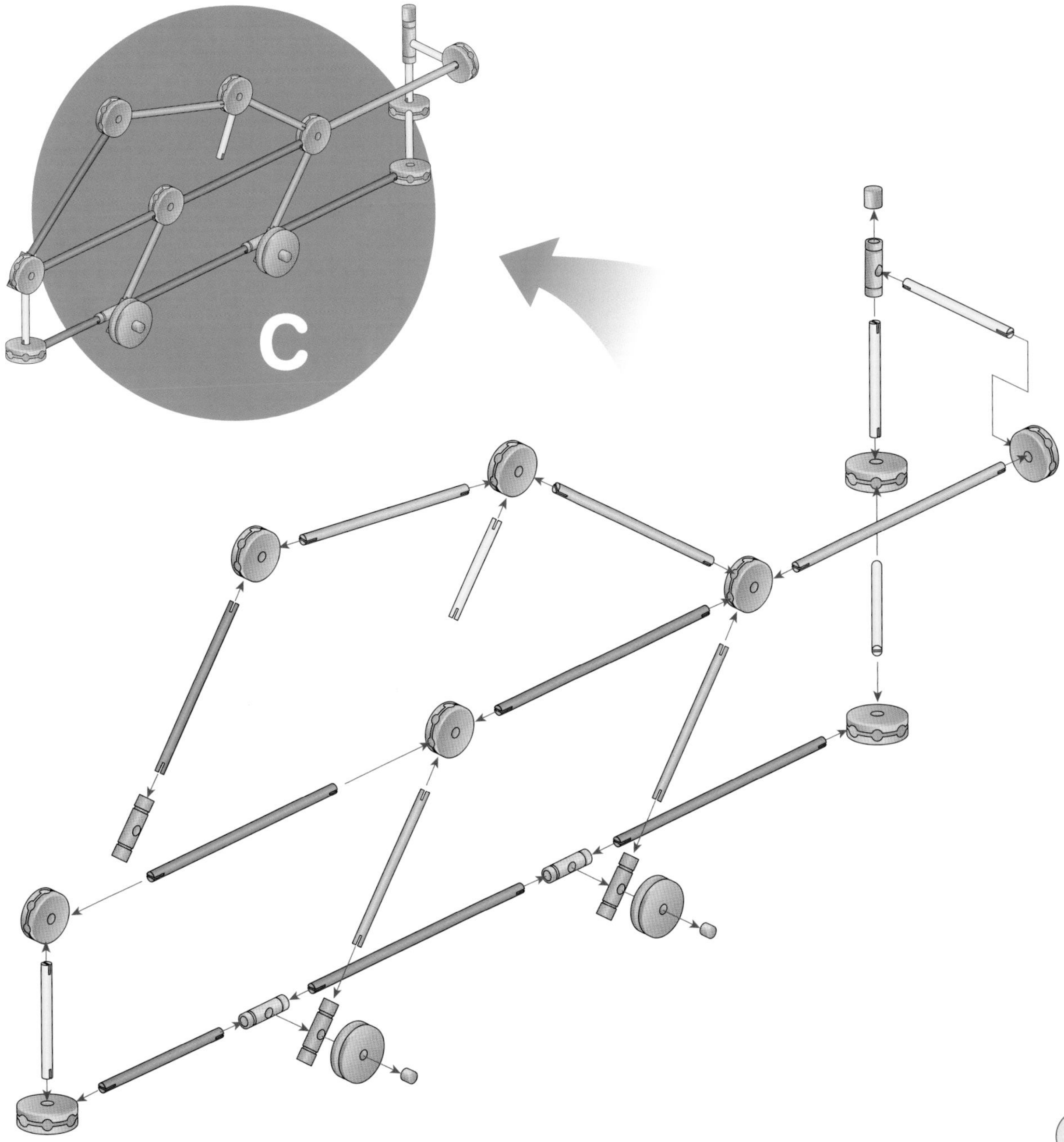
C

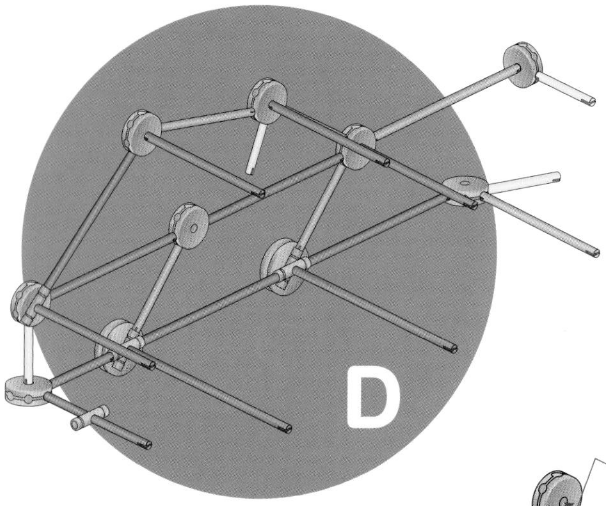
D

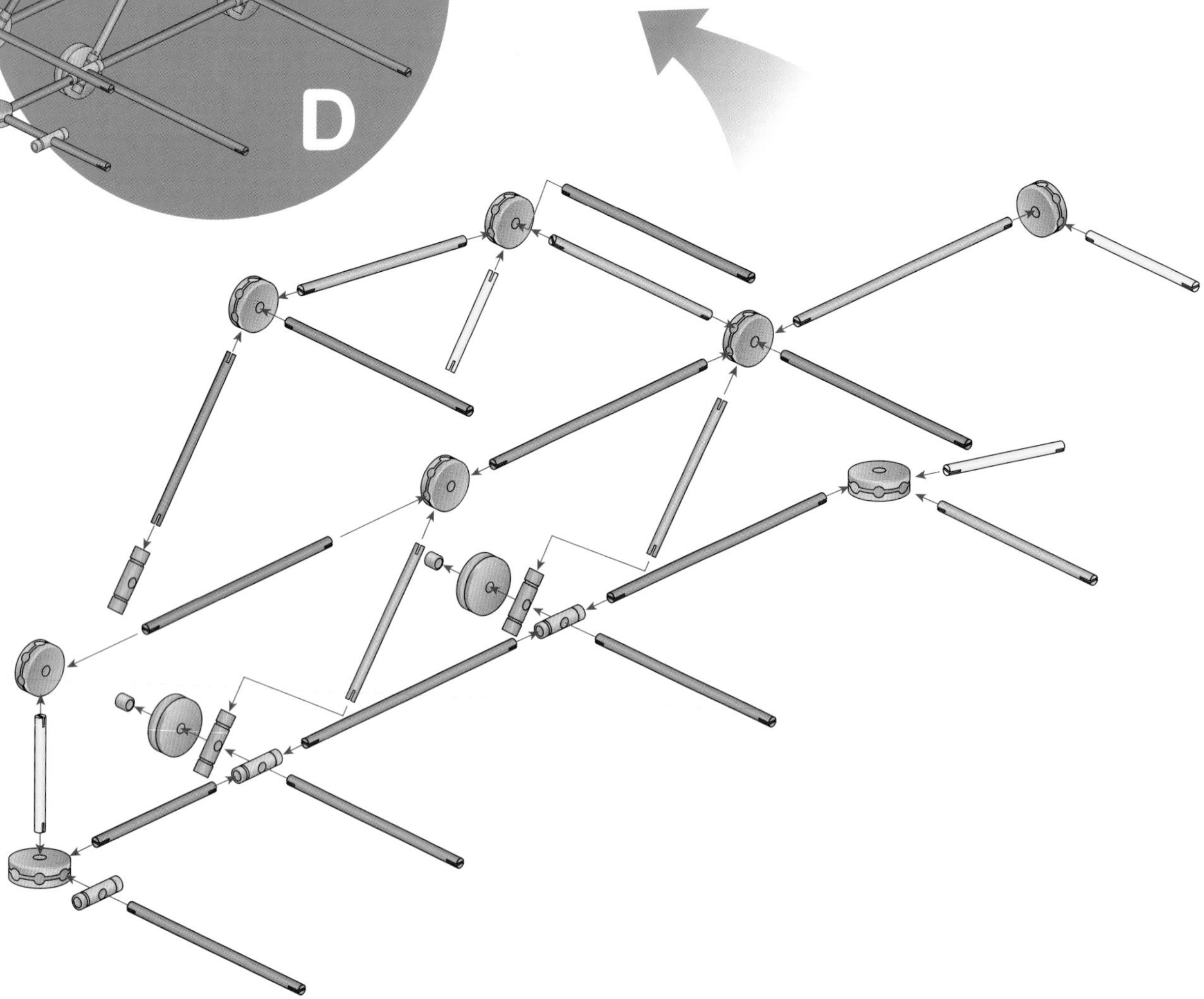

Train Scene

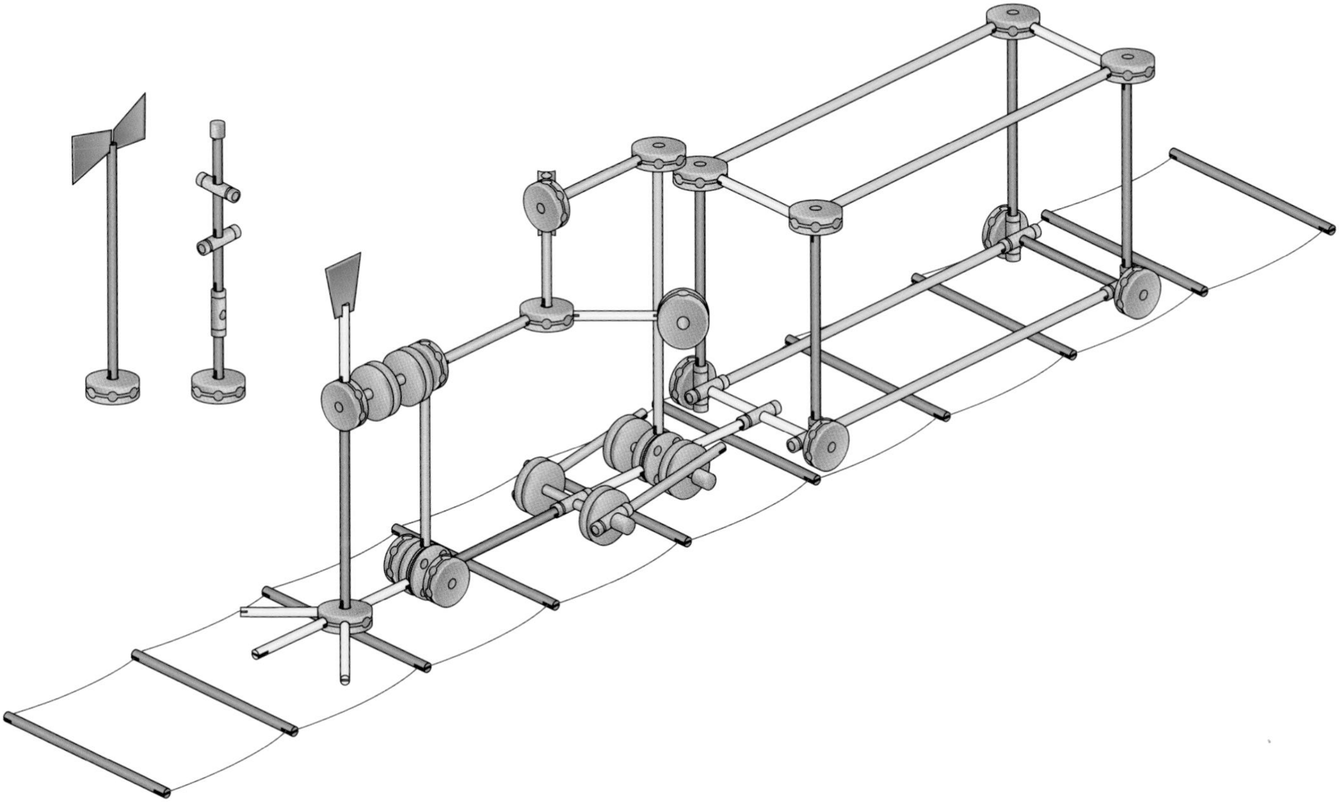

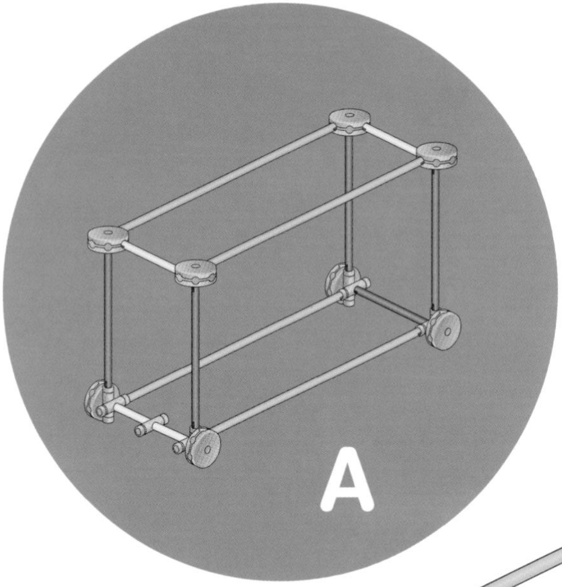
A

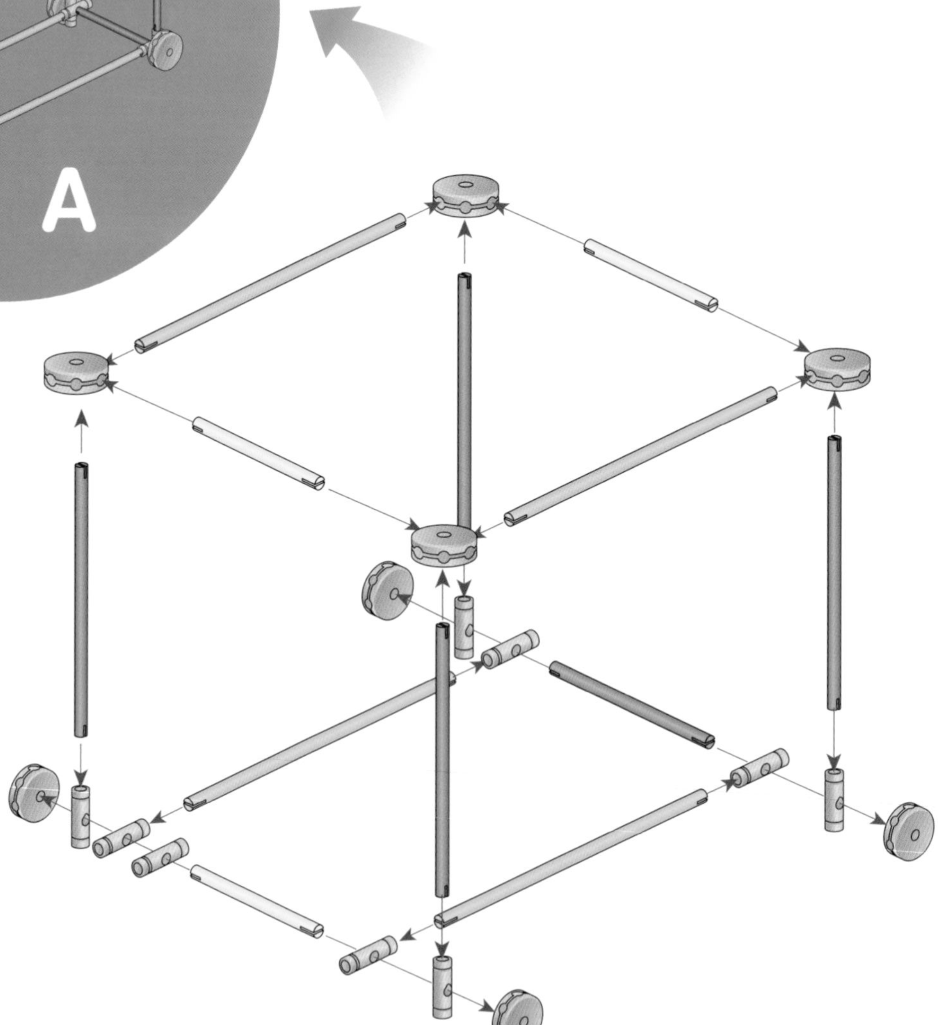

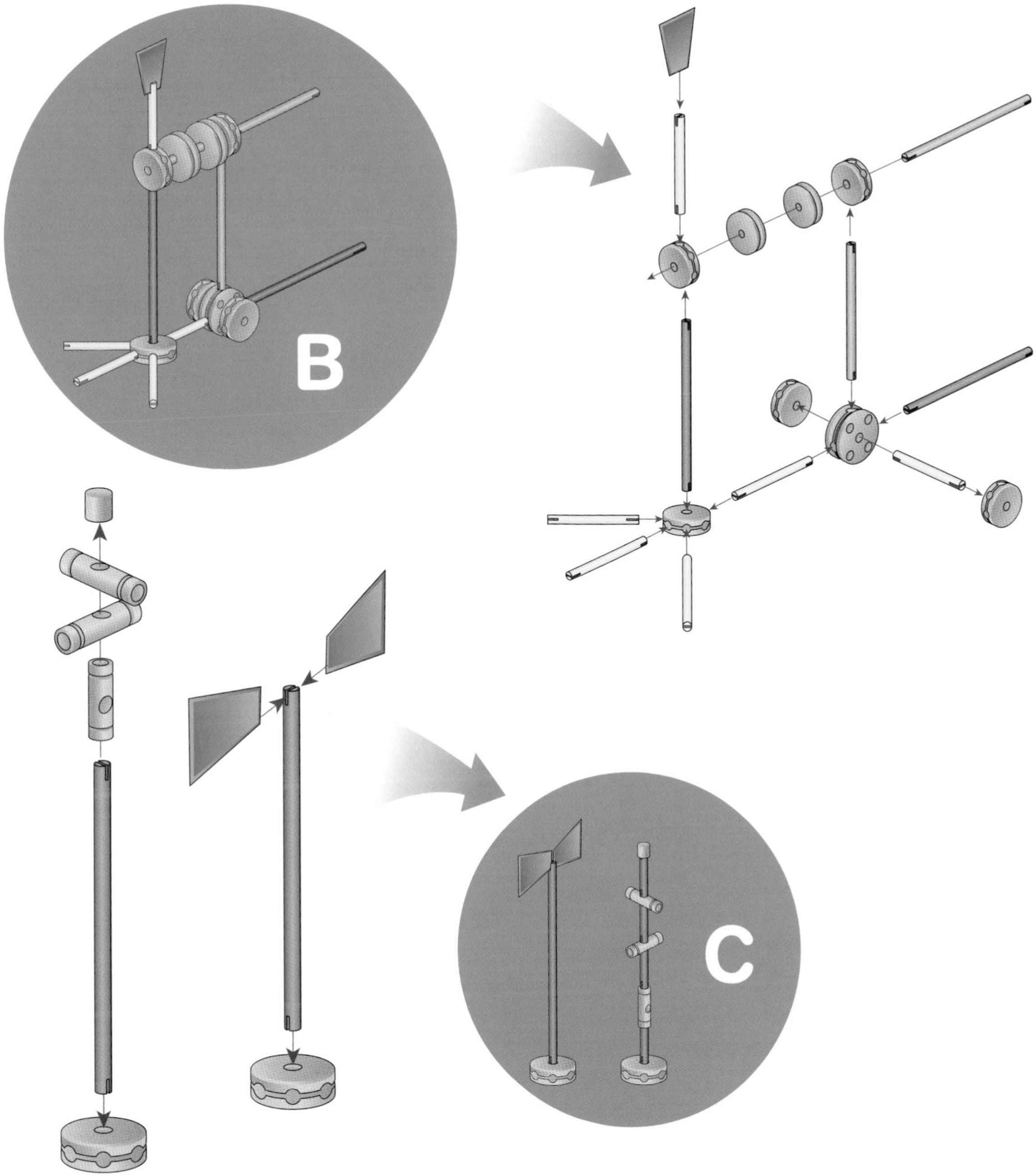
B
C

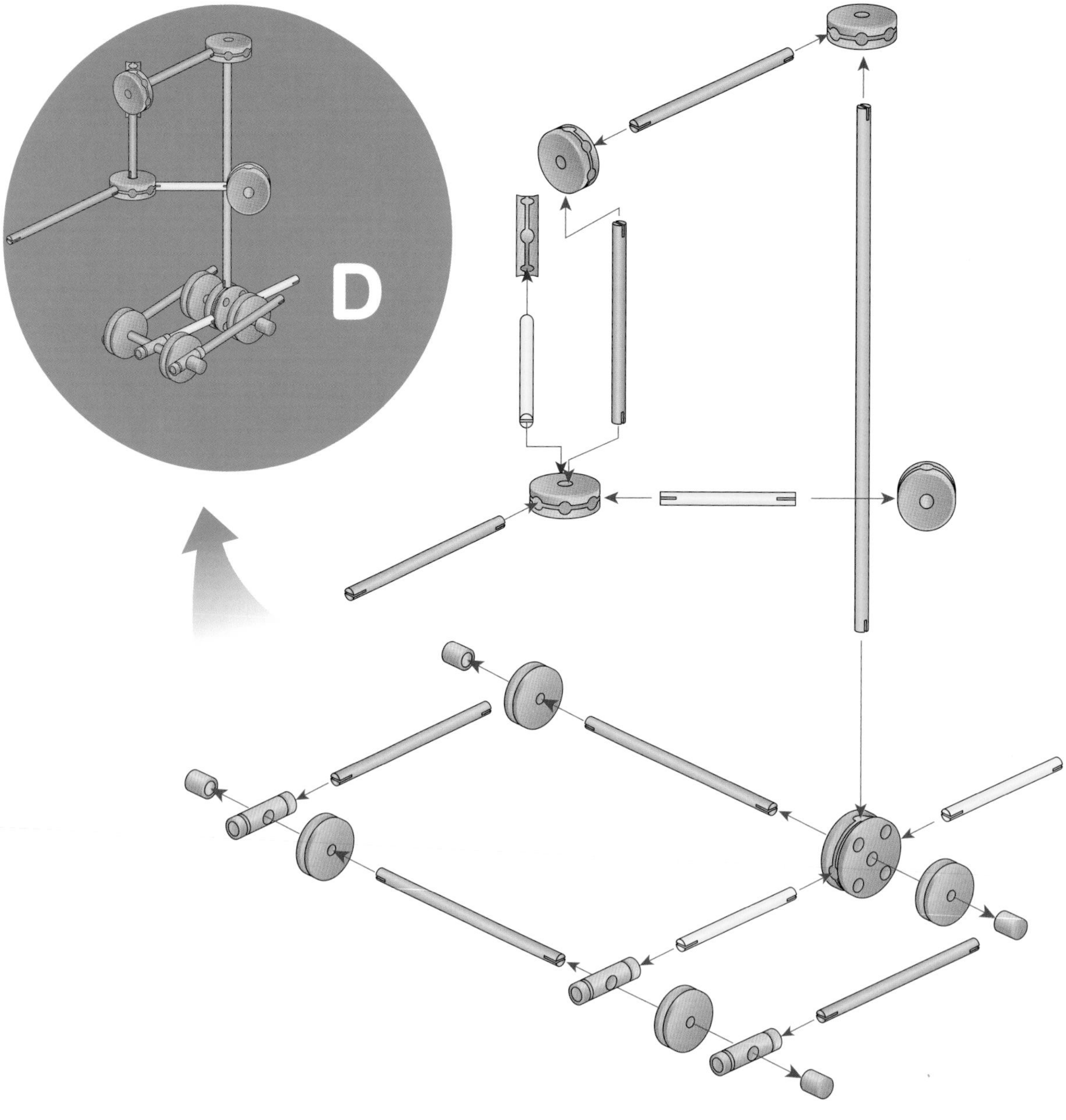
D

Pirate Ship

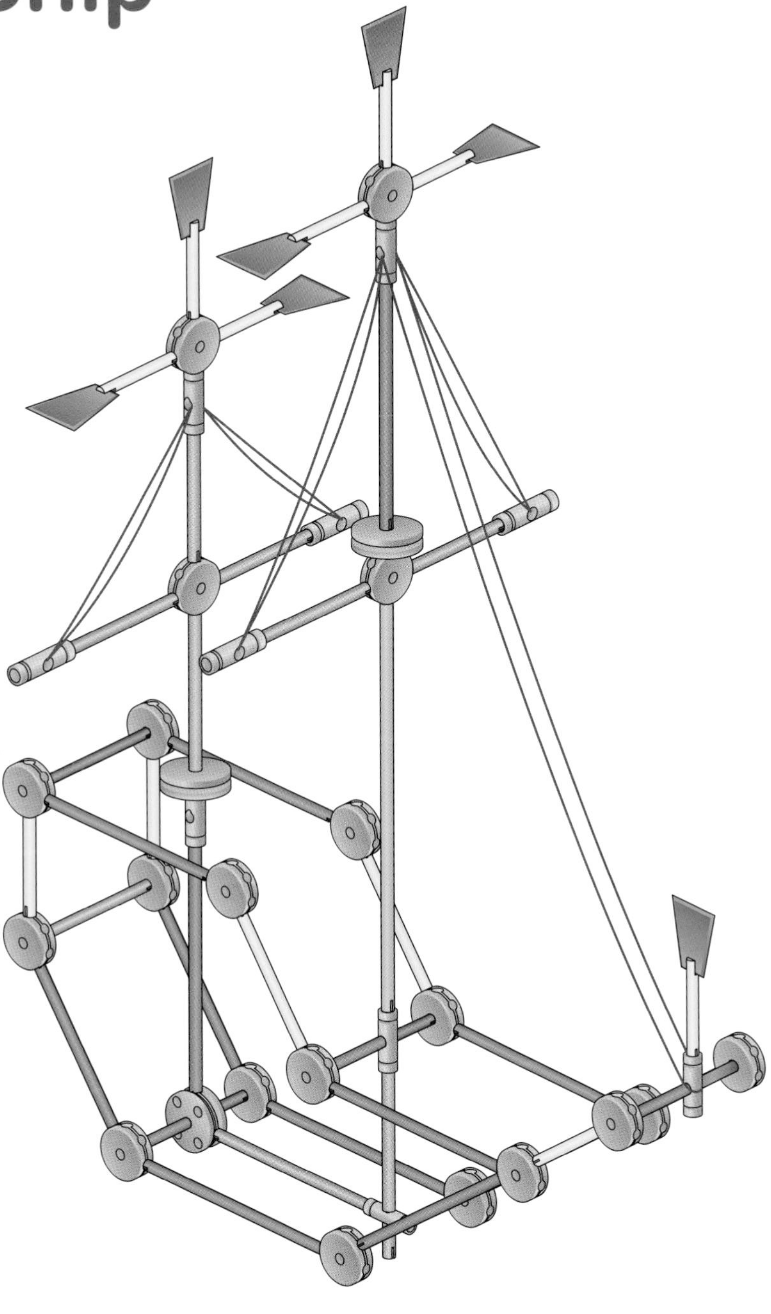

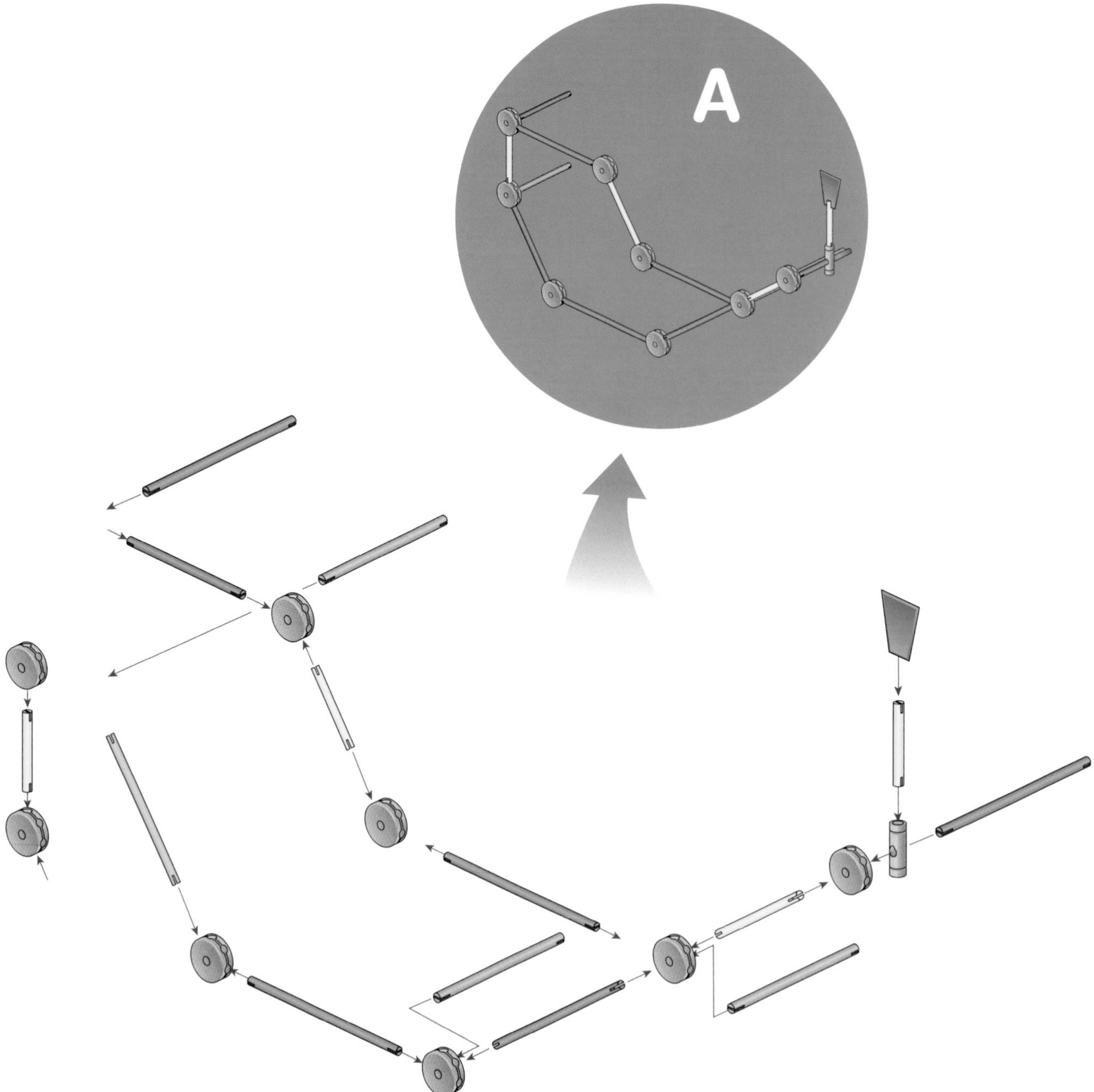
A

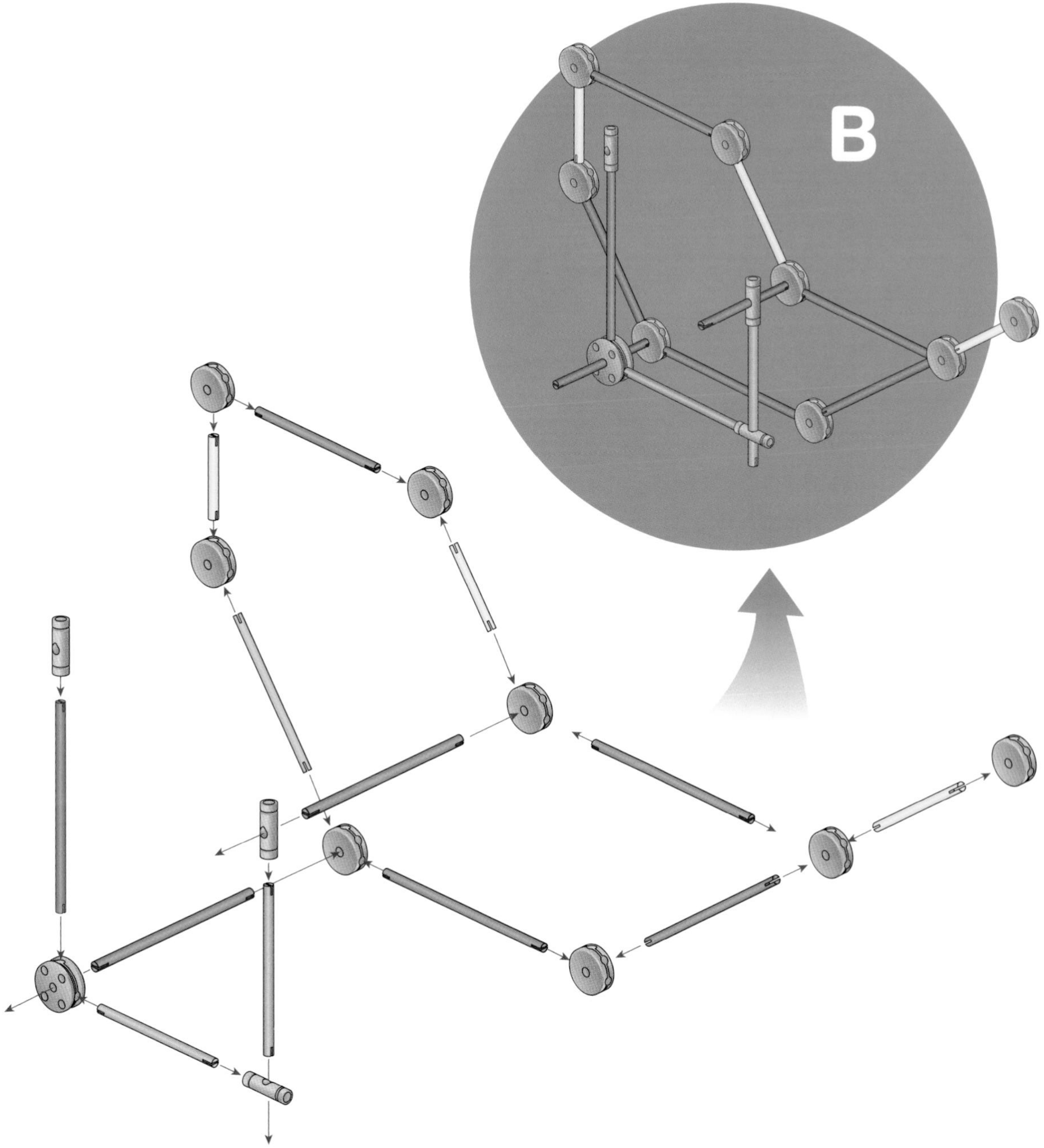
B

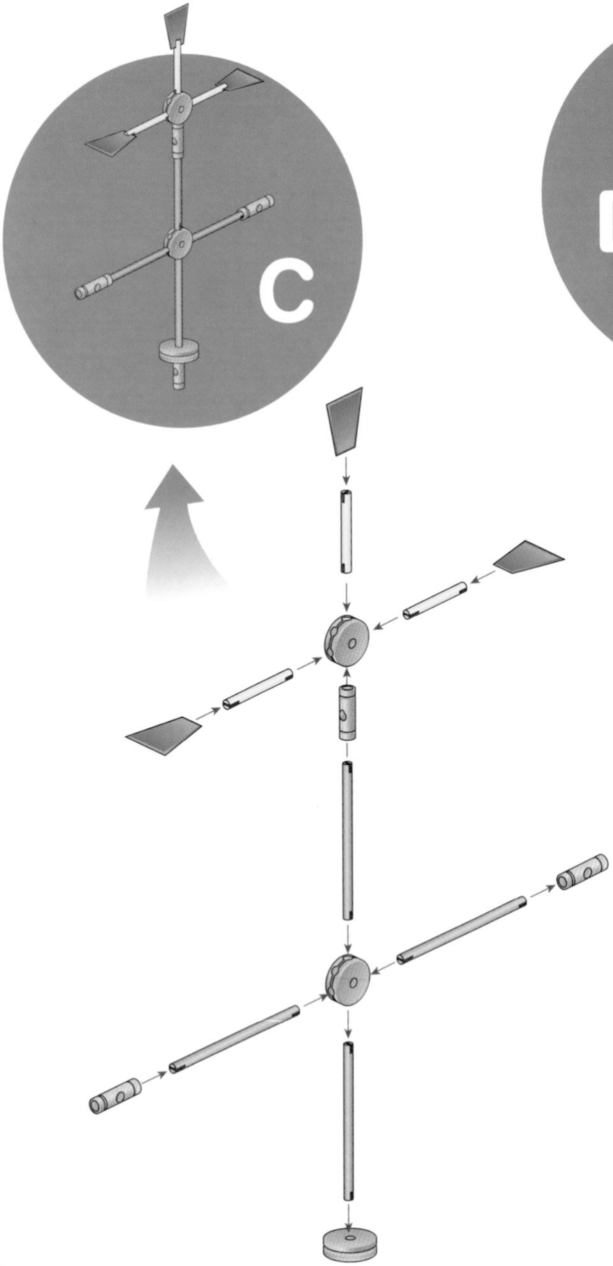
C

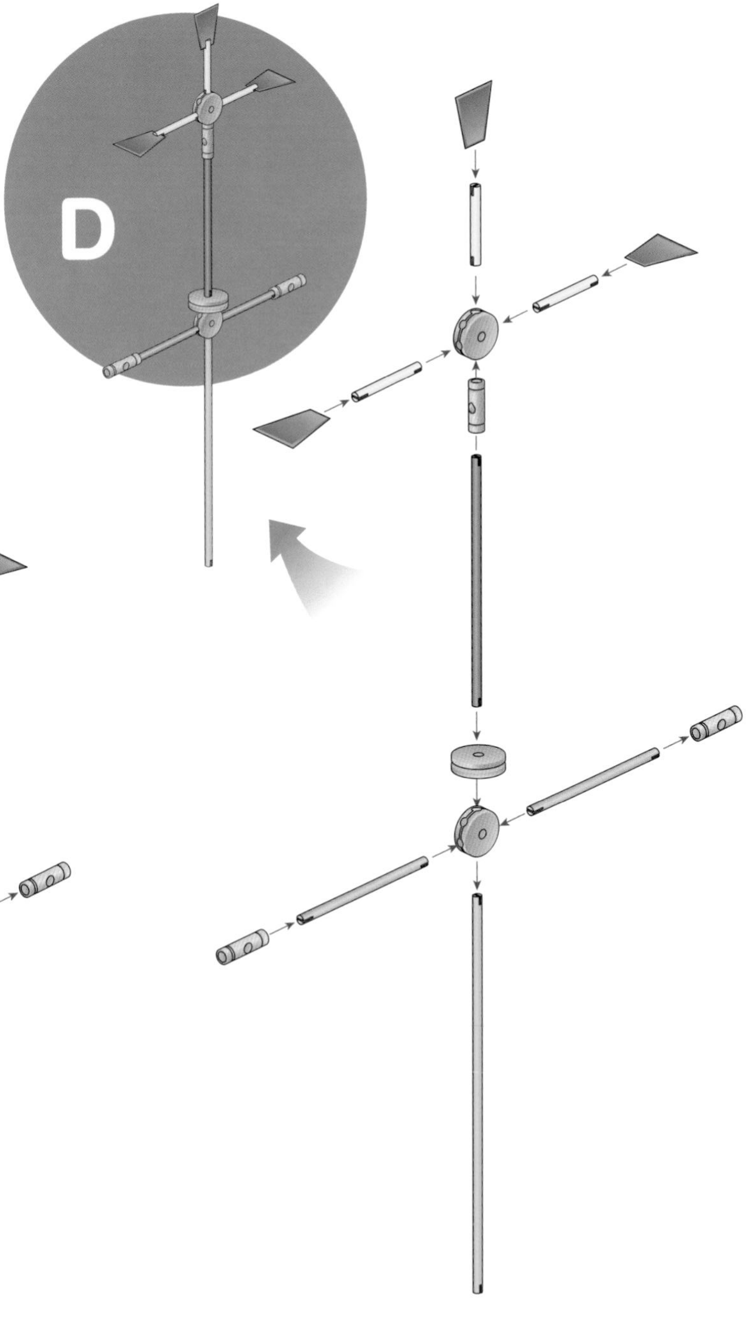
D

Fan Car

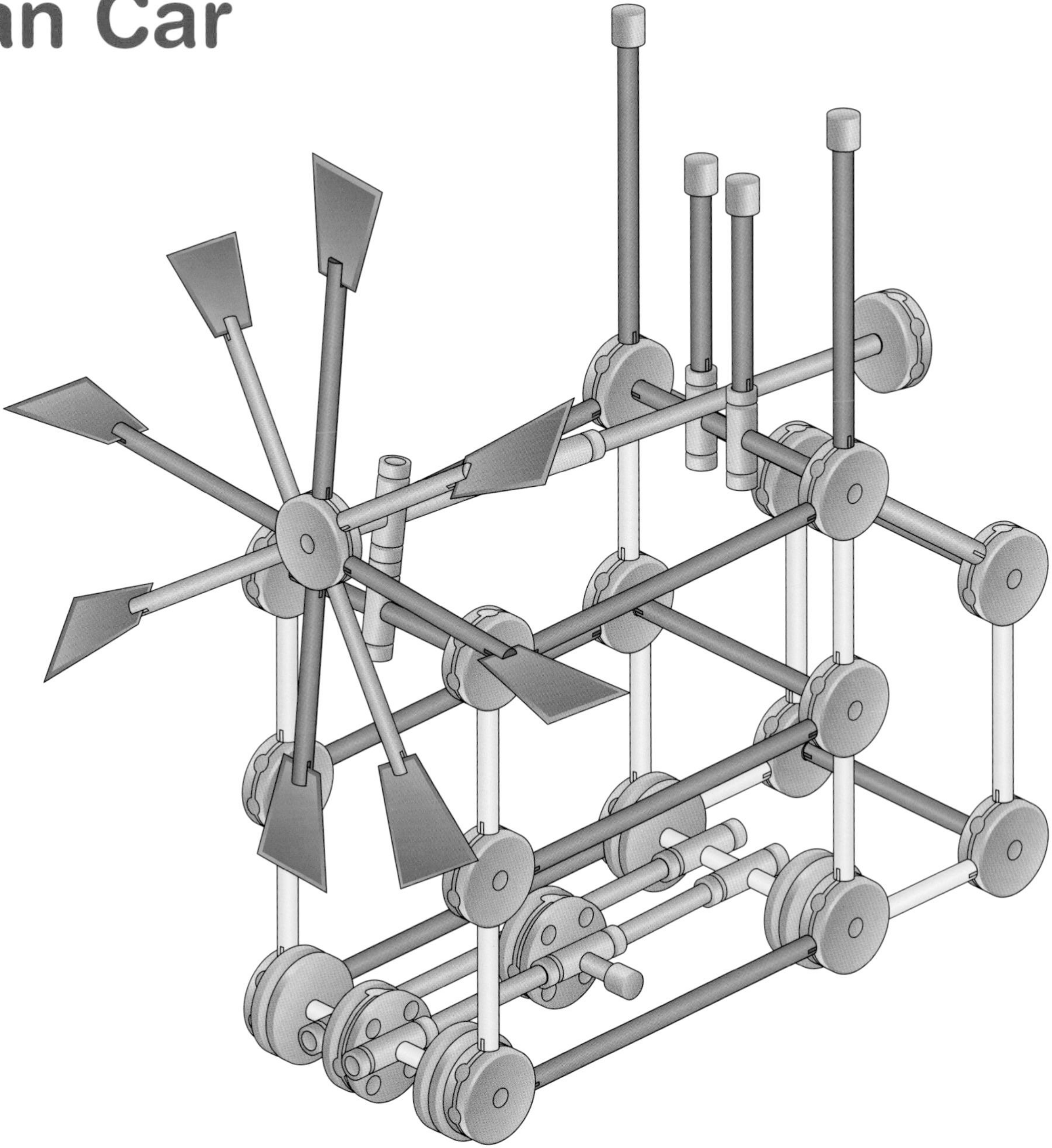

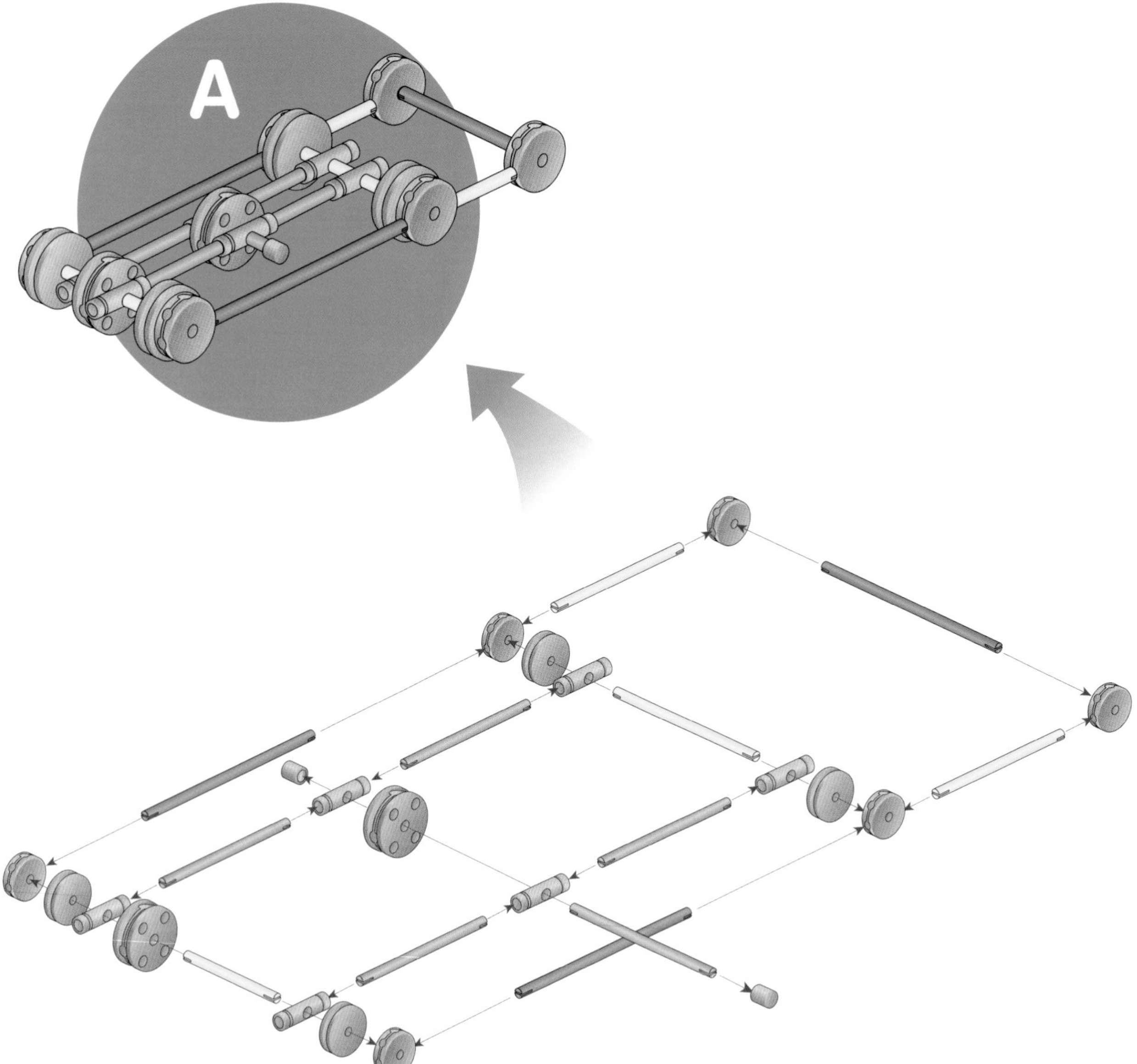
A

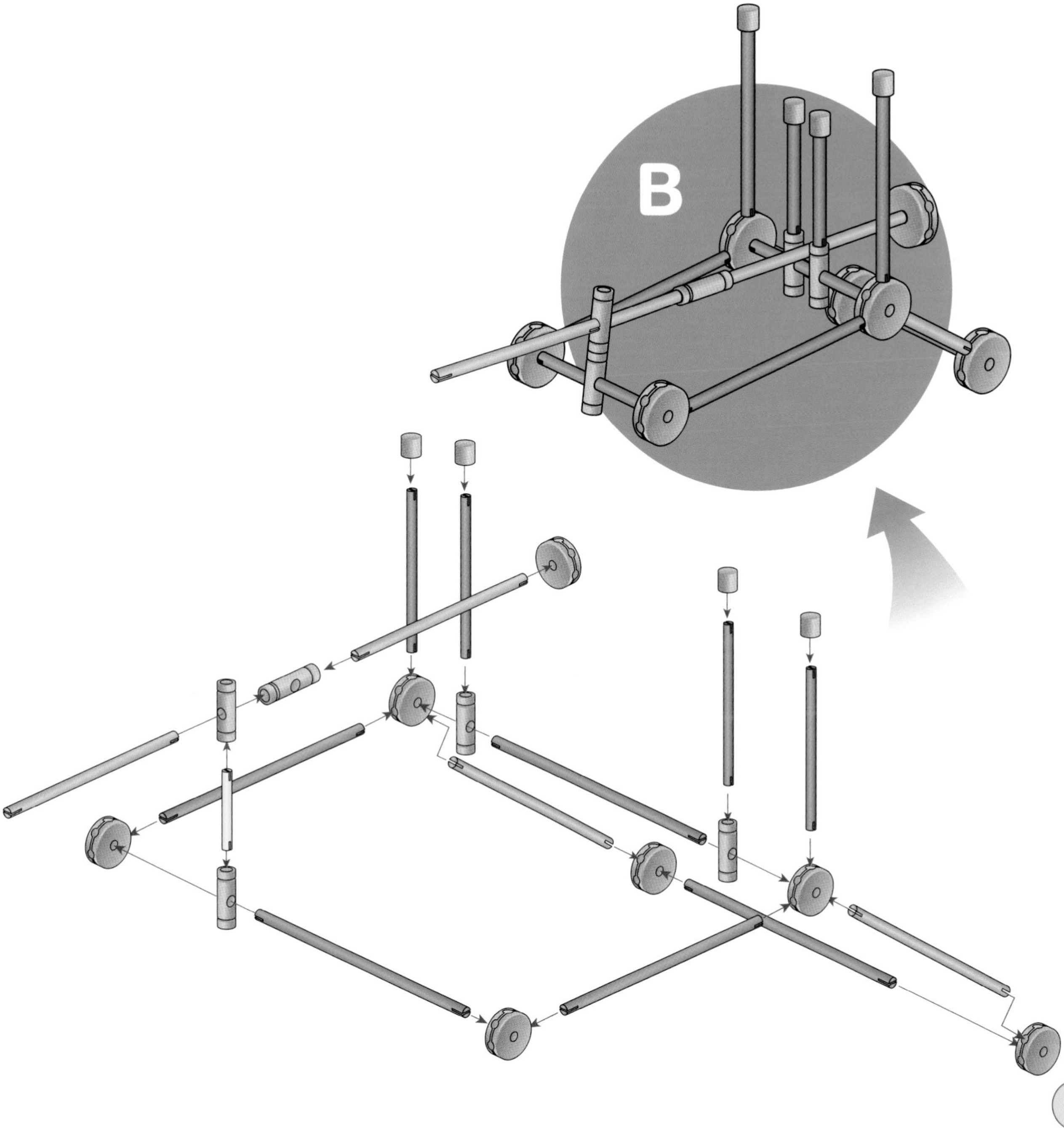
B

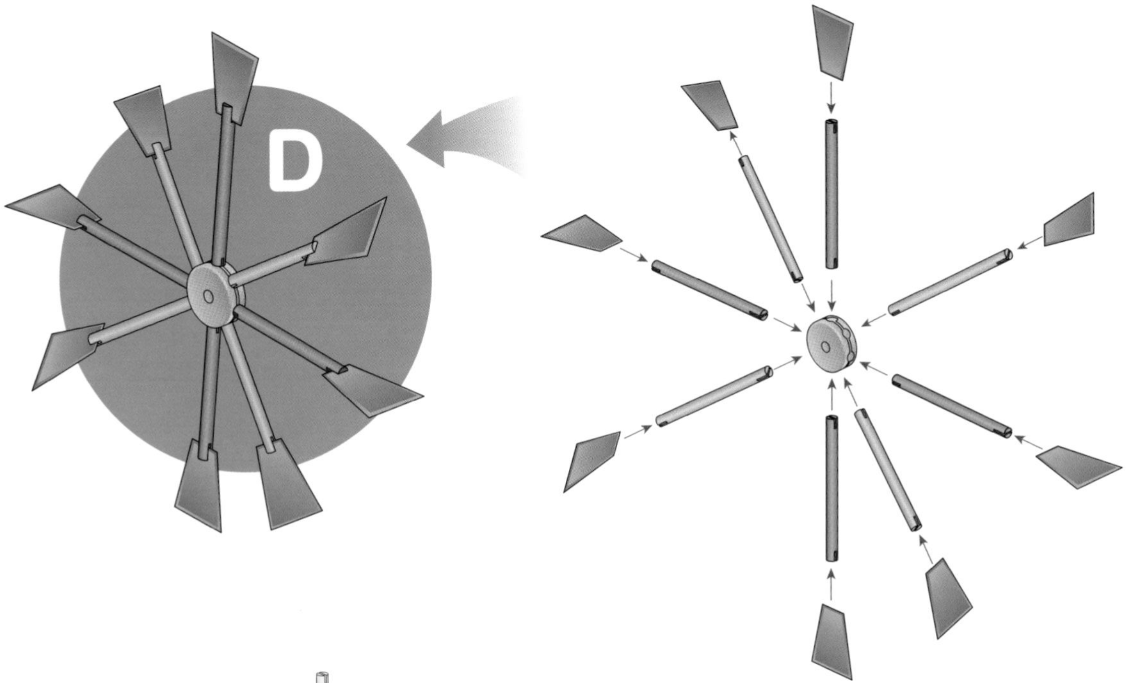
D

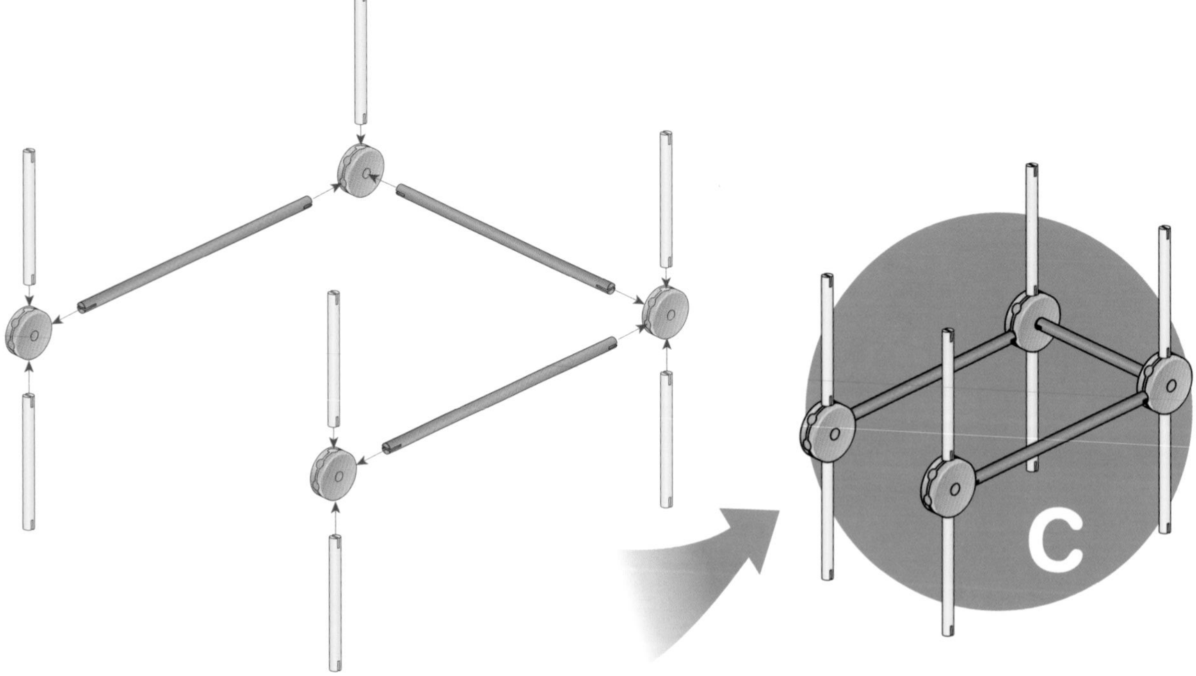
C

Elevator

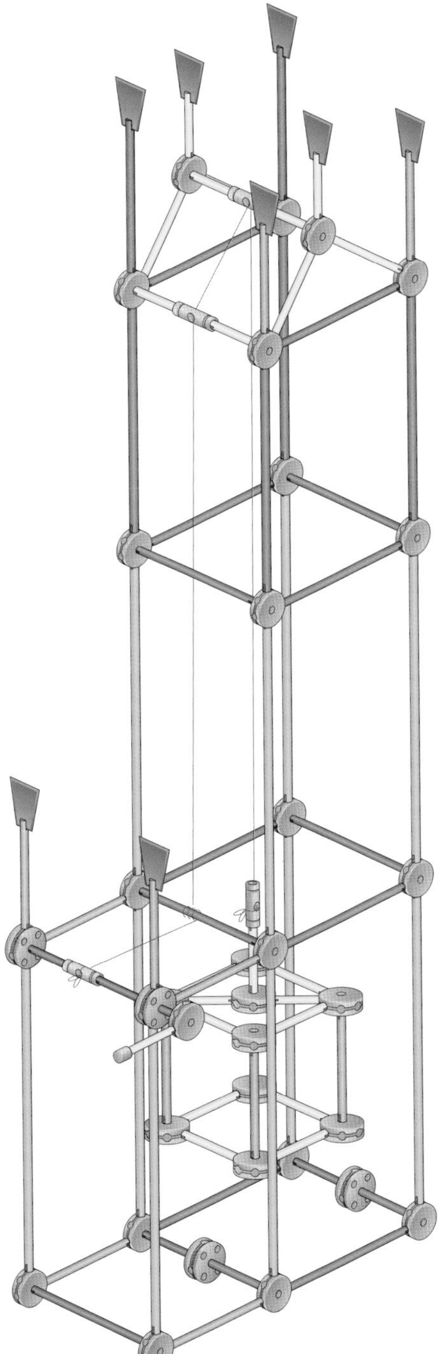

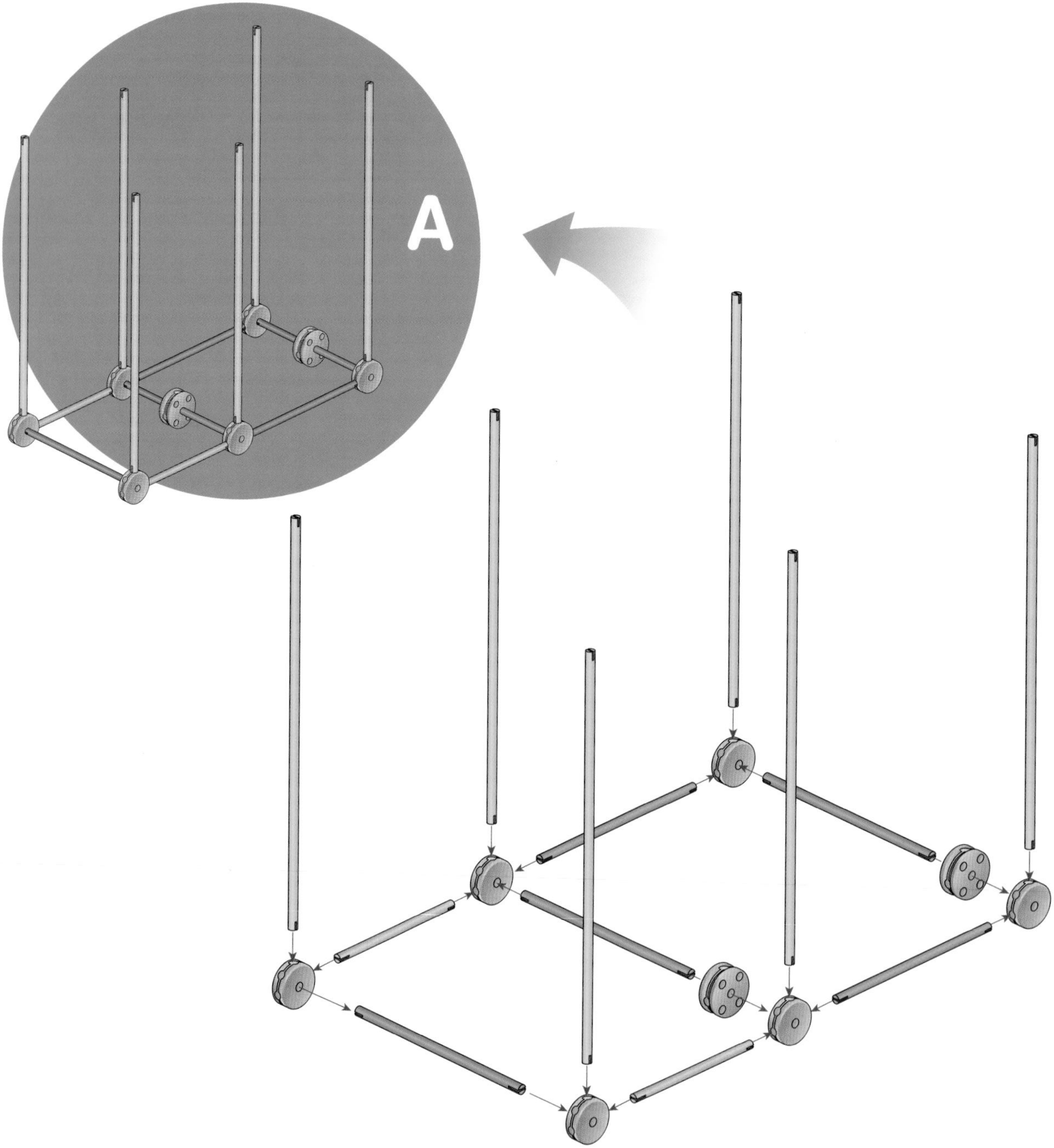
A

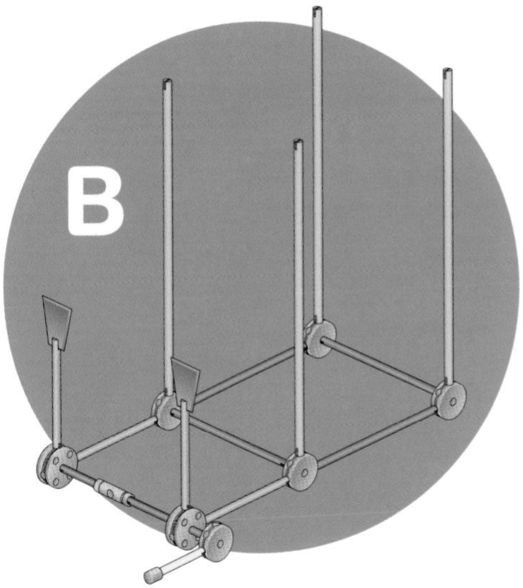
B

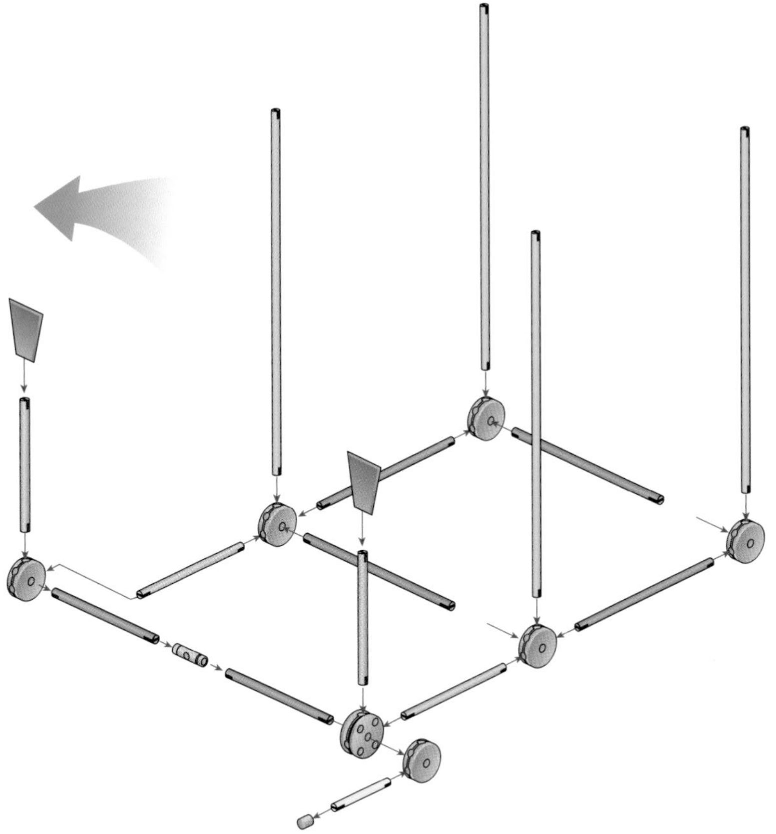

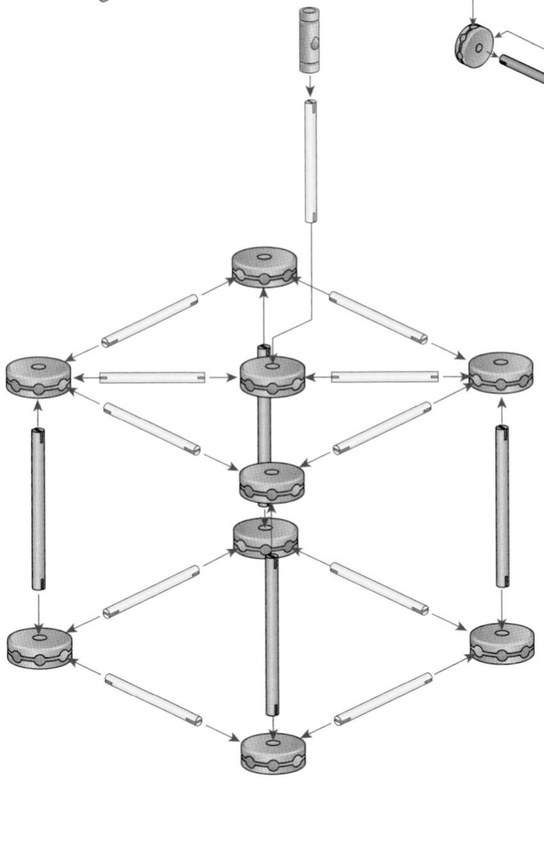

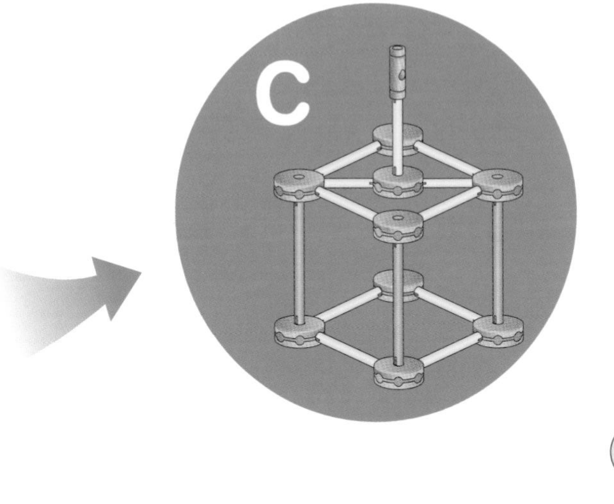
C

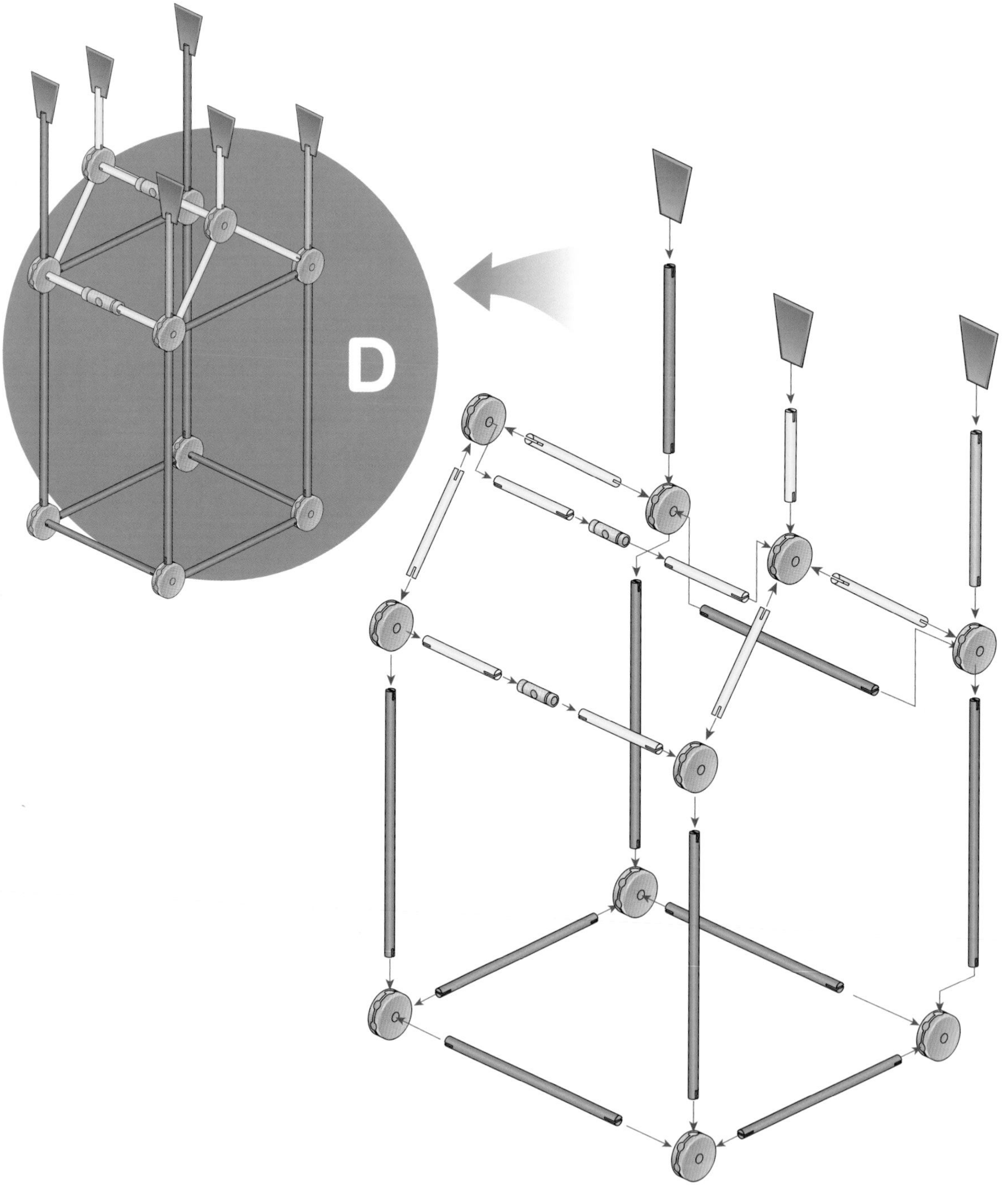
D

Crane

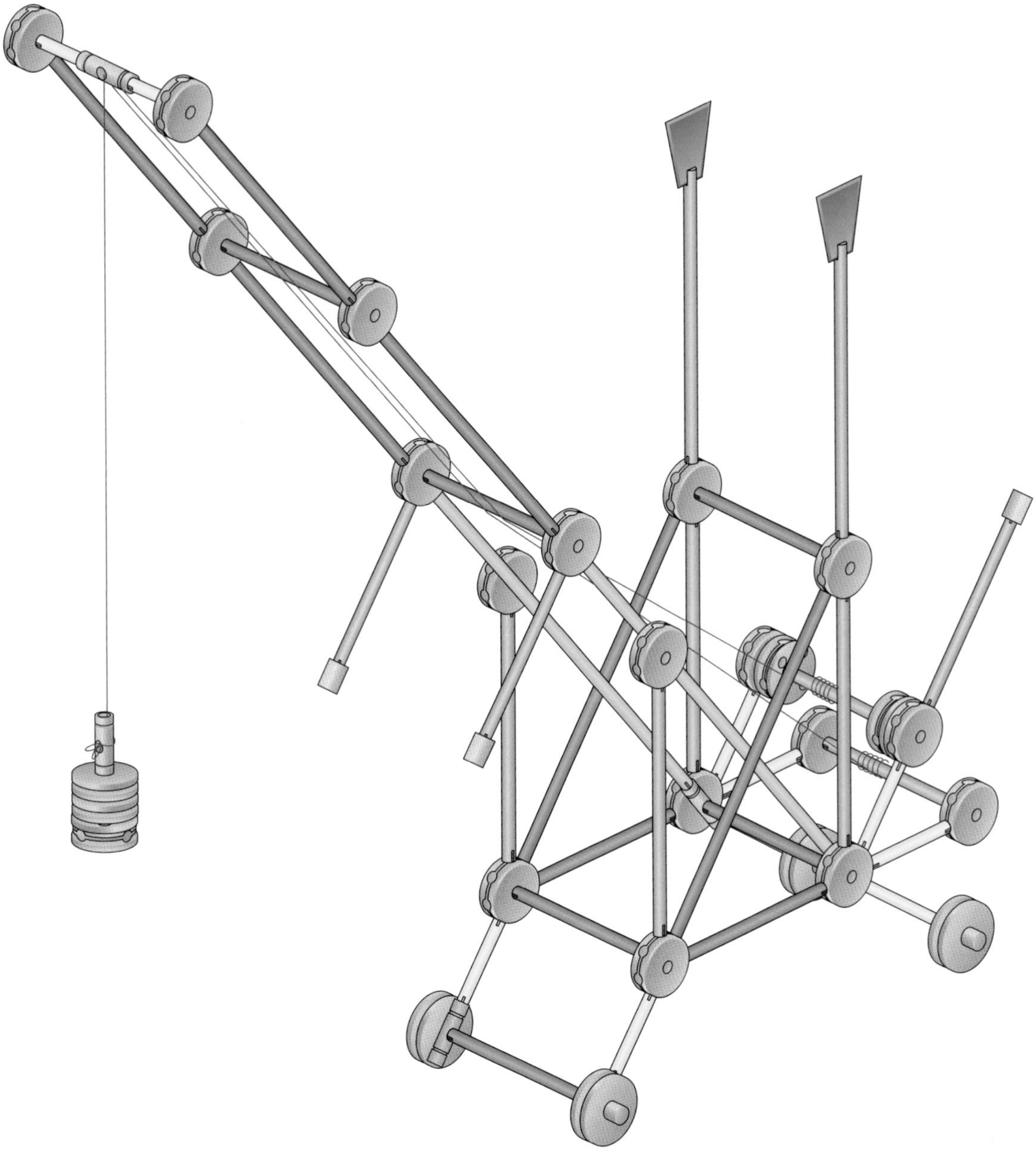

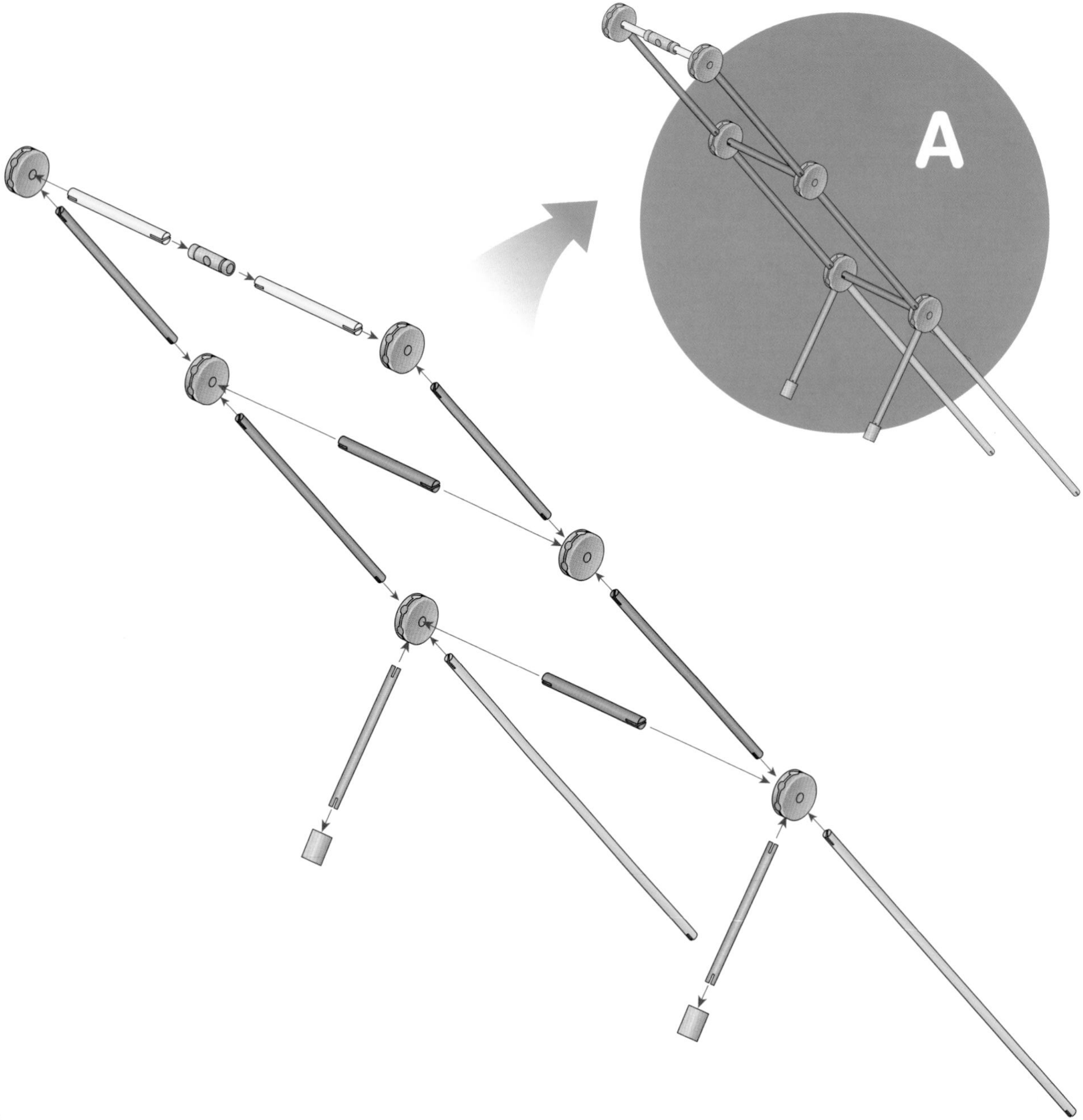
A

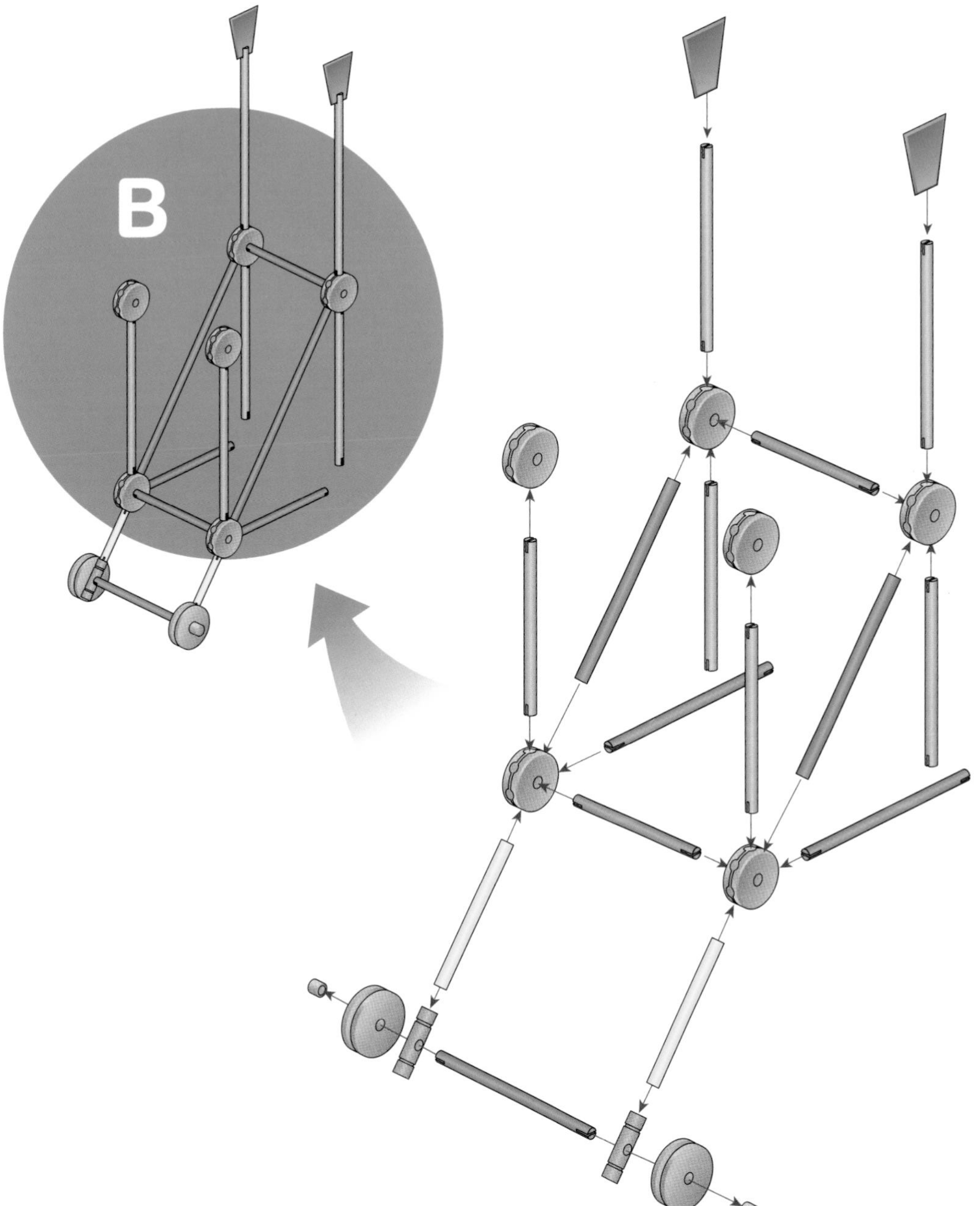
B

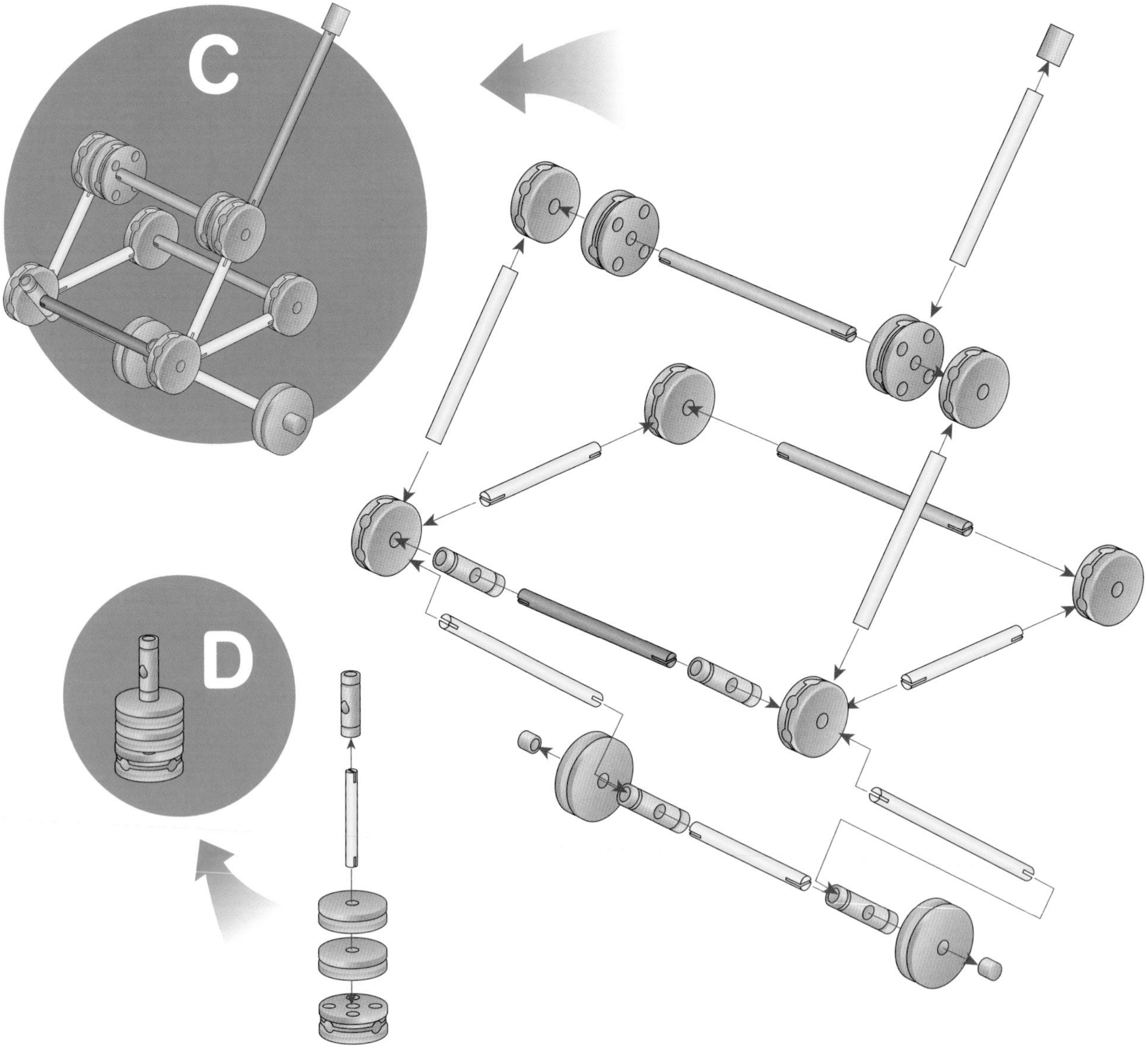
C
D

Scorpion

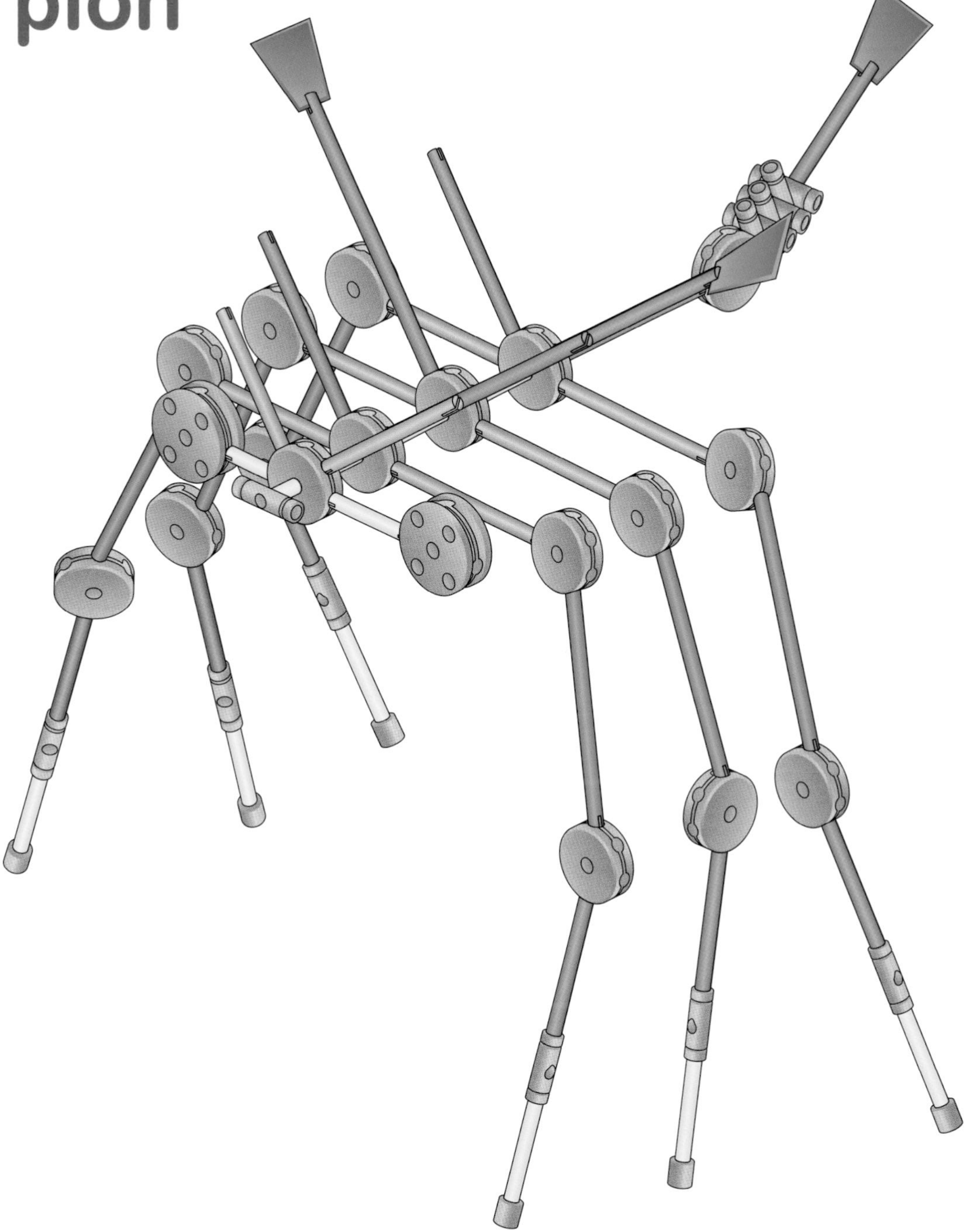

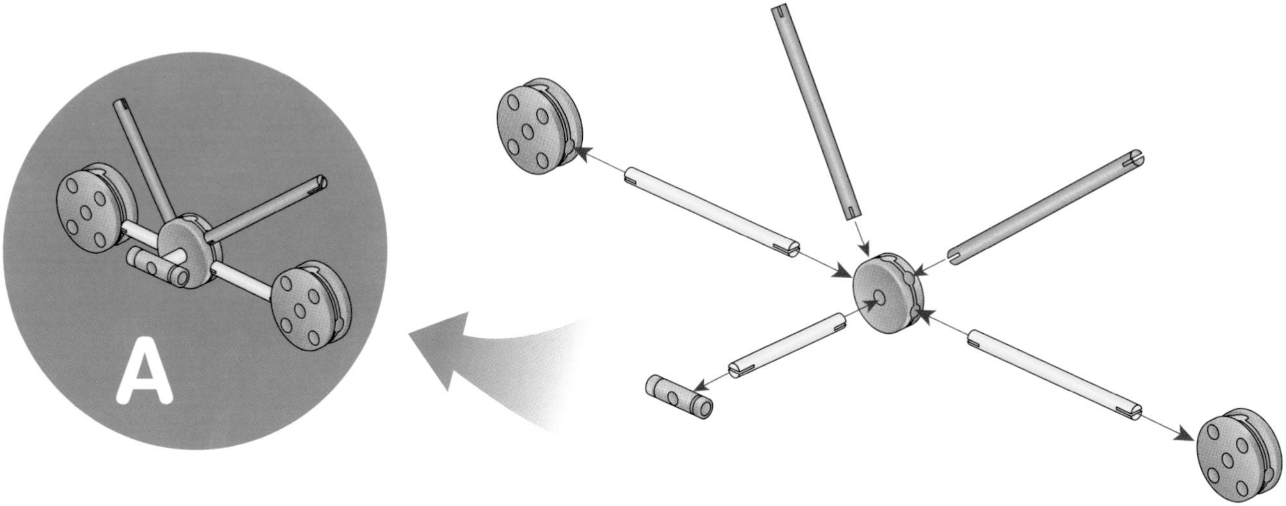
A

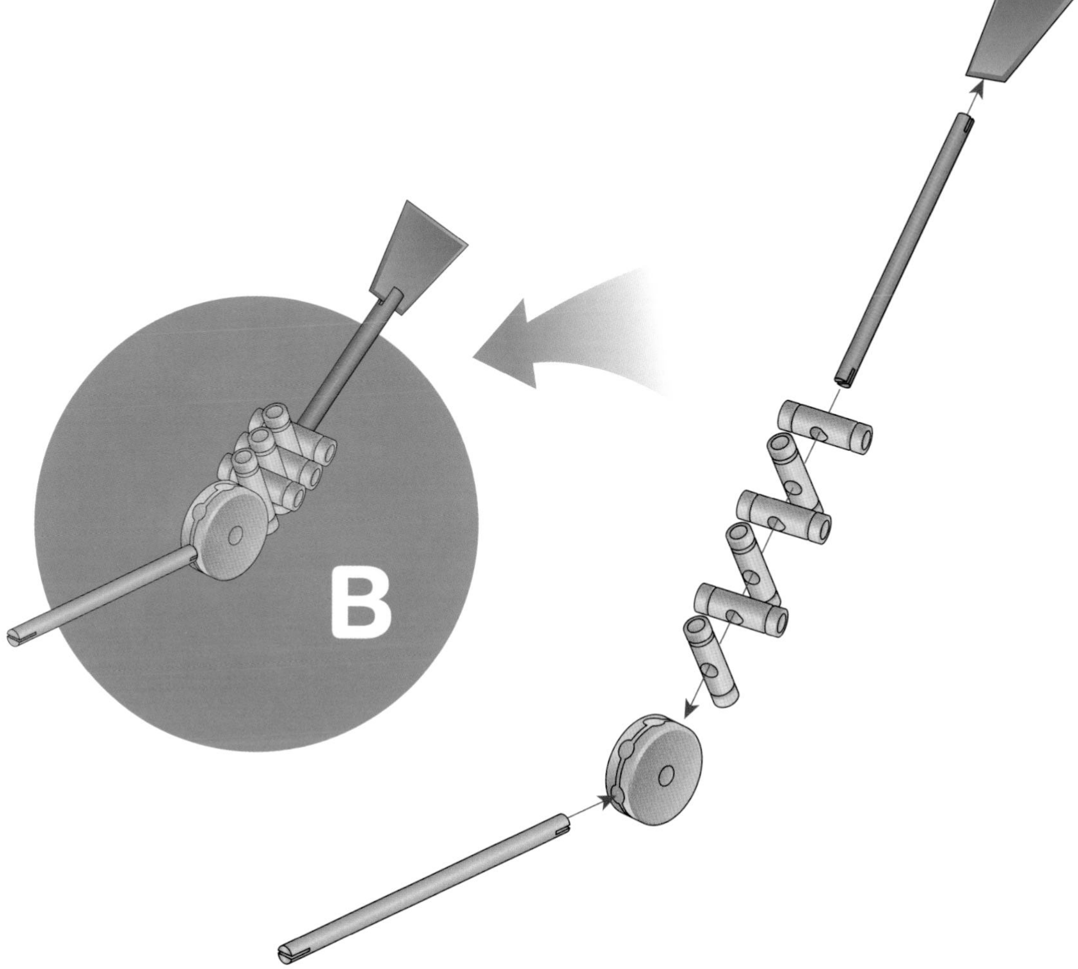
B

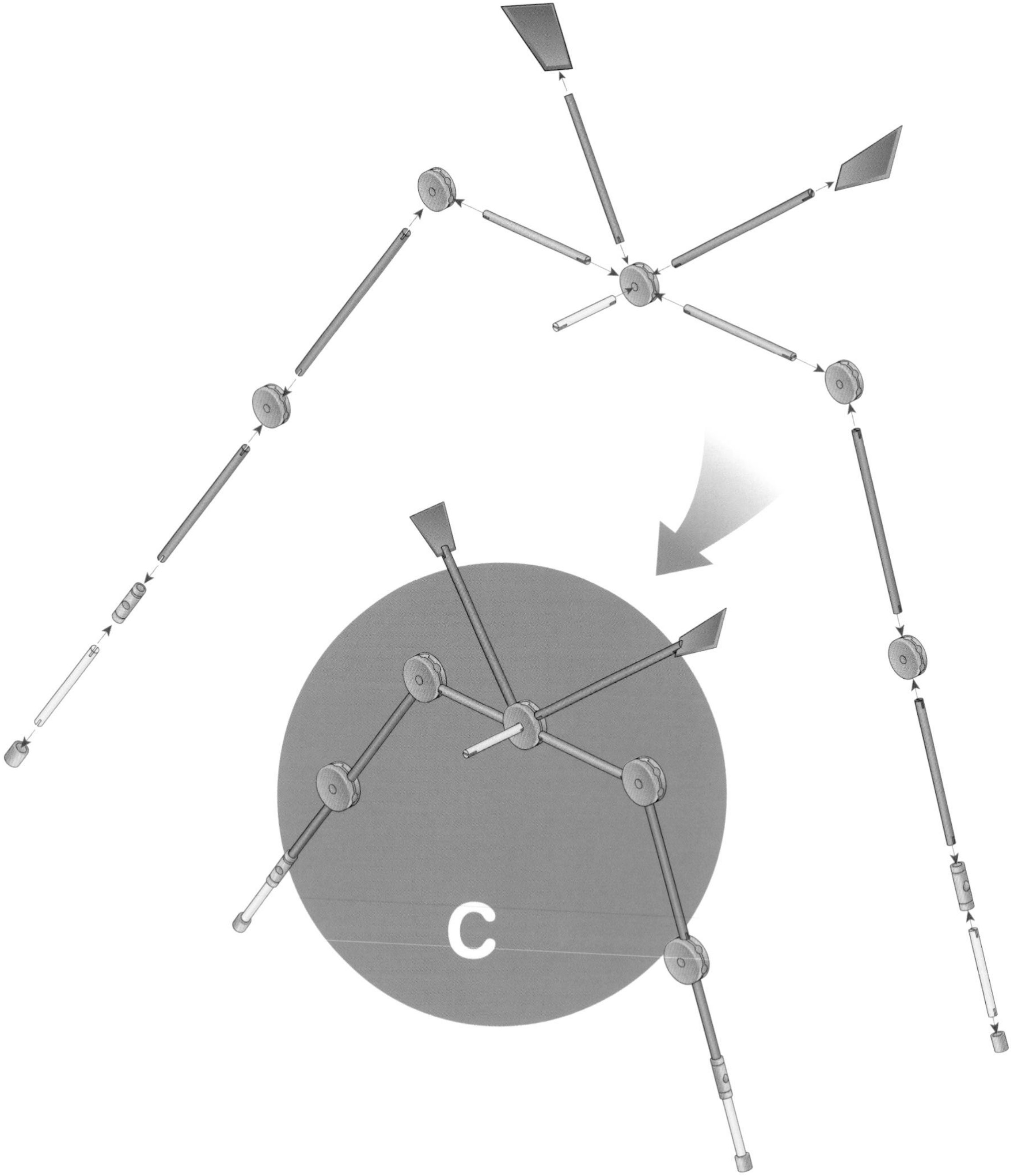
C

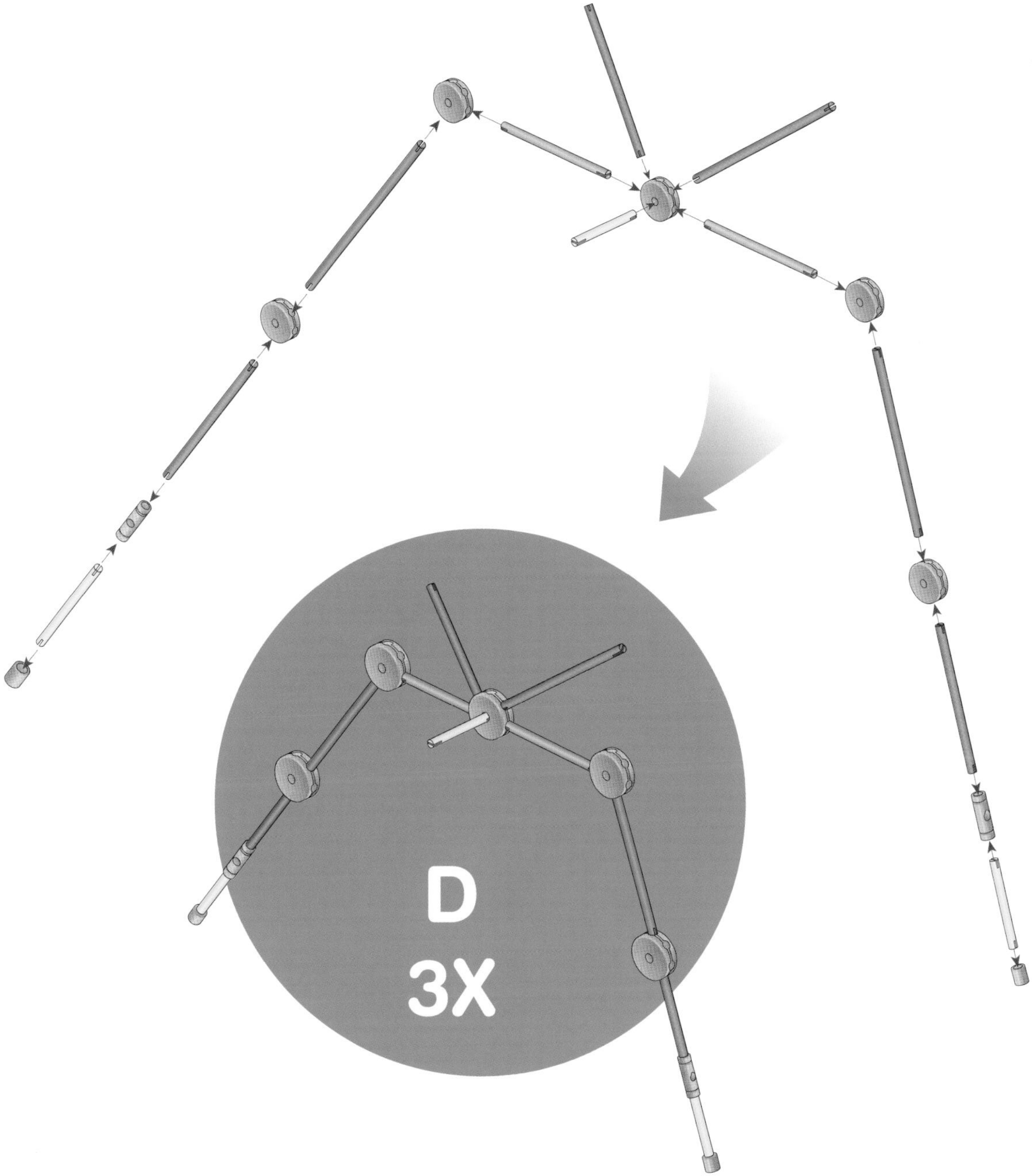
D
3X

Space Buggy

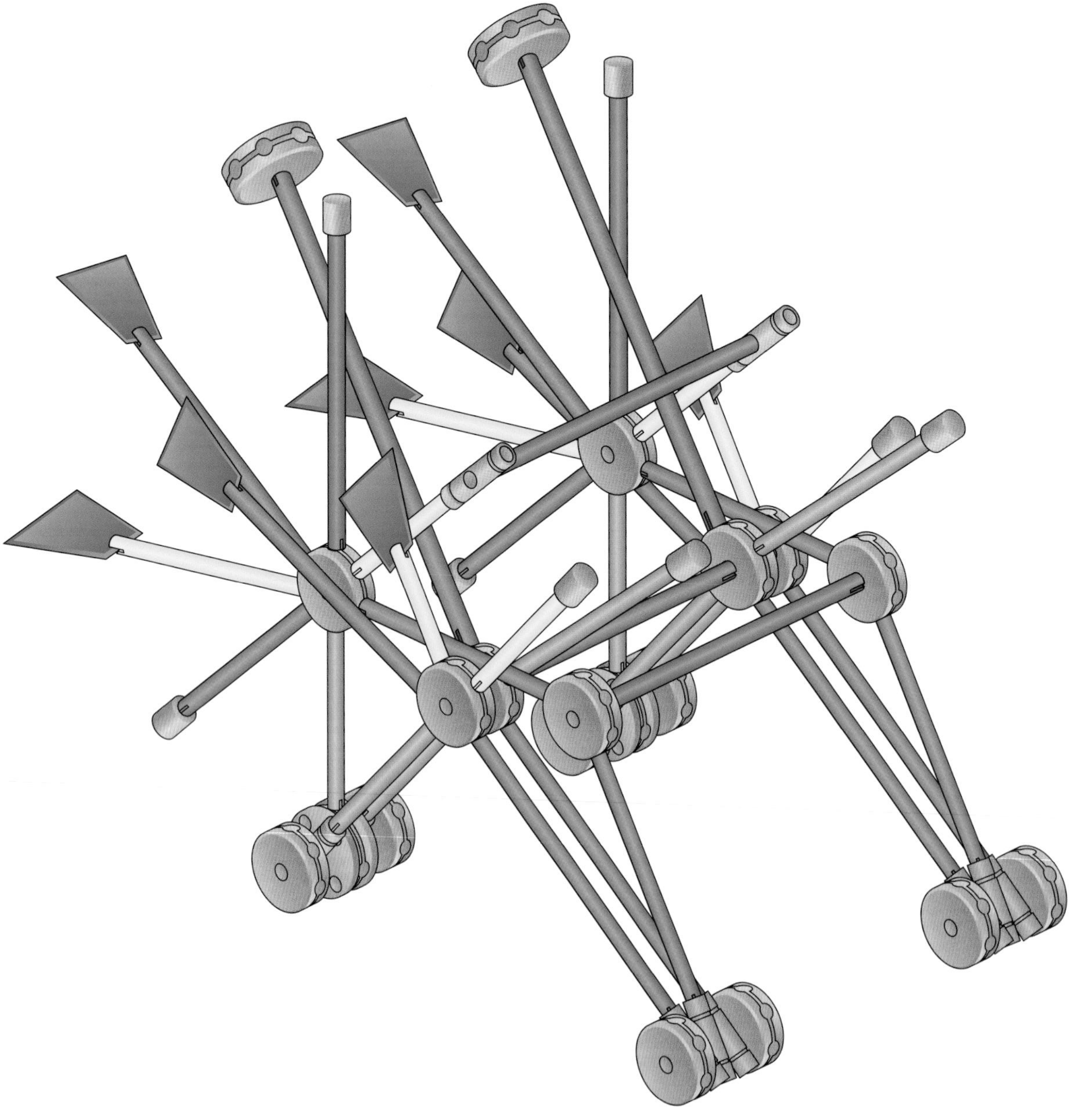

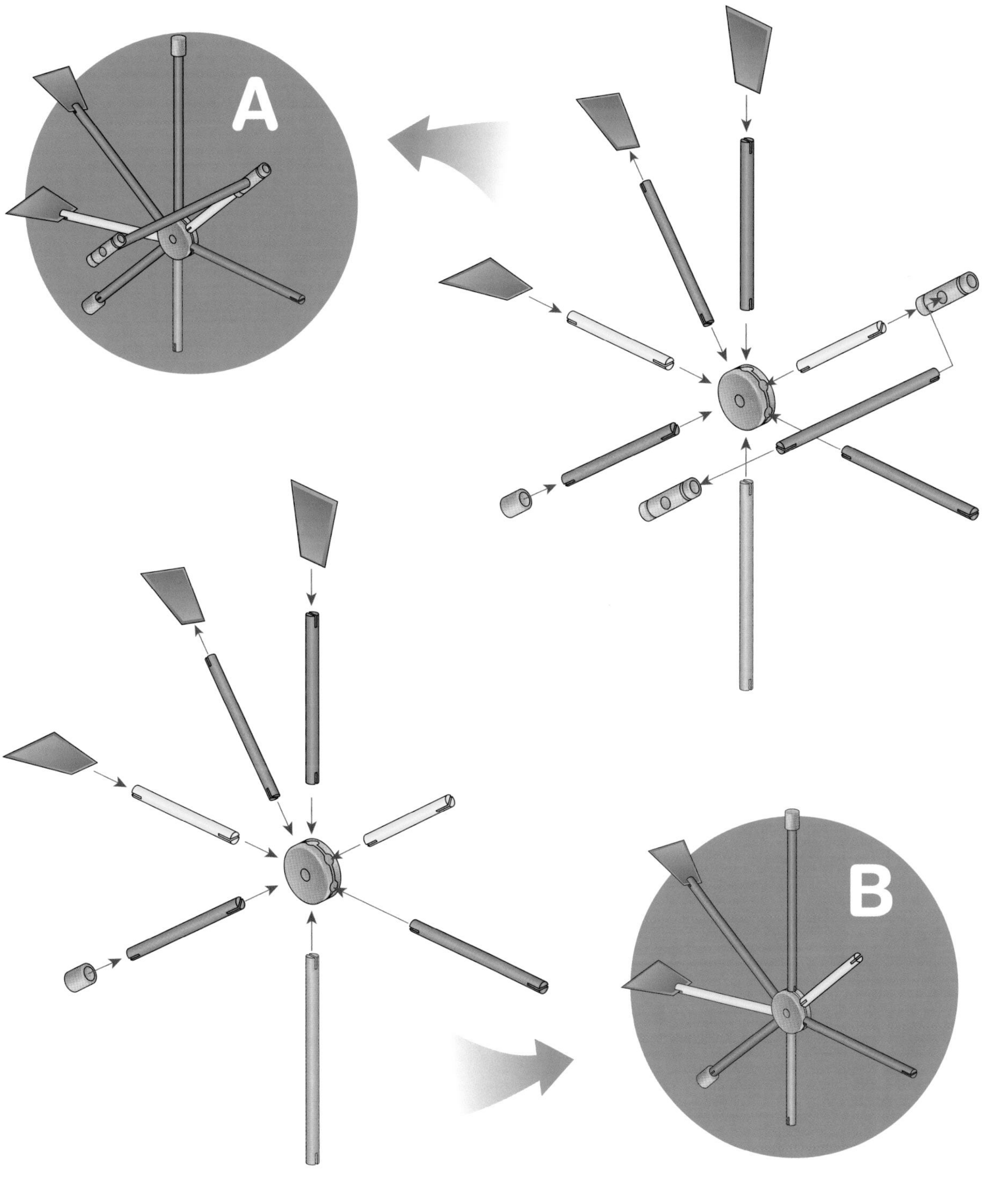
A
B

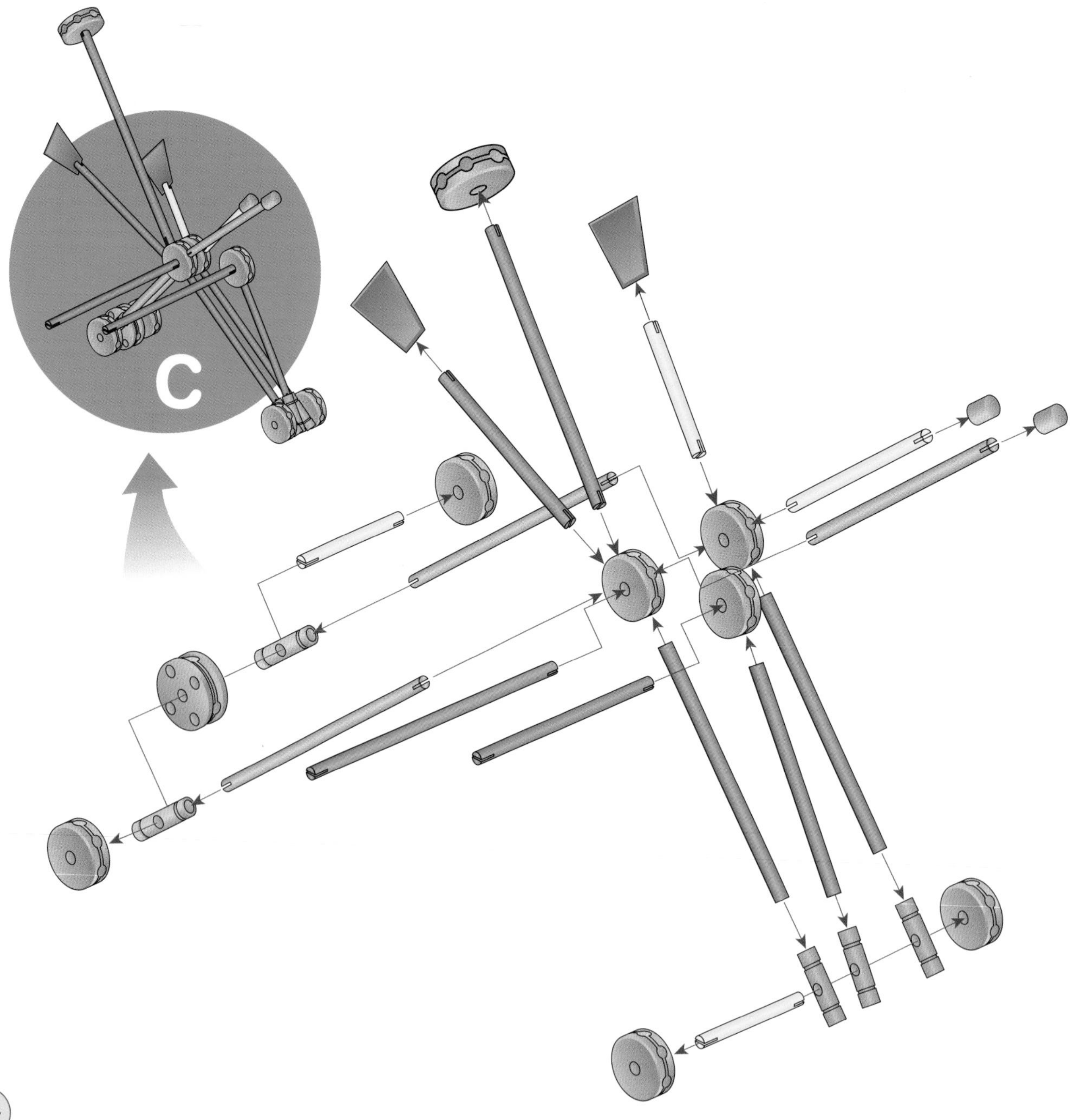
C

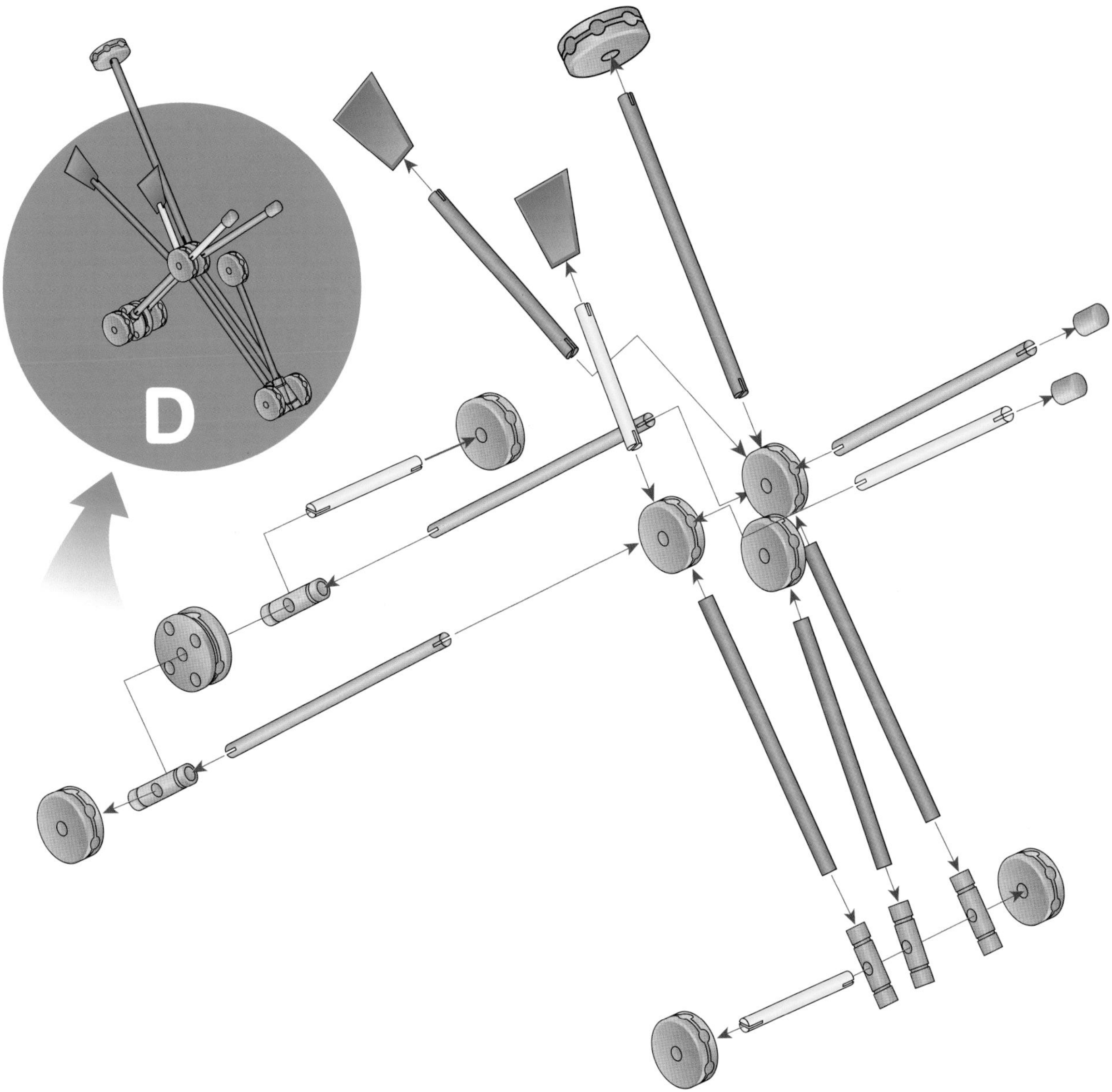
D

Space Alien

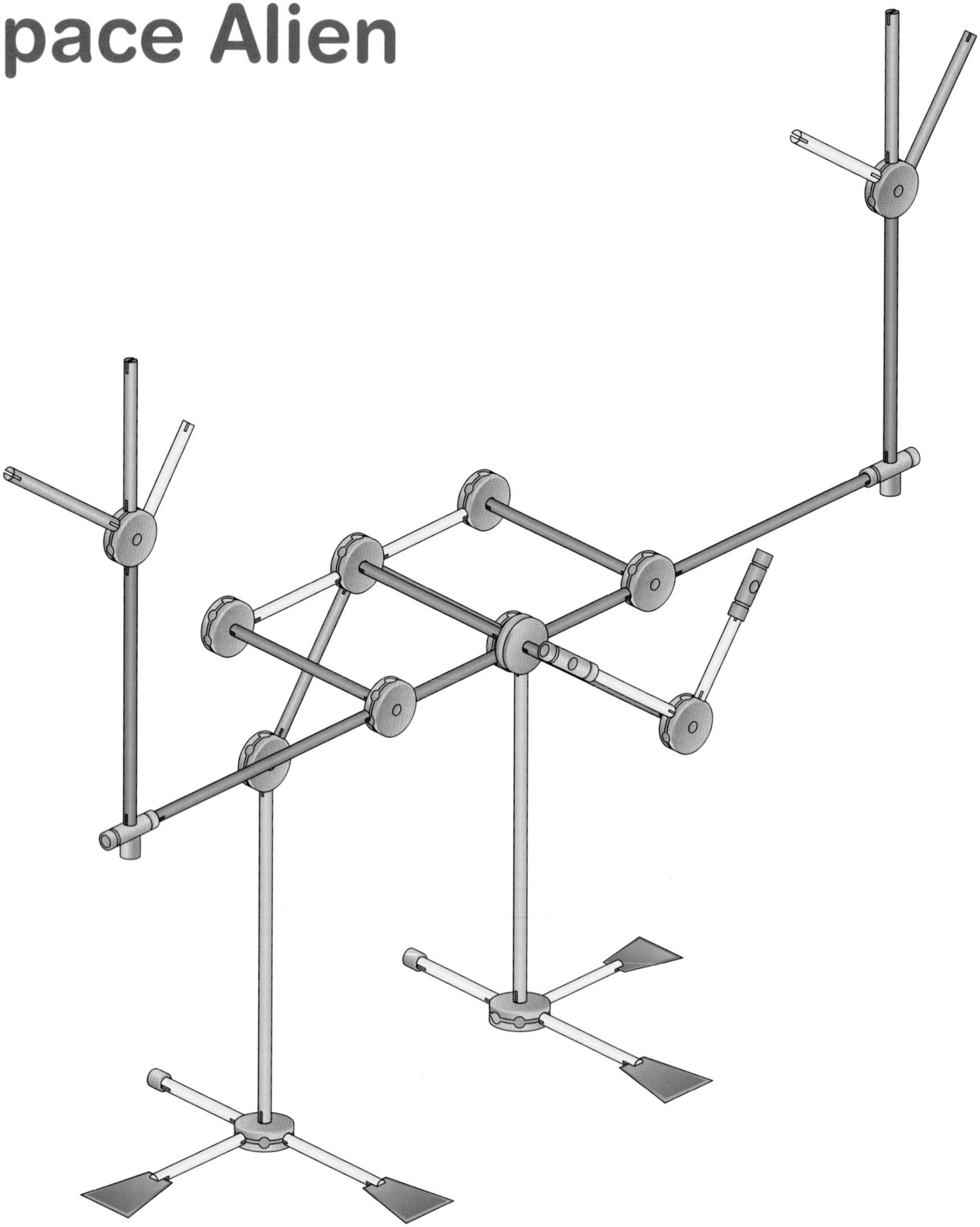

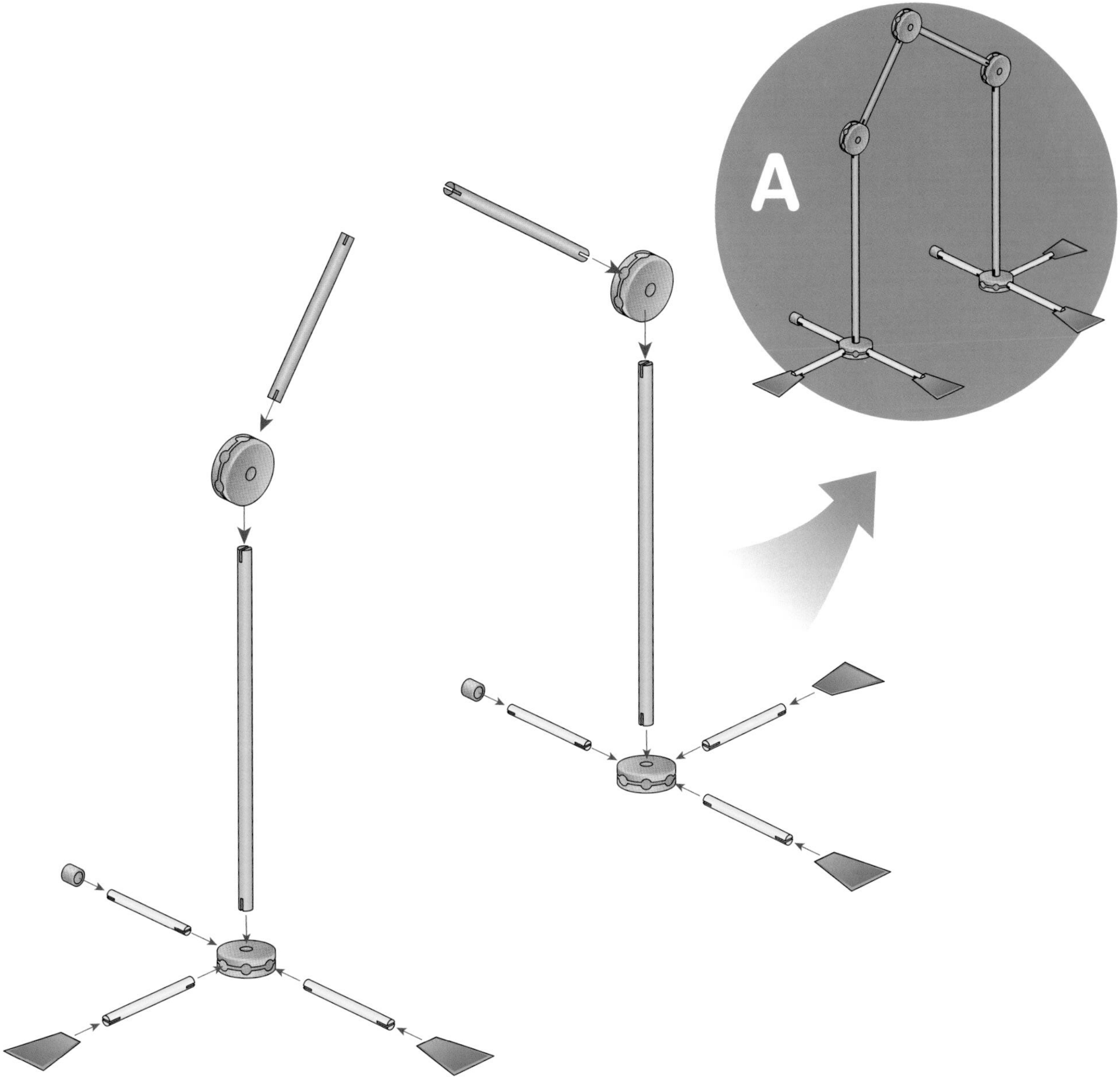
A

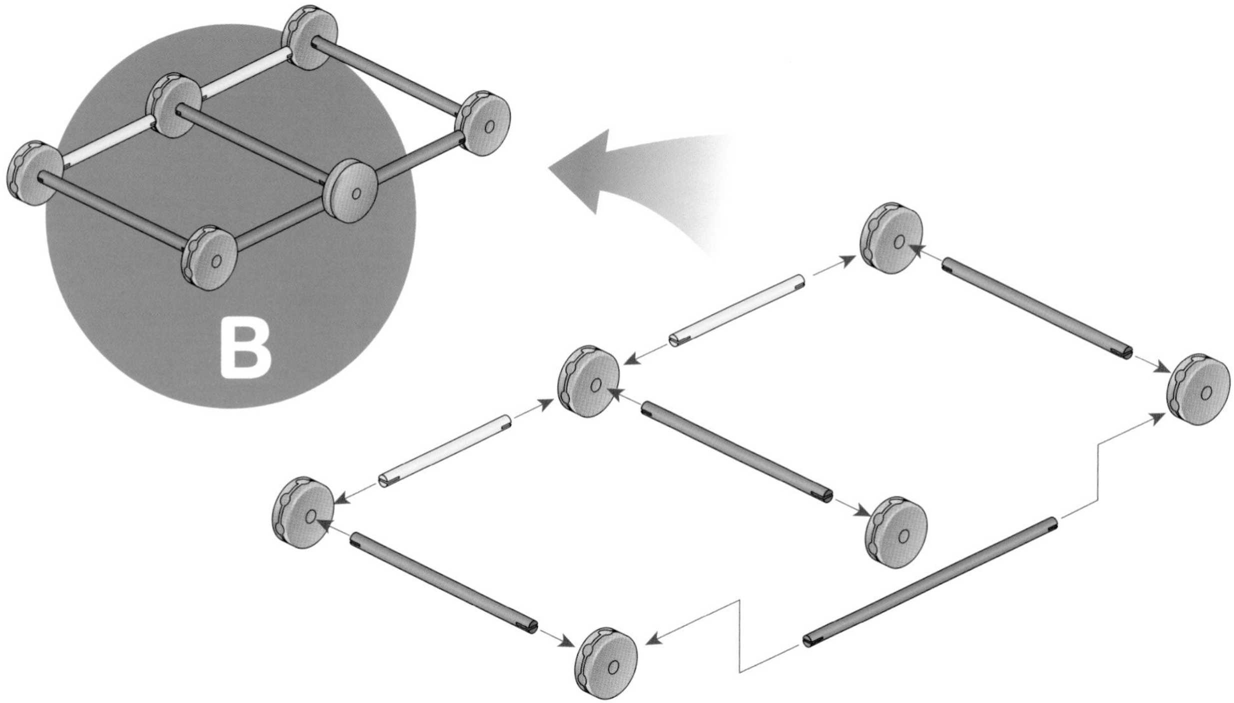
B

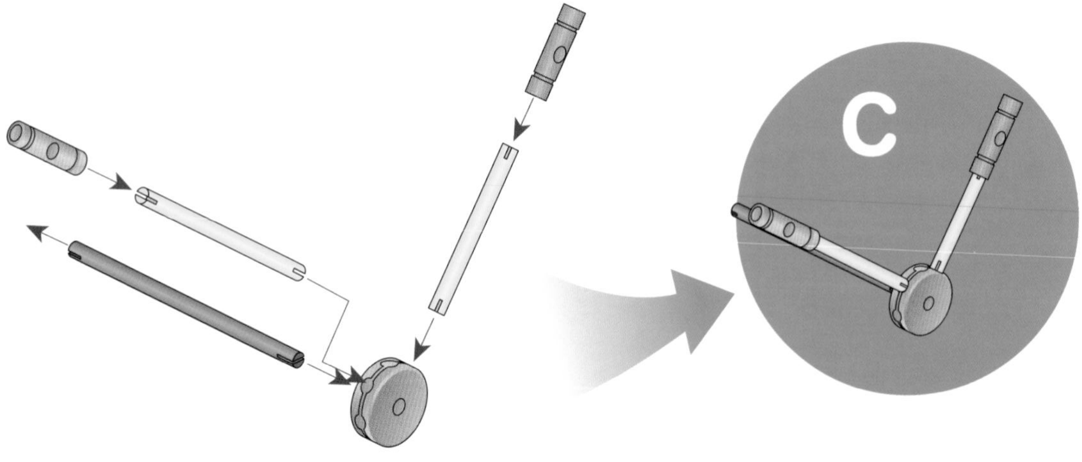
C

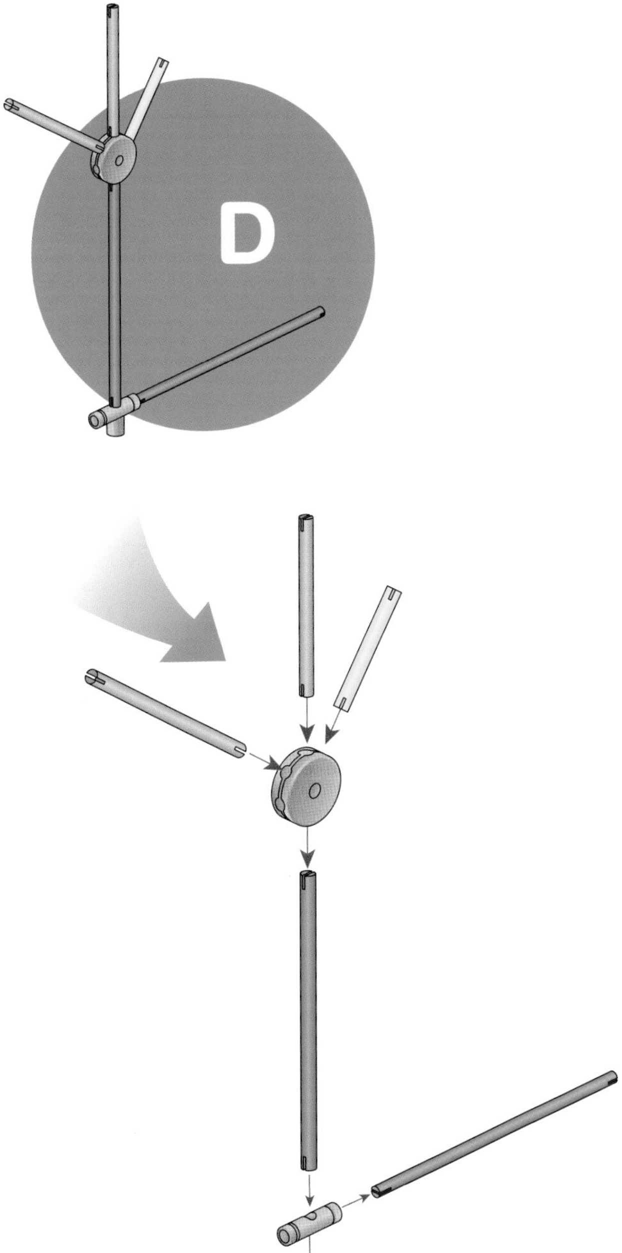
D

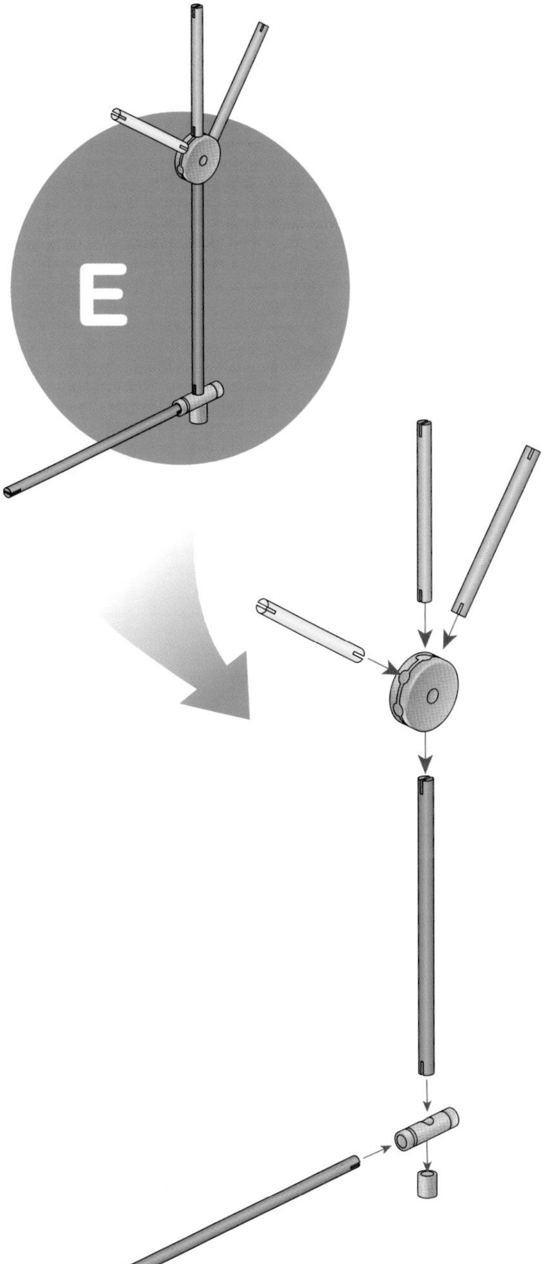
E

Flower Garden

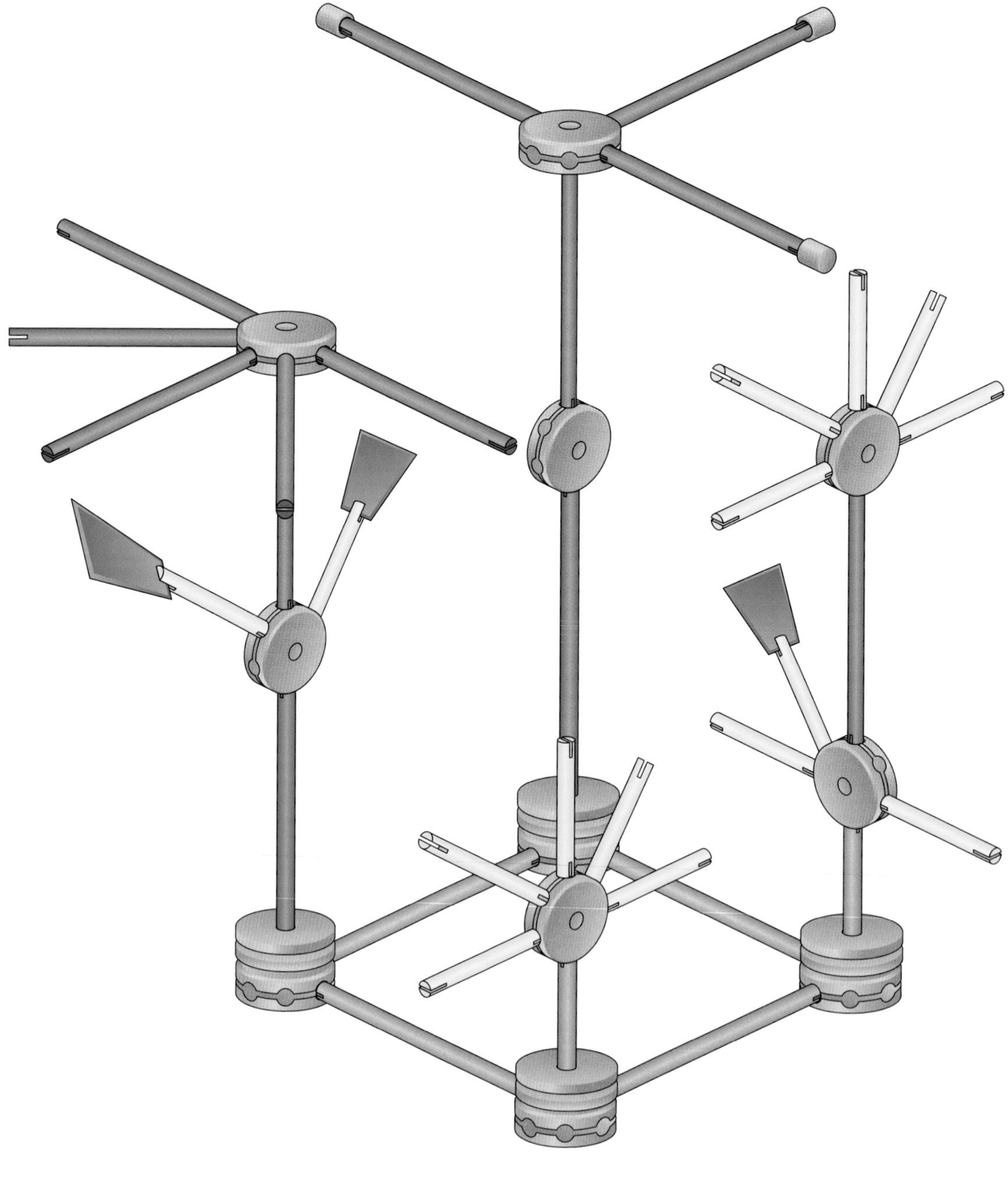

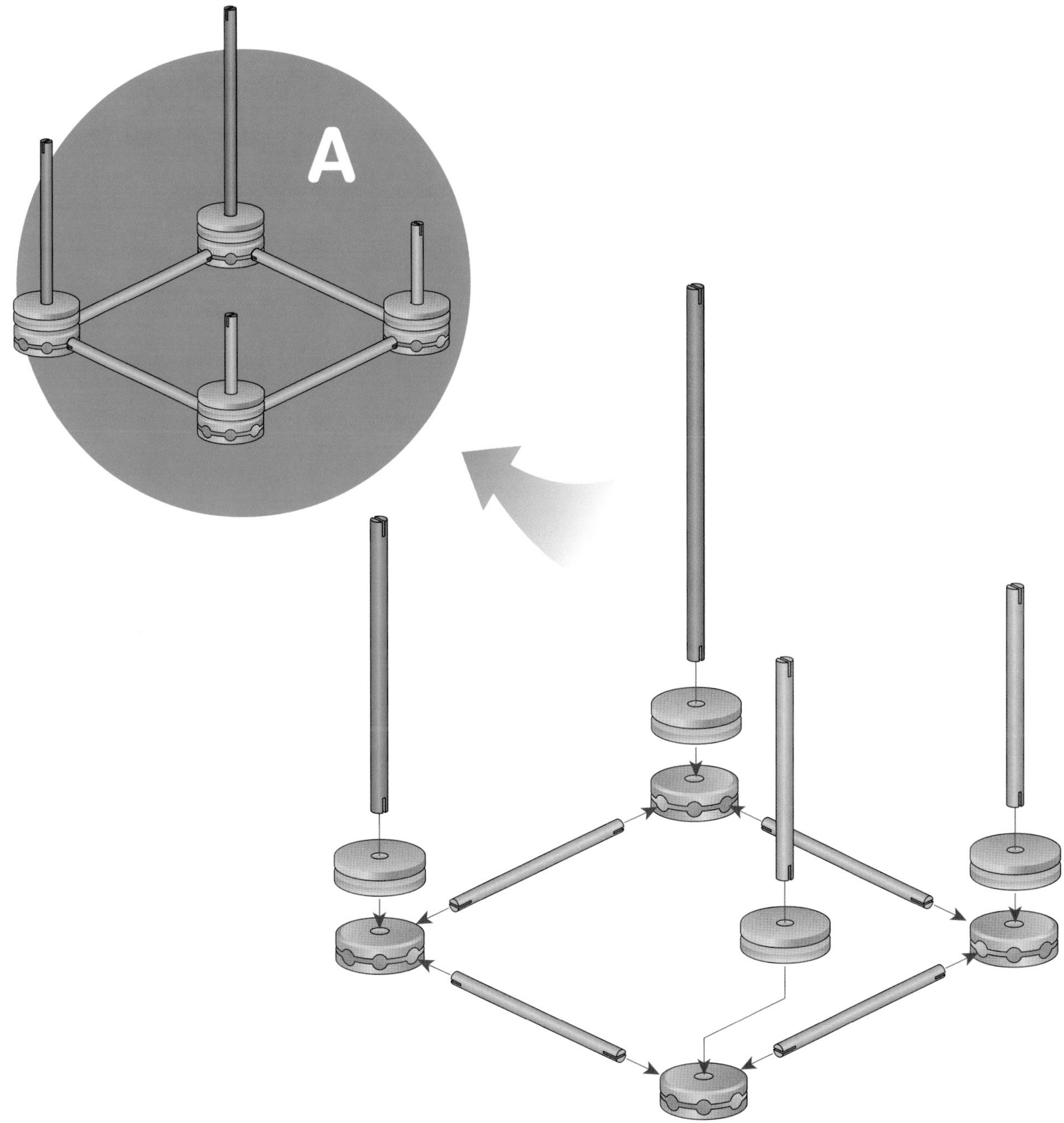
A

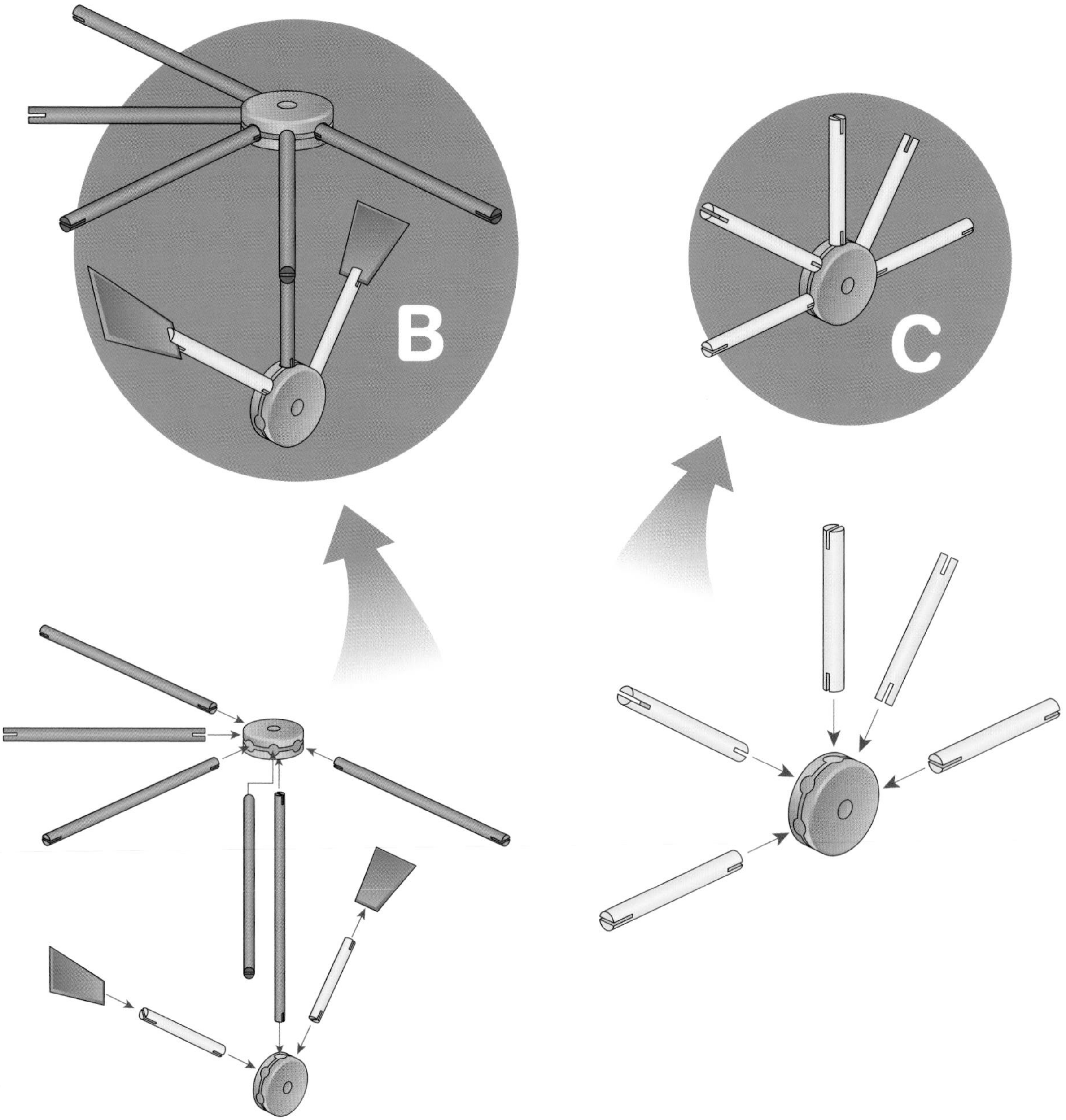
B
C

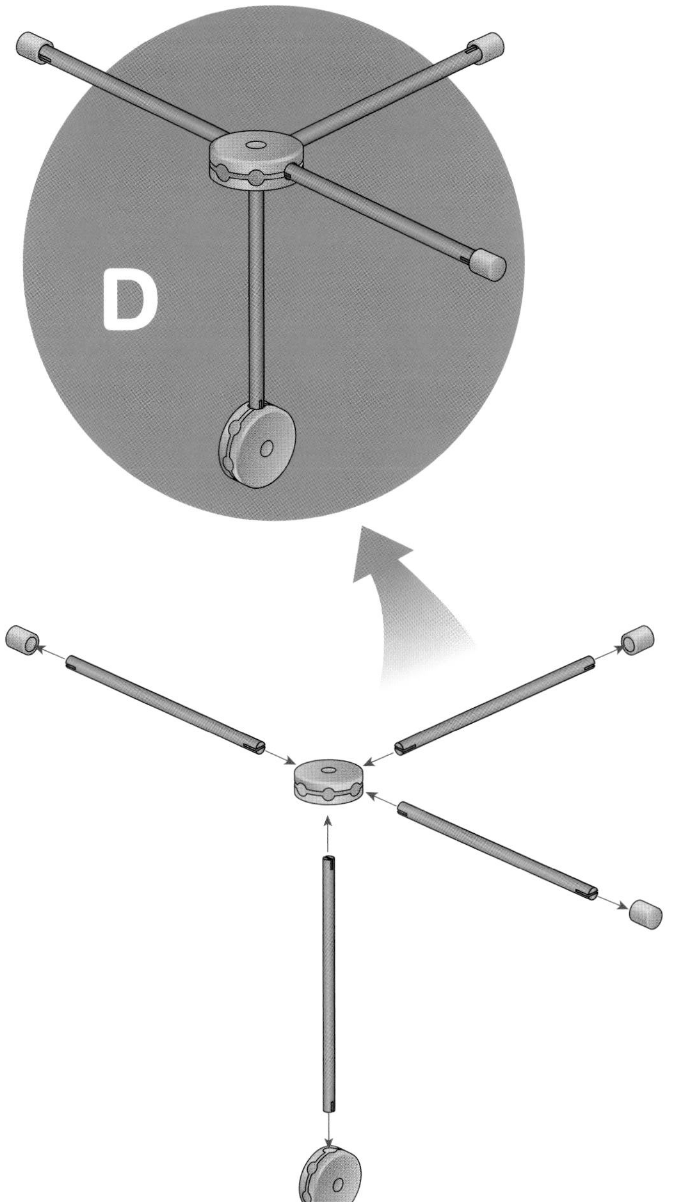
D

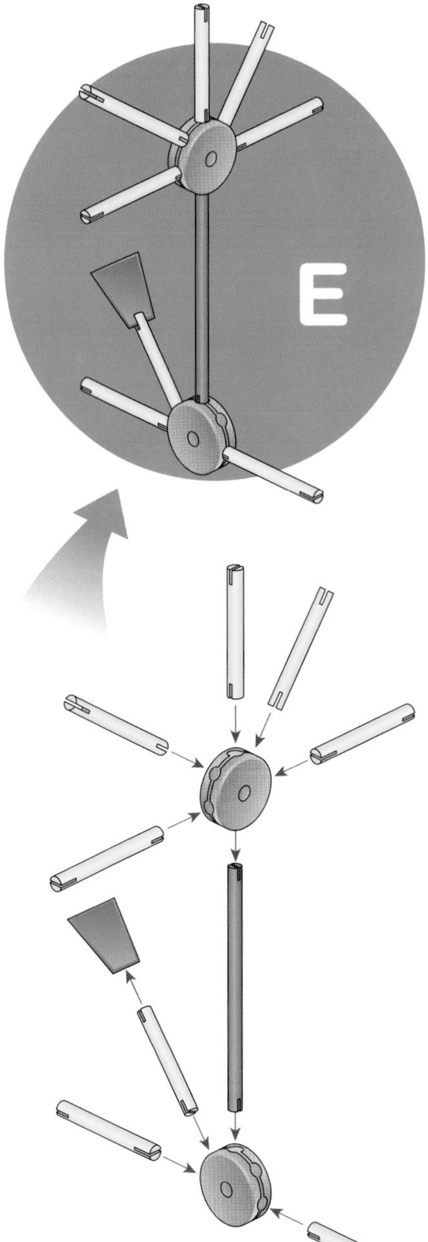
E

Pinwheel

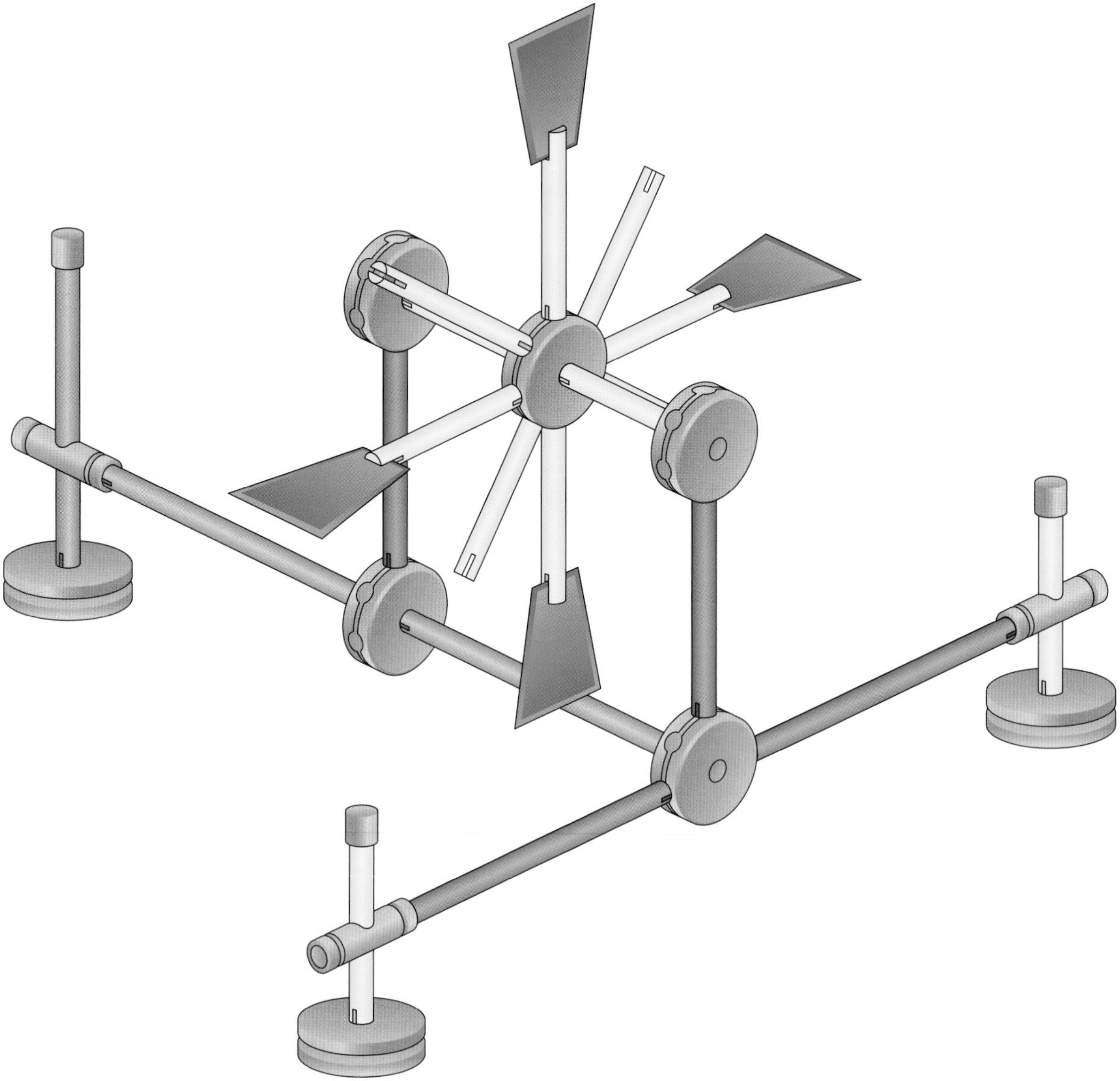

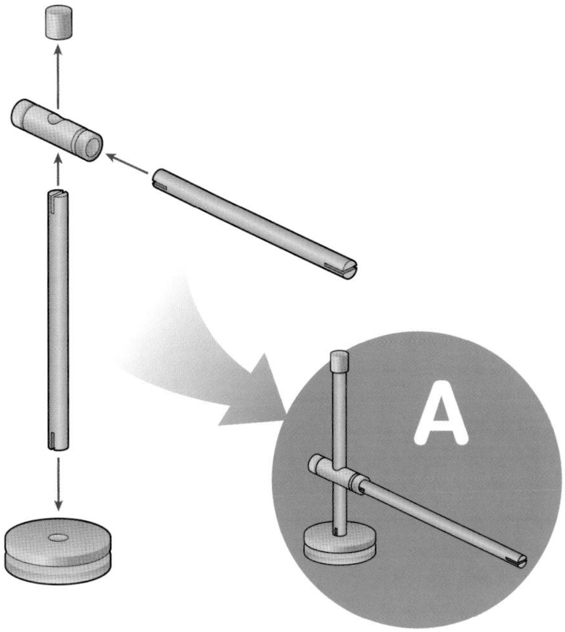
A

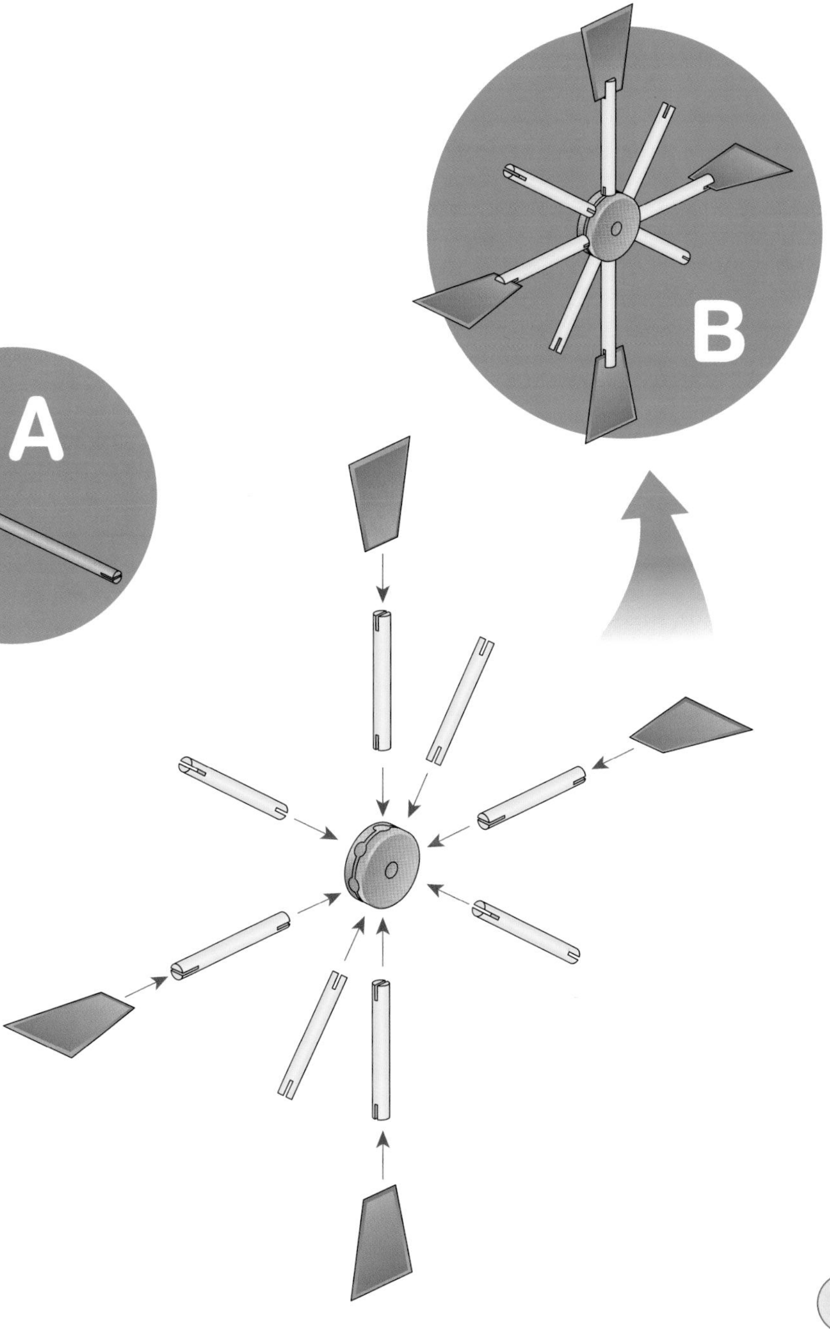
B

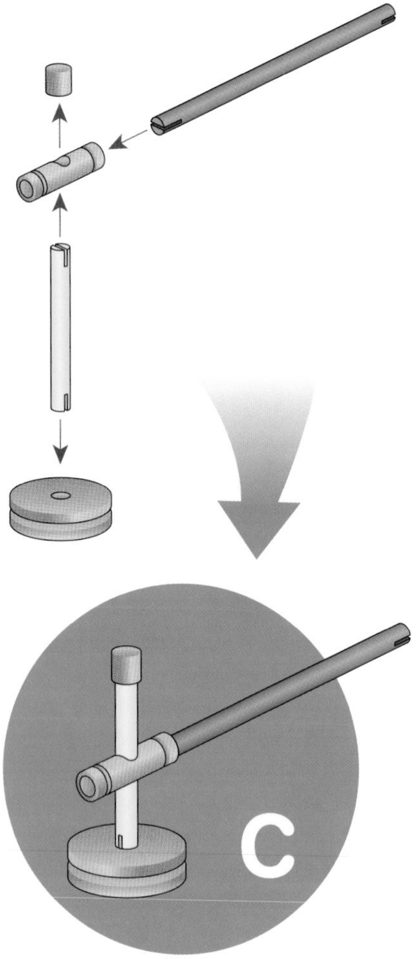
C

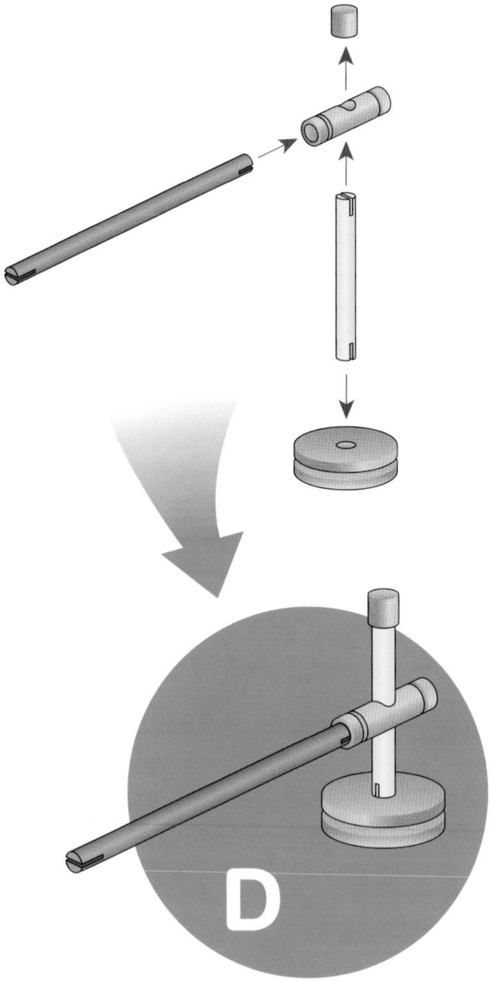
D

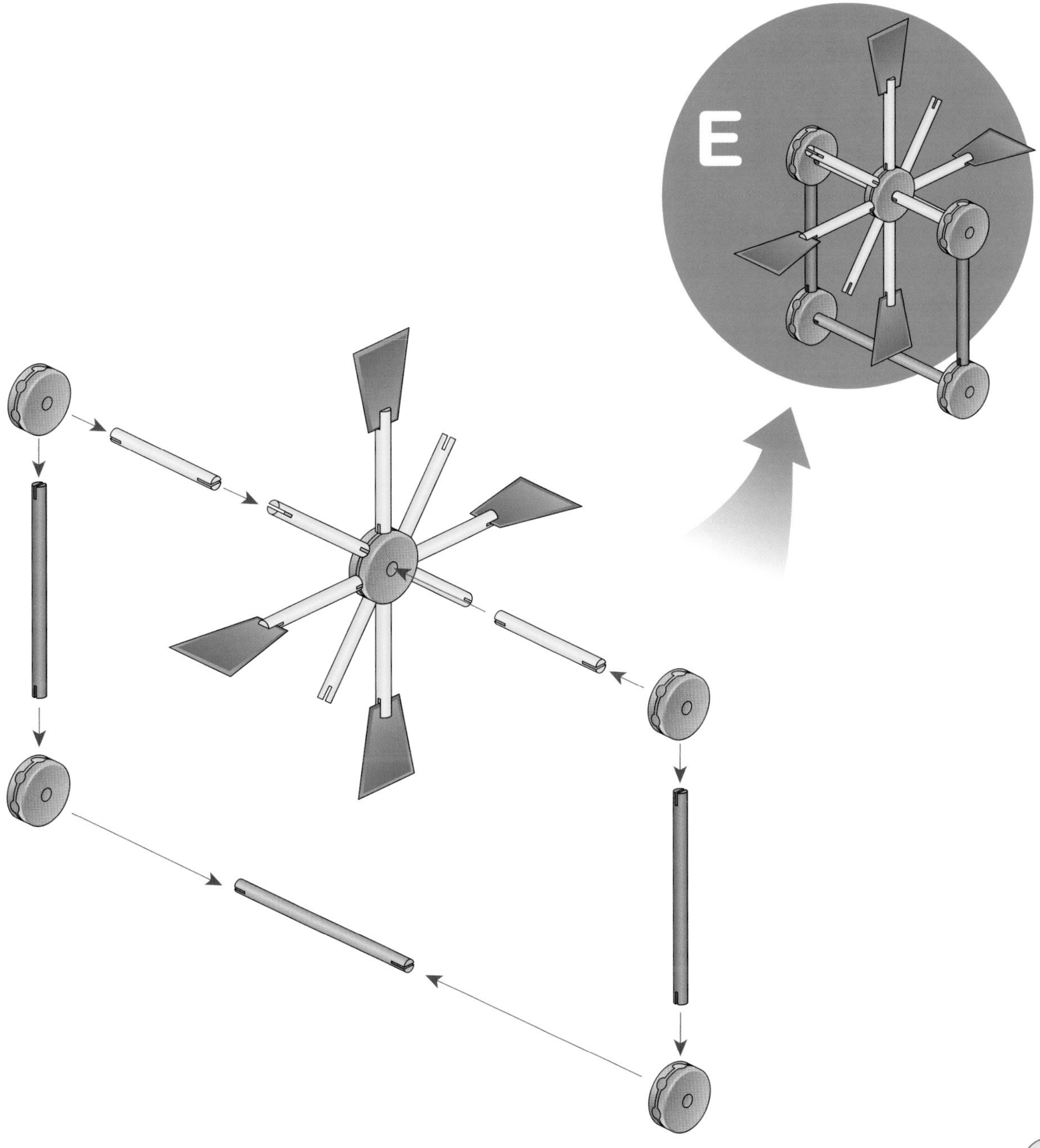
E

Ferris Wheel

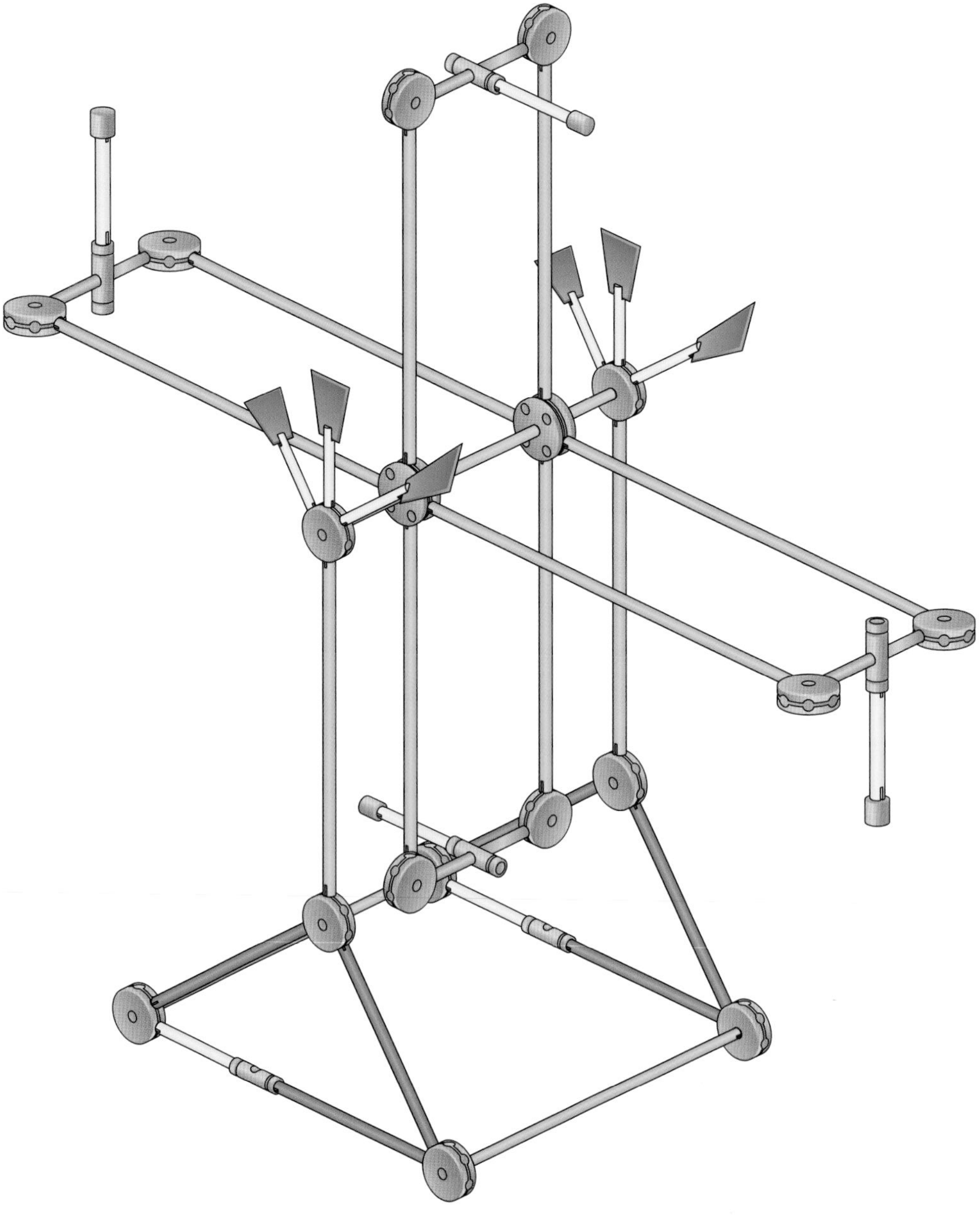

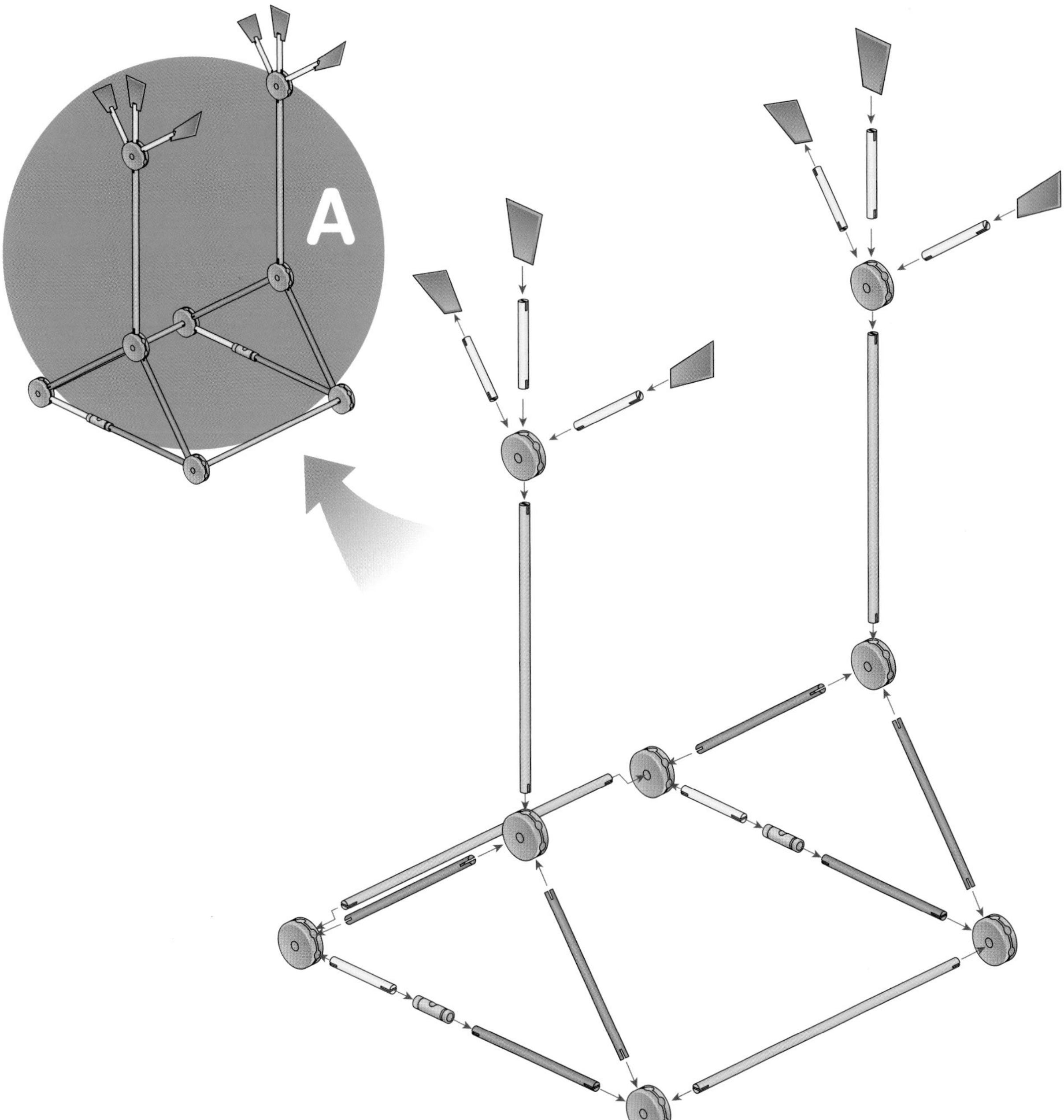
A

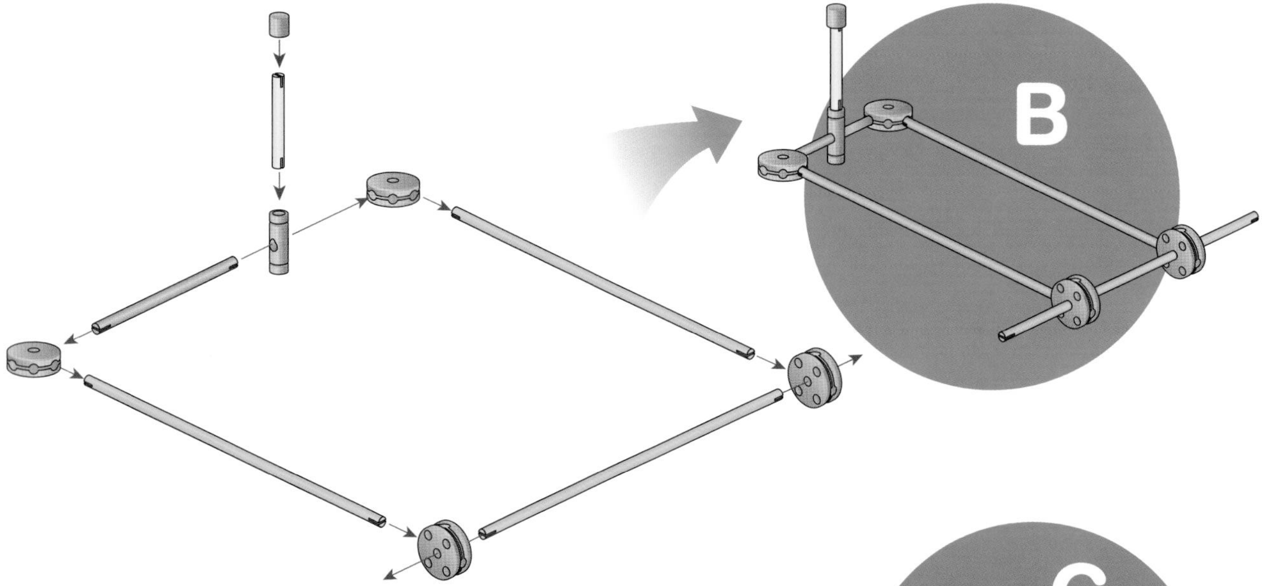
B

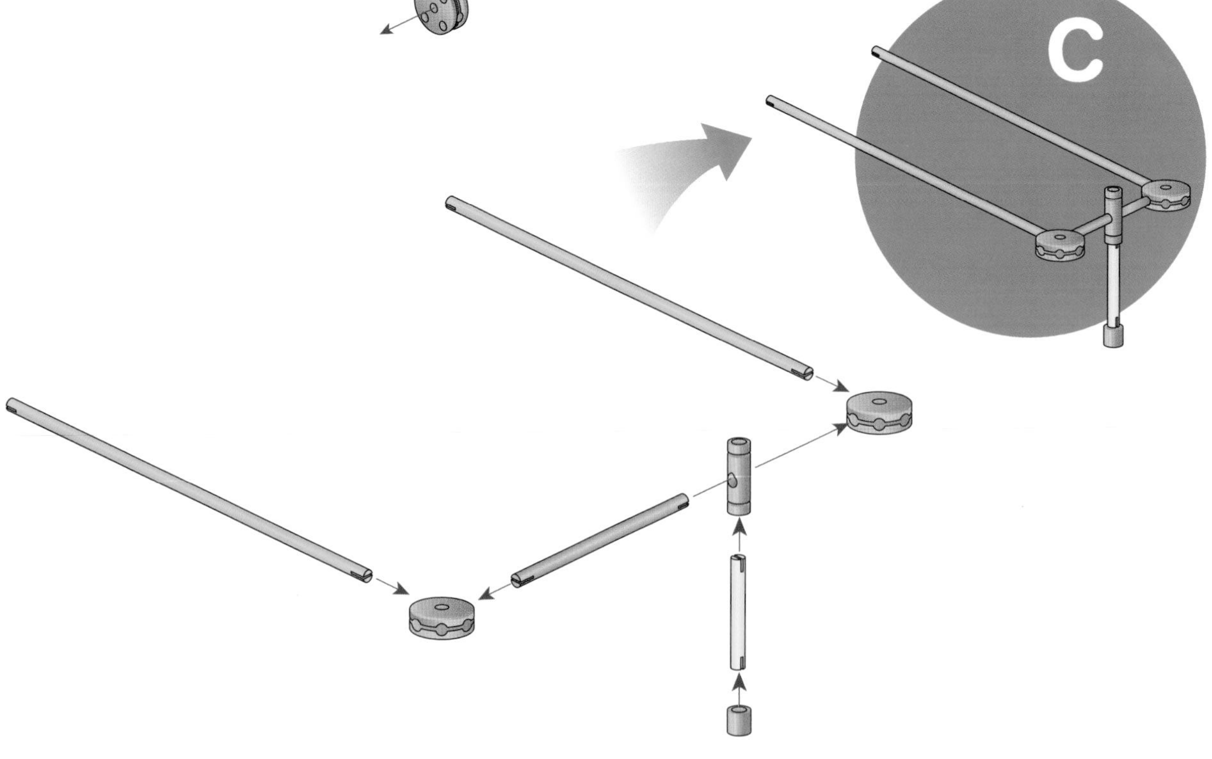
C

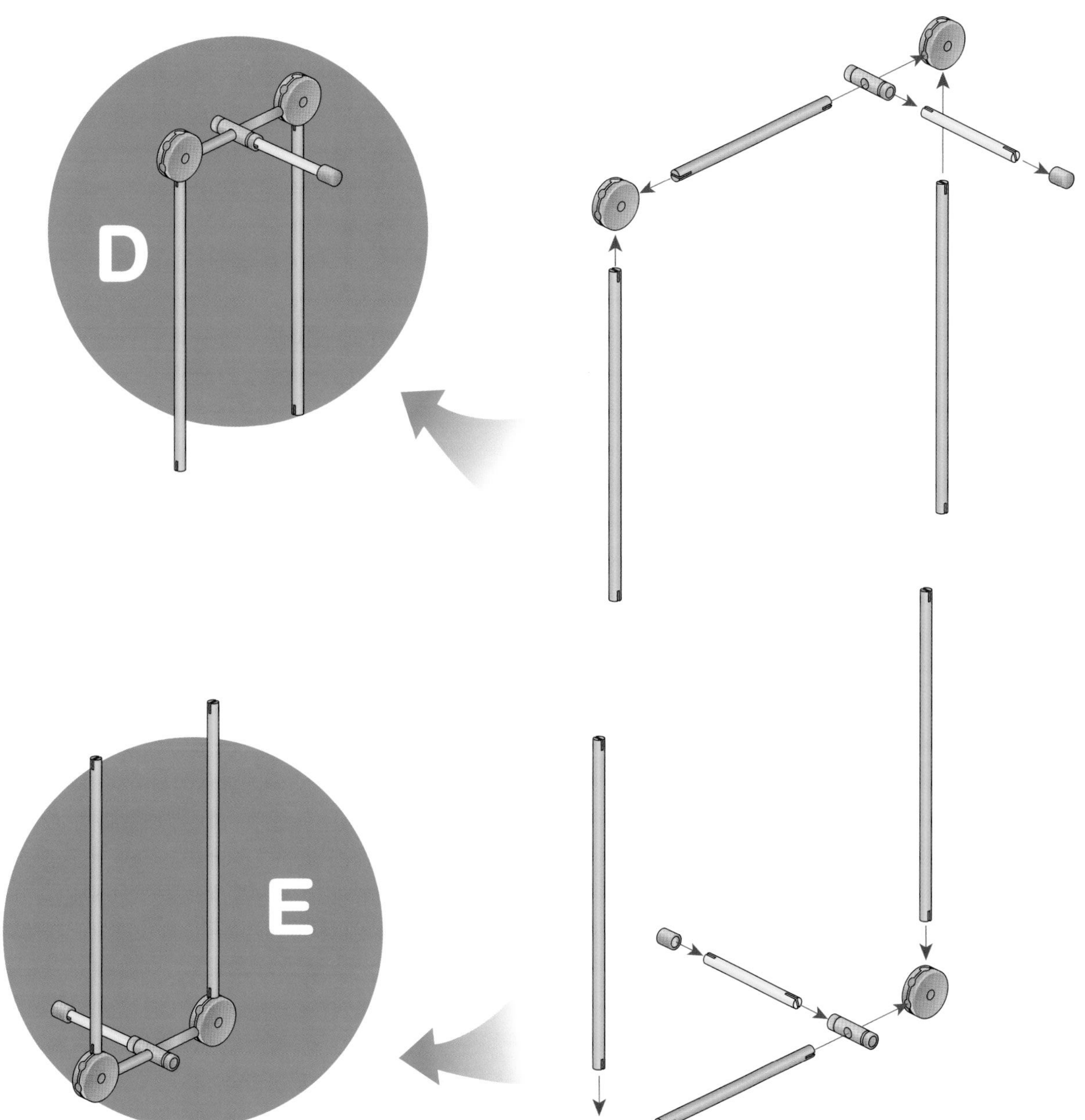
D
E

Big Ferris Wheel

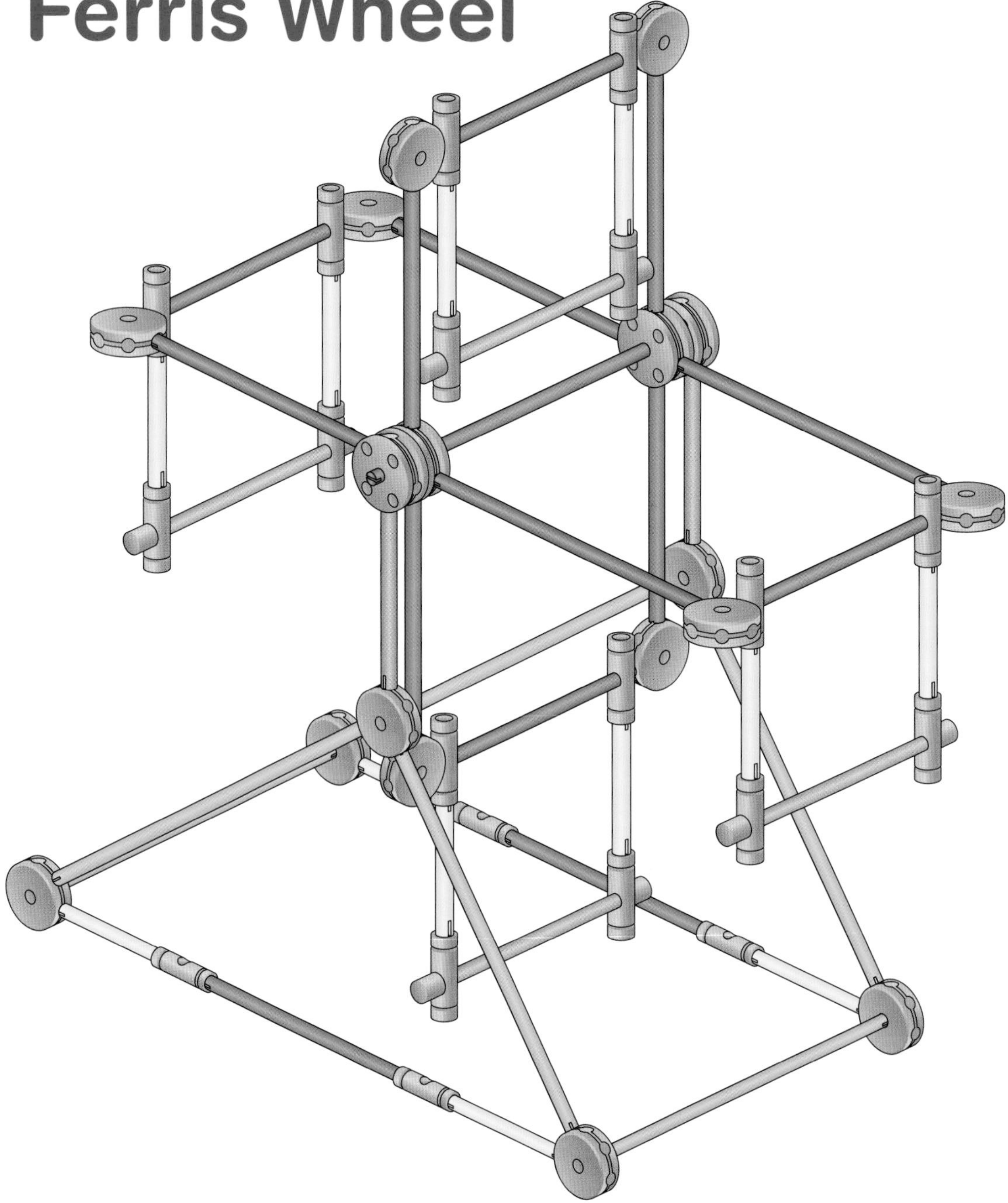

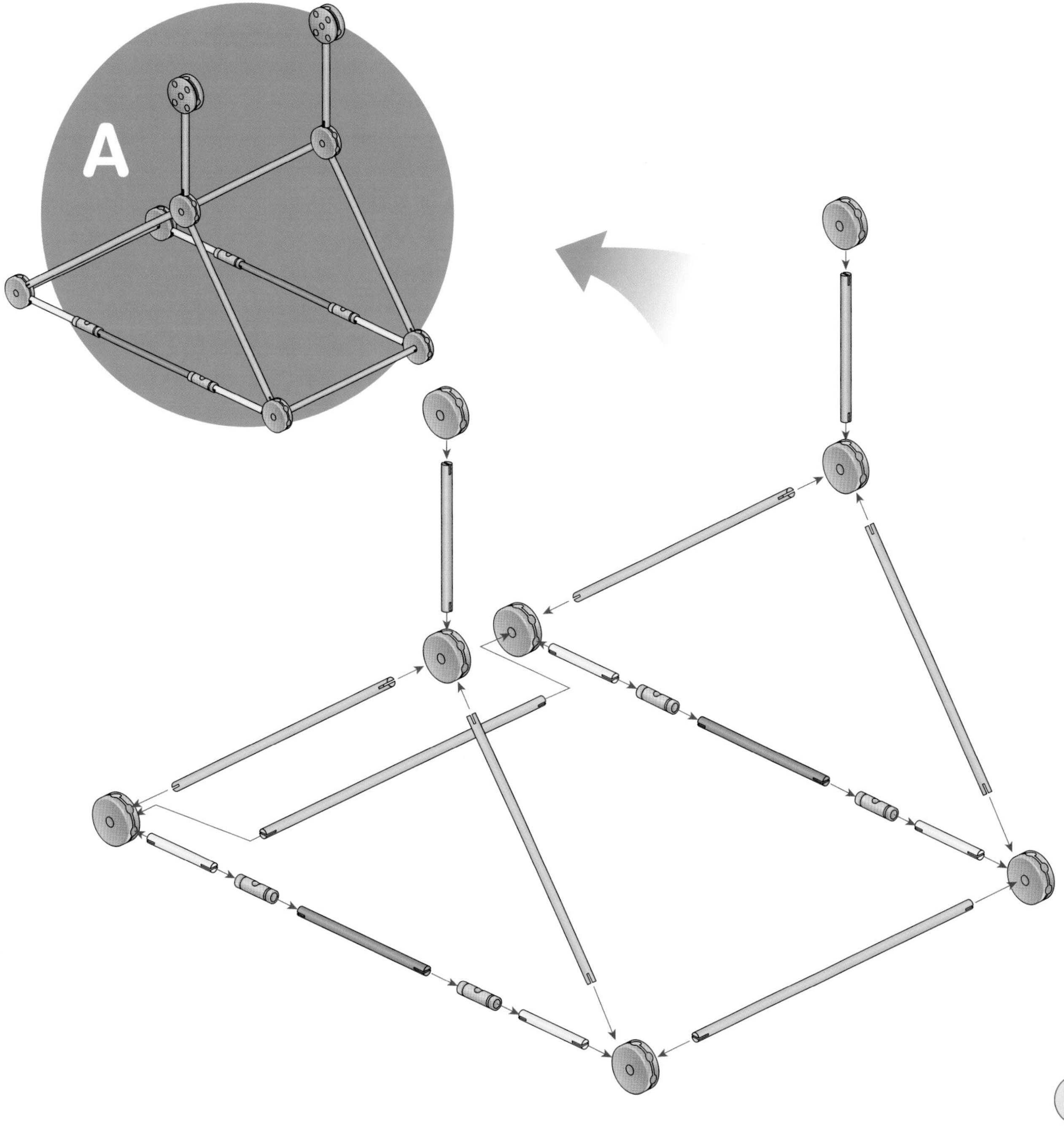
A

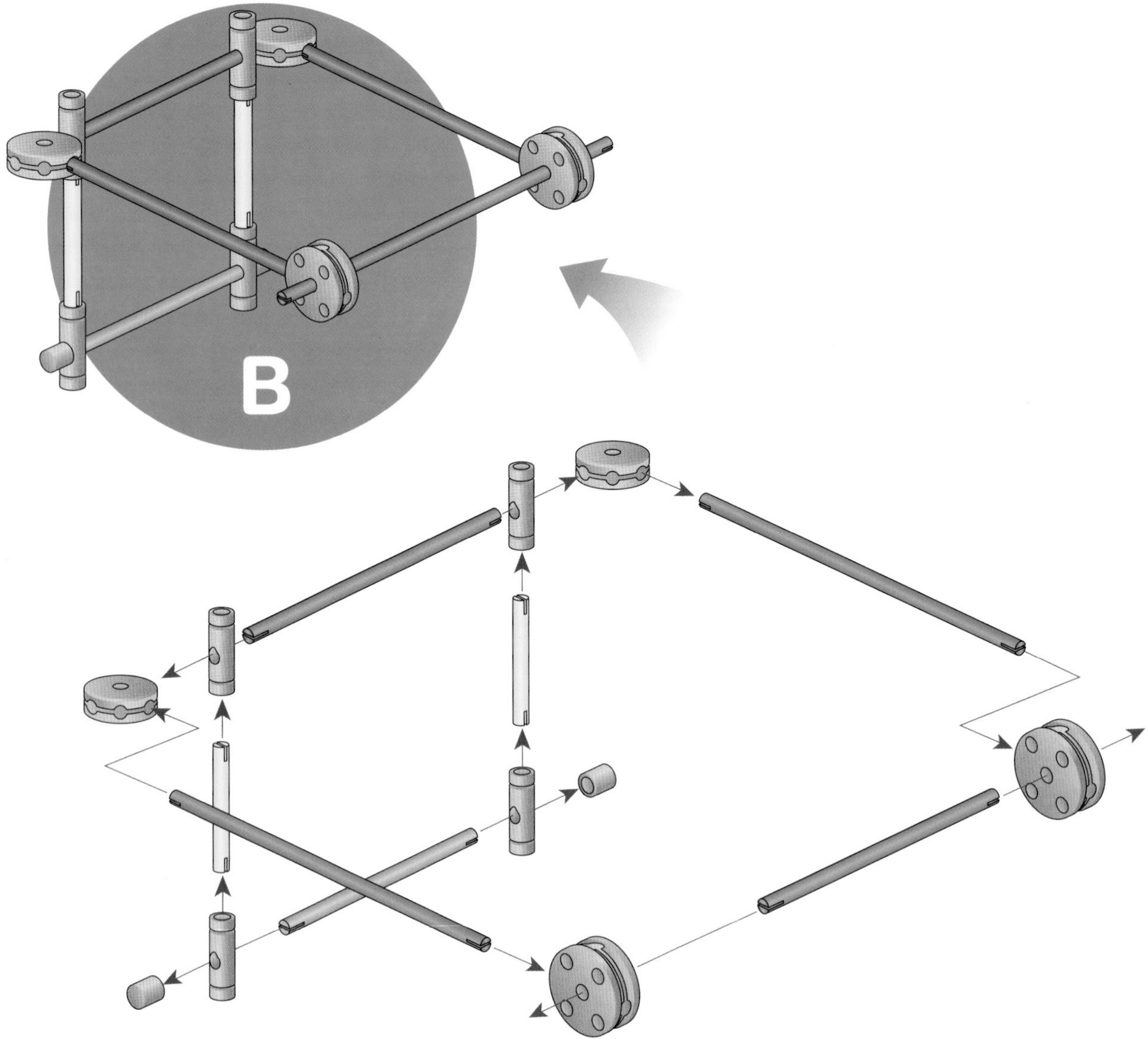
B

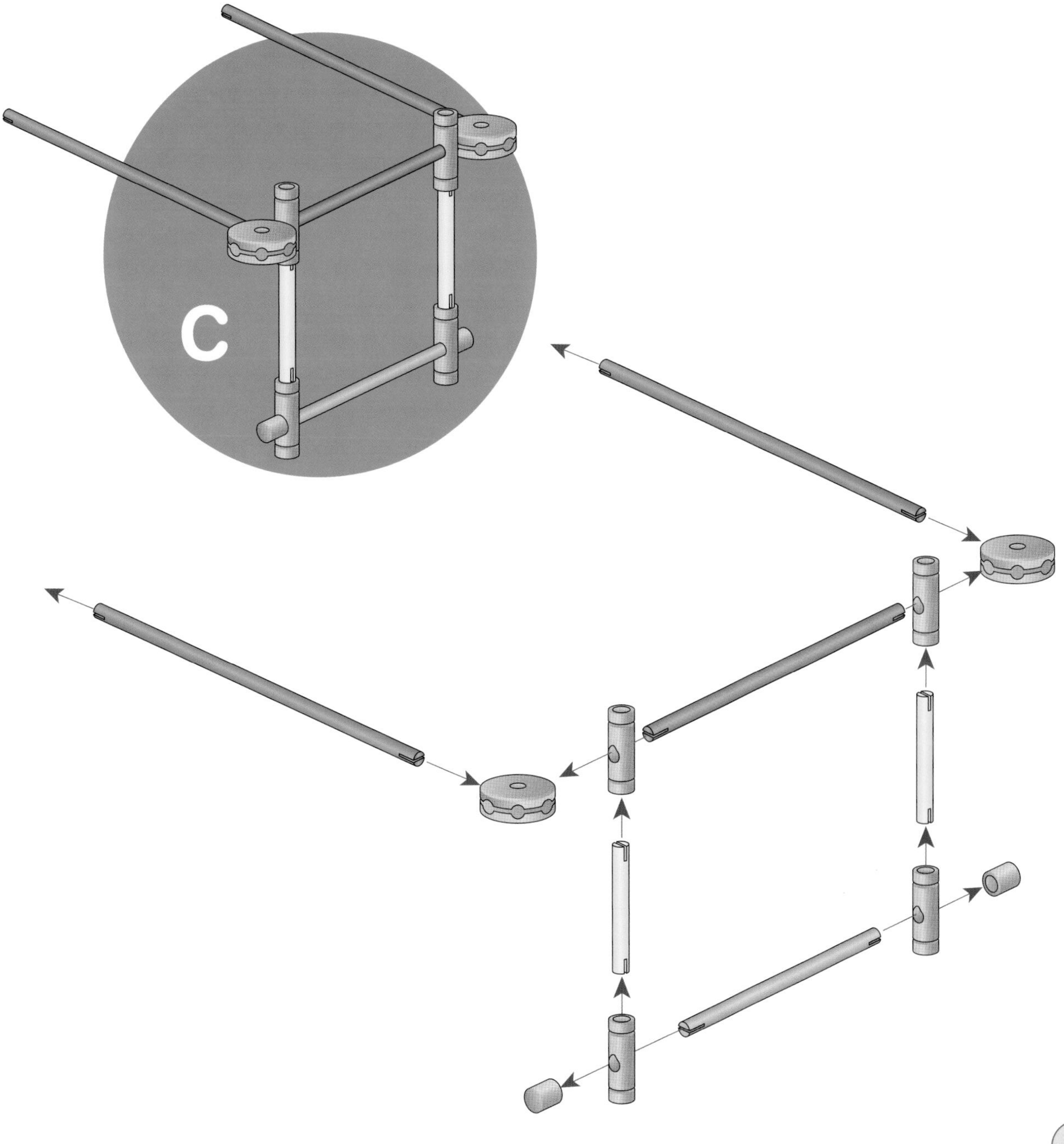
C

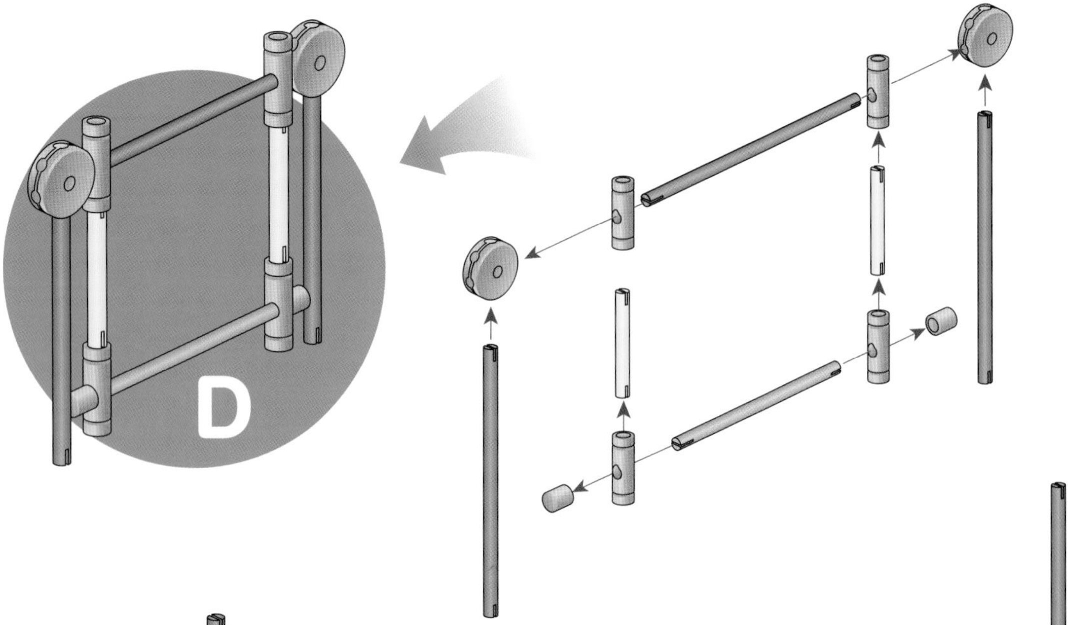
D
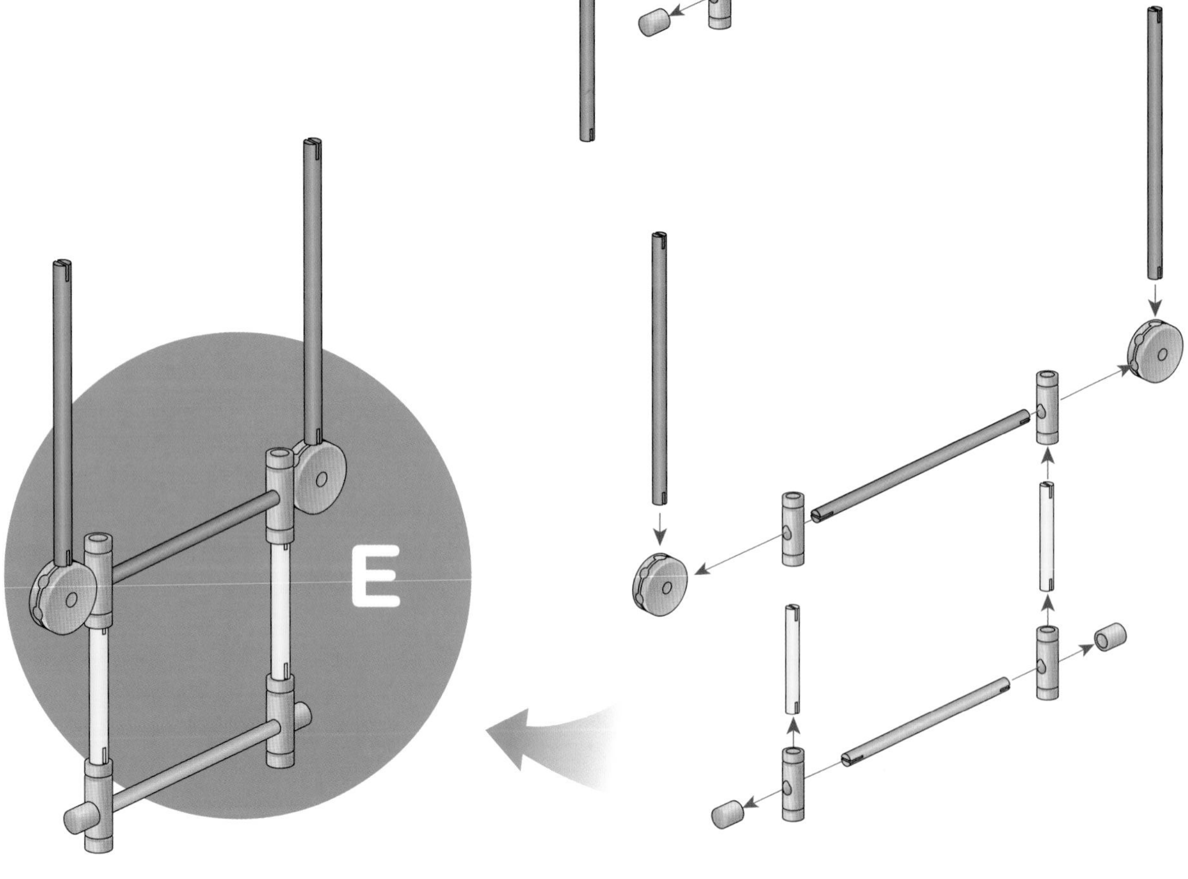
E

Jumbo Jet

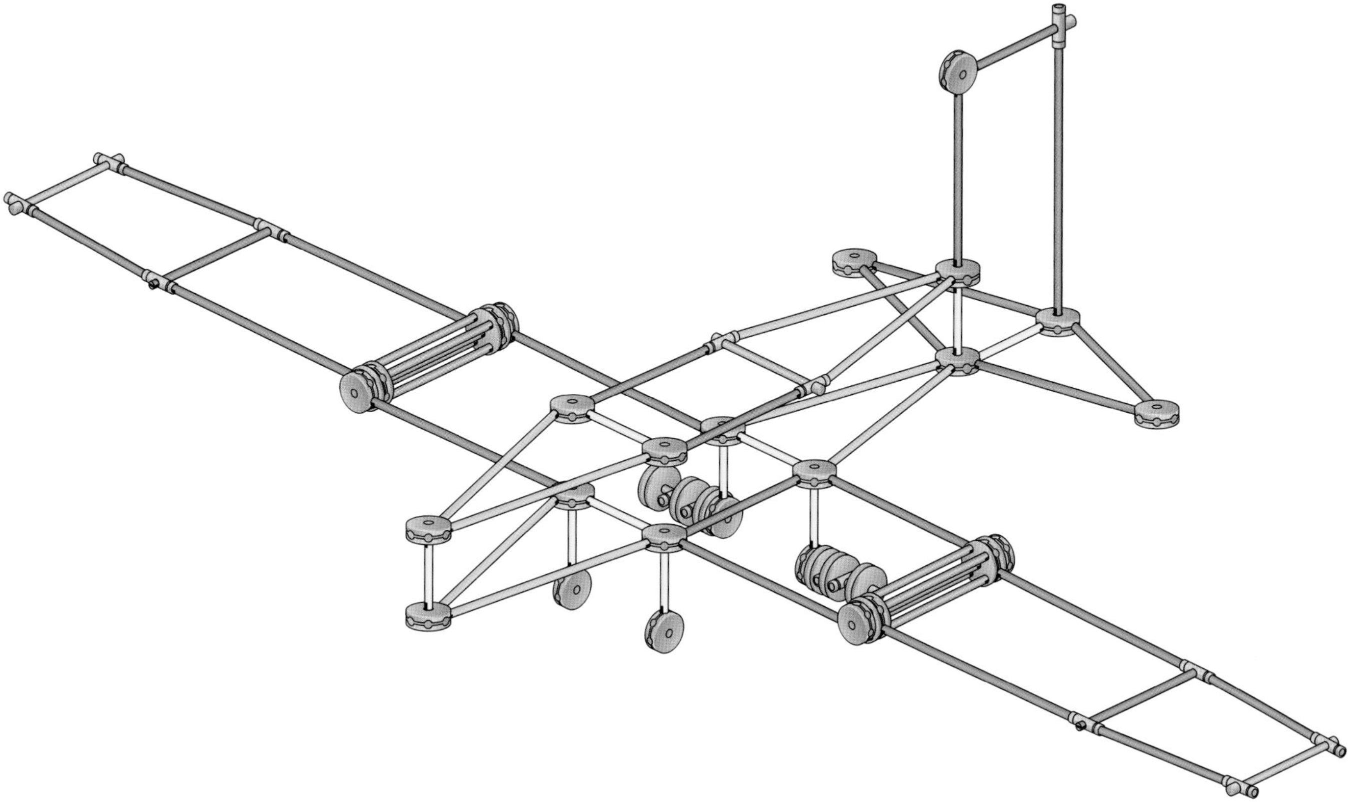

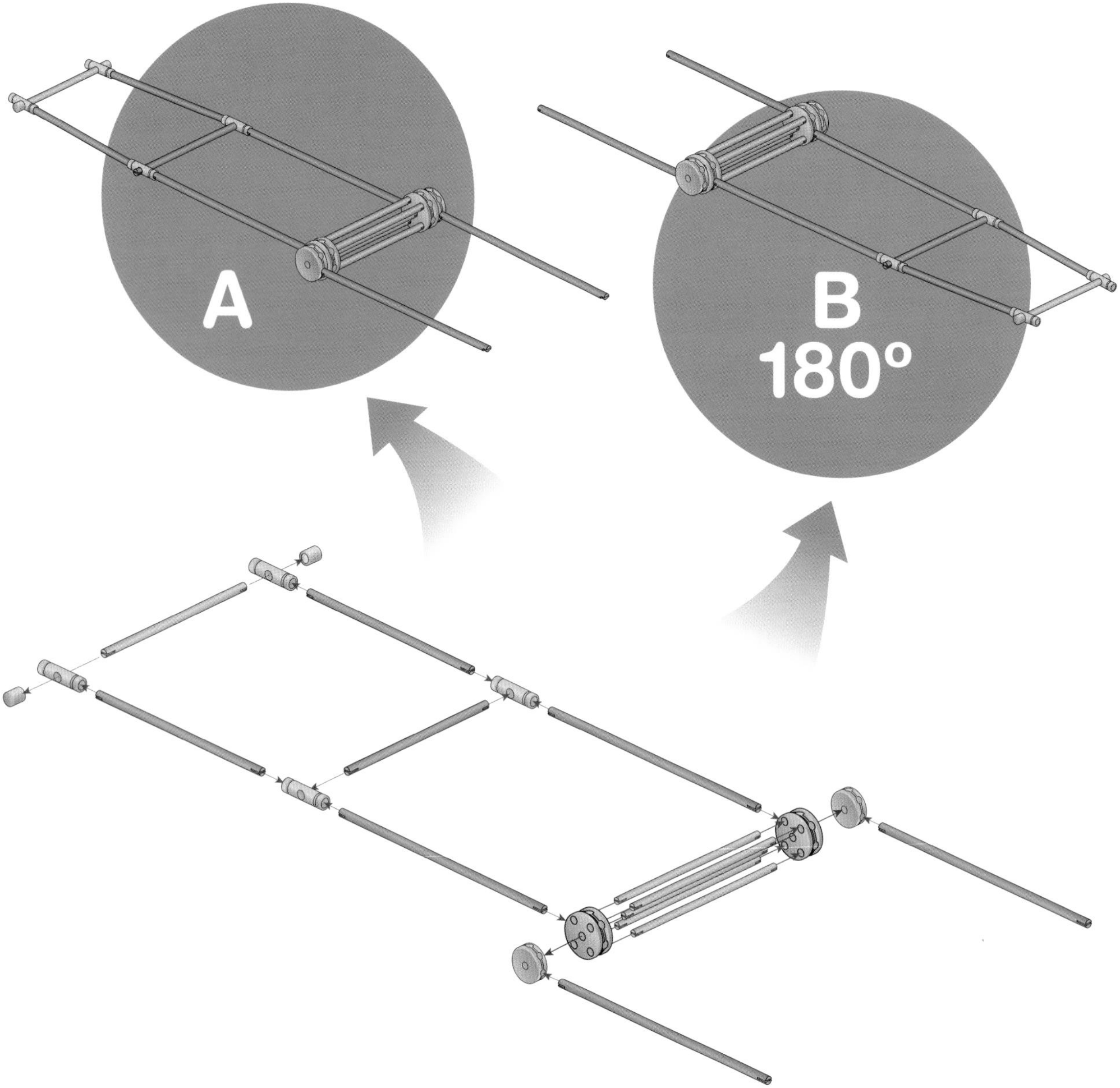
A
B
180°

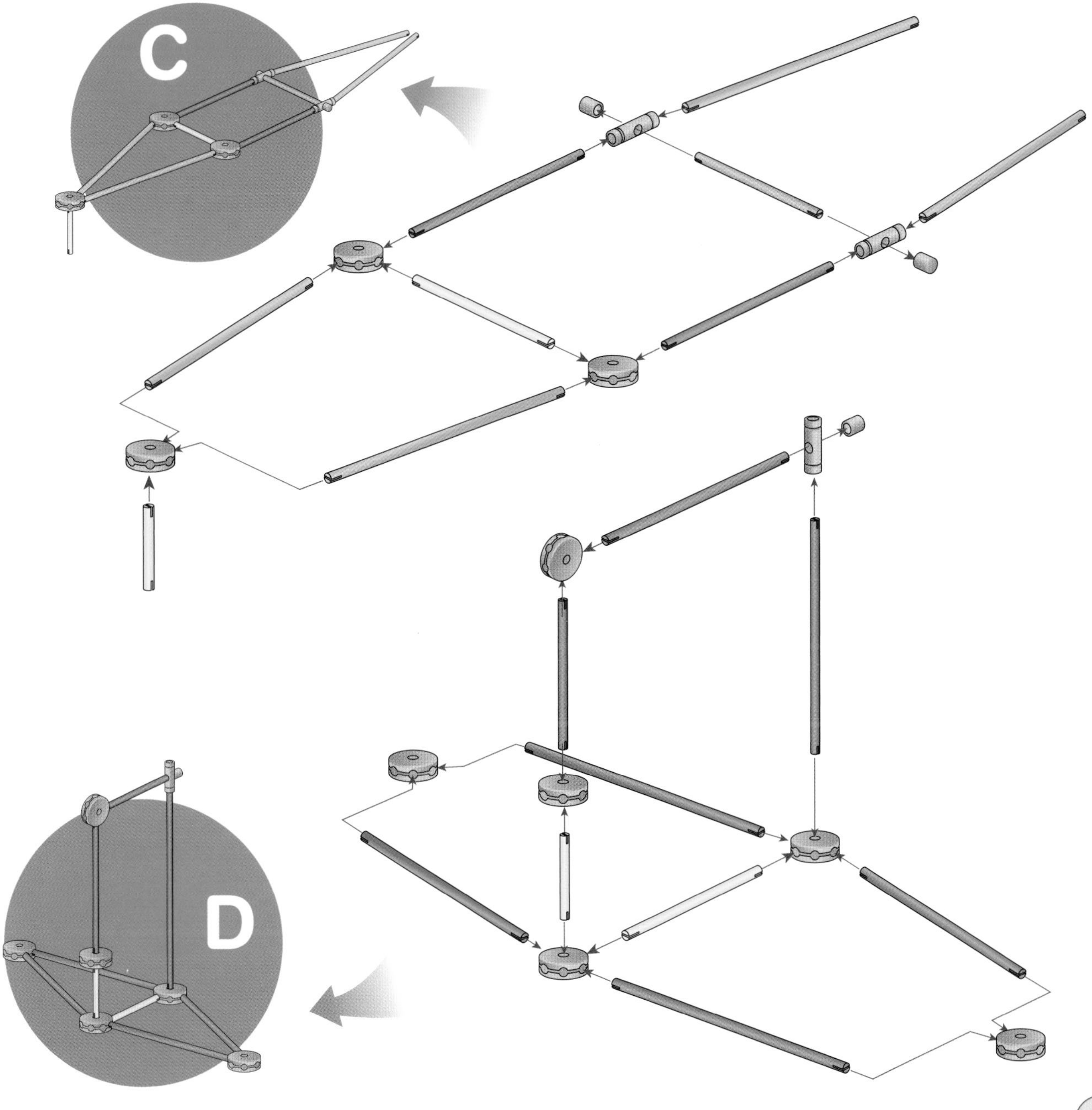
C
D

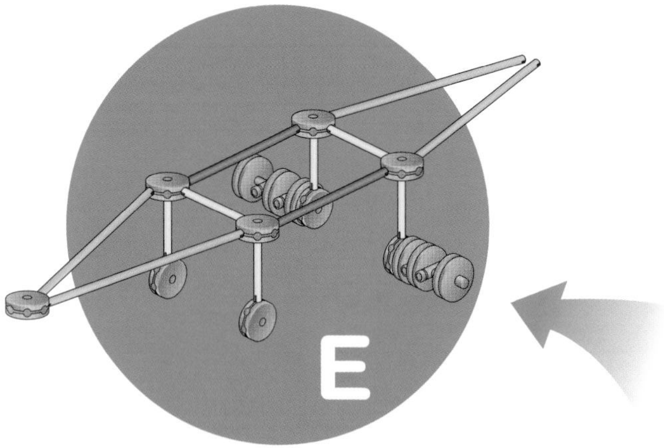
E

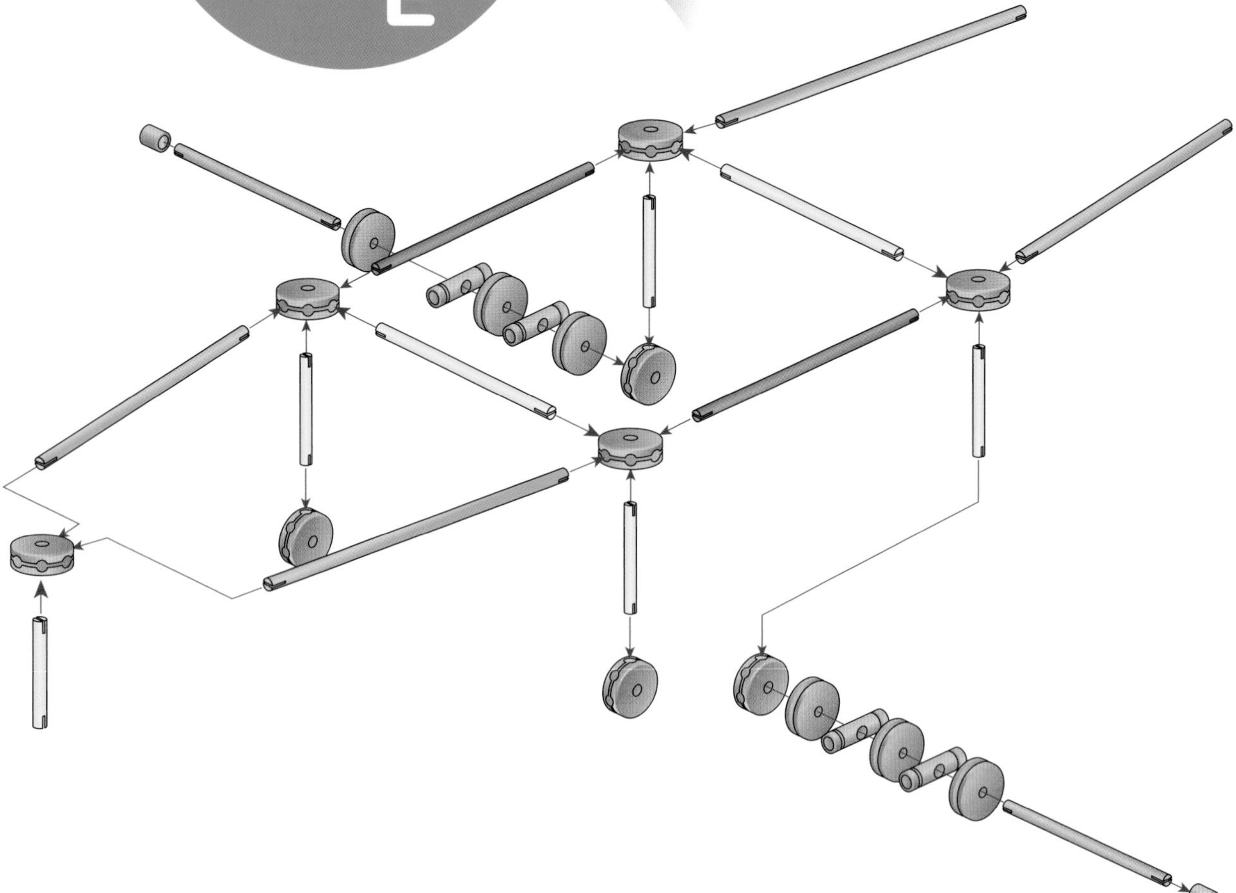

Swing Set

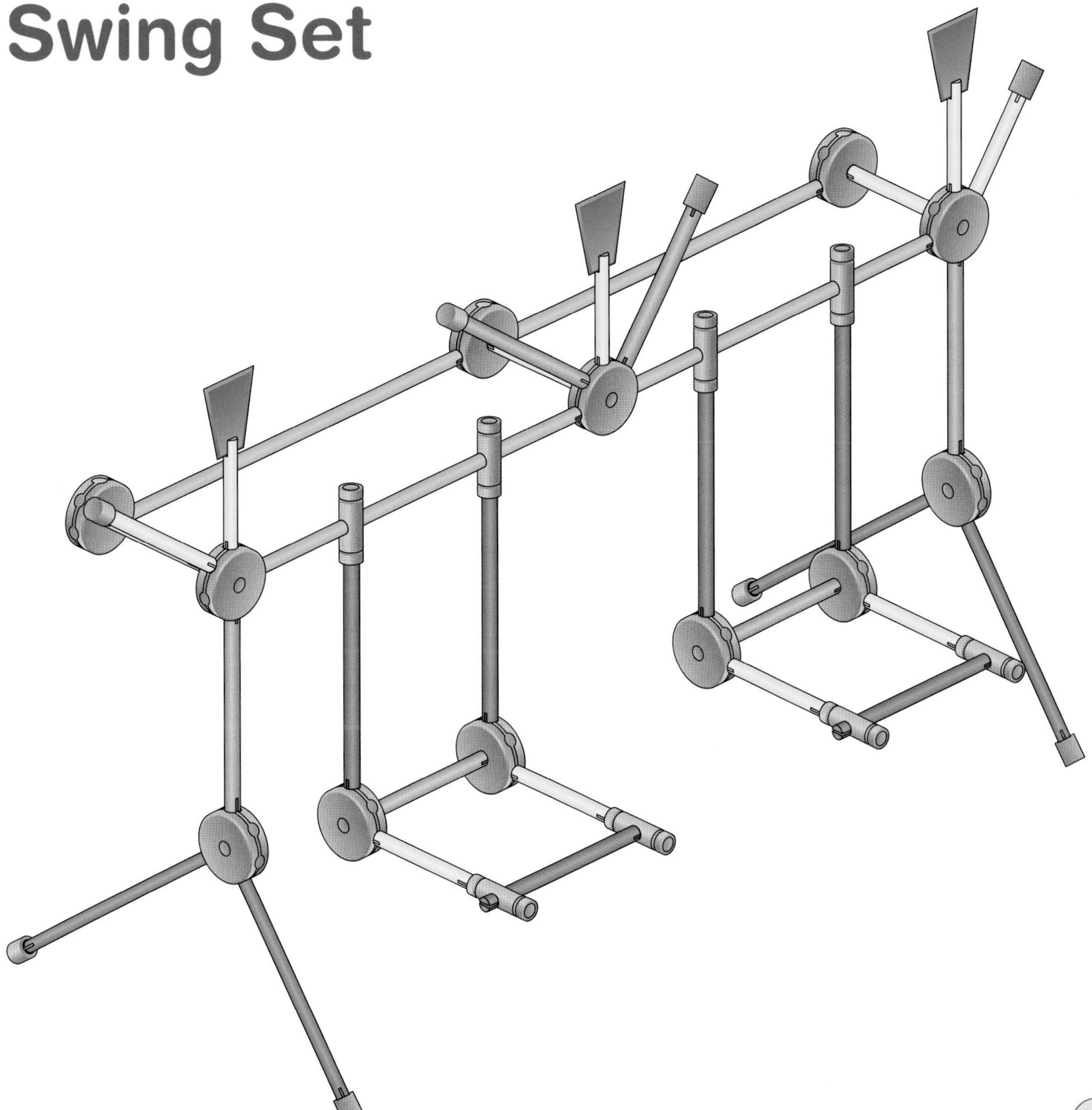

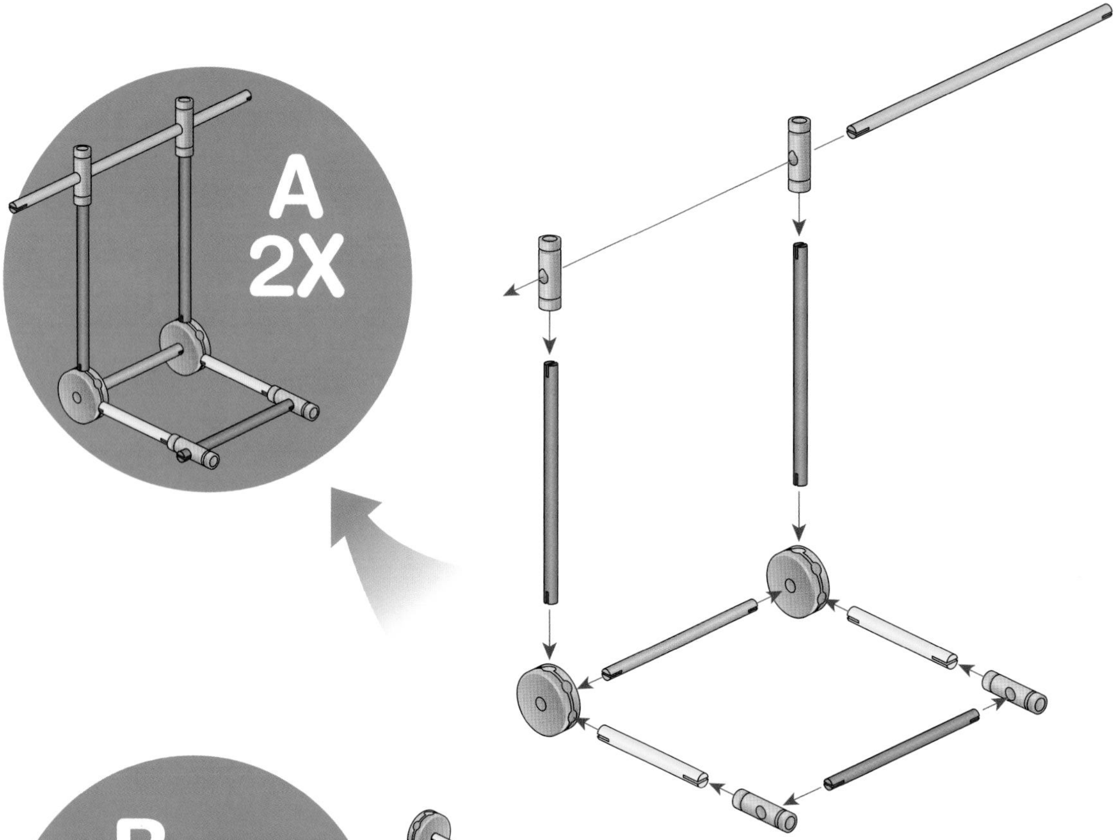
A
2X

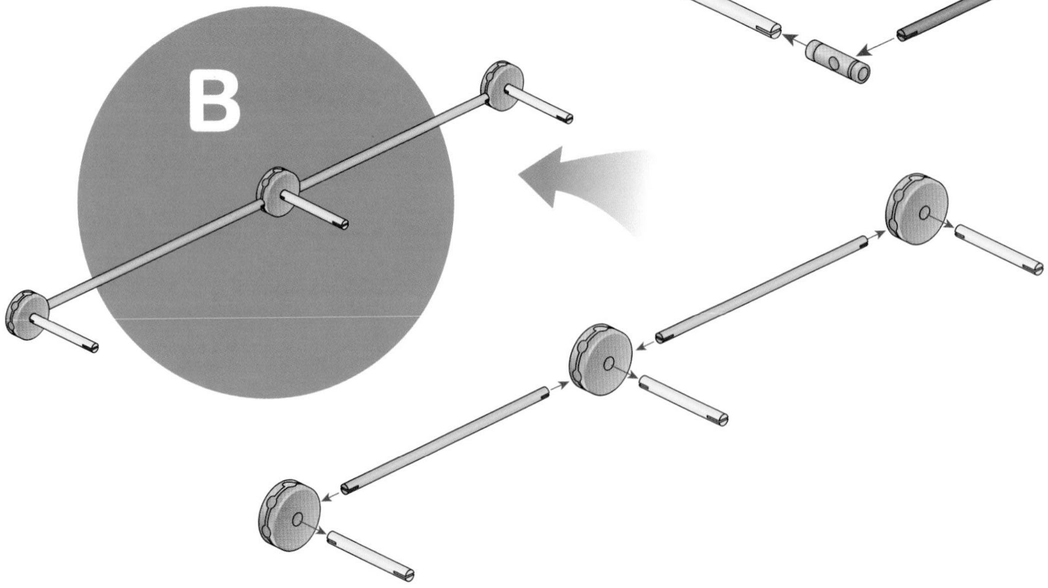
B

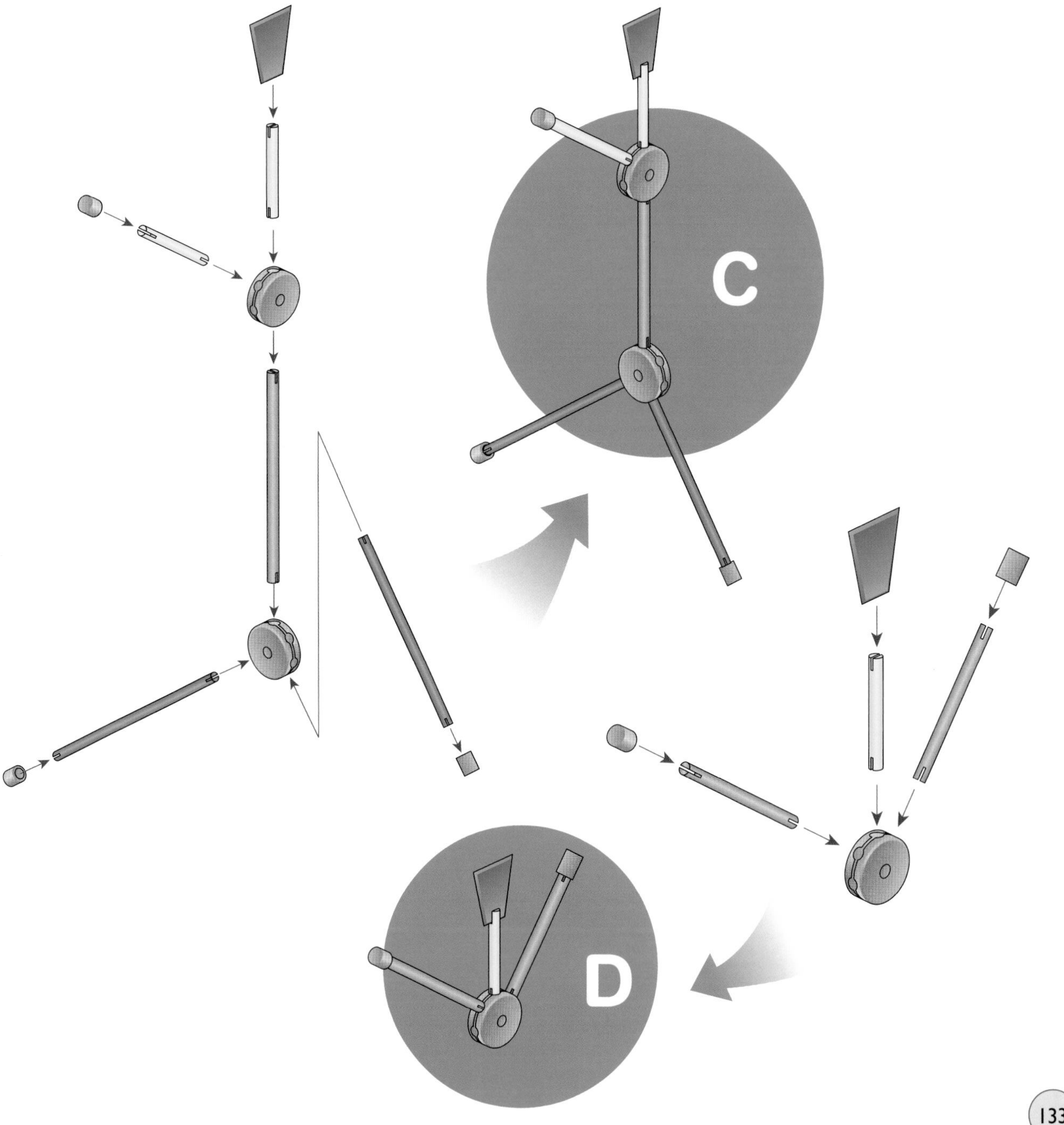
C
D

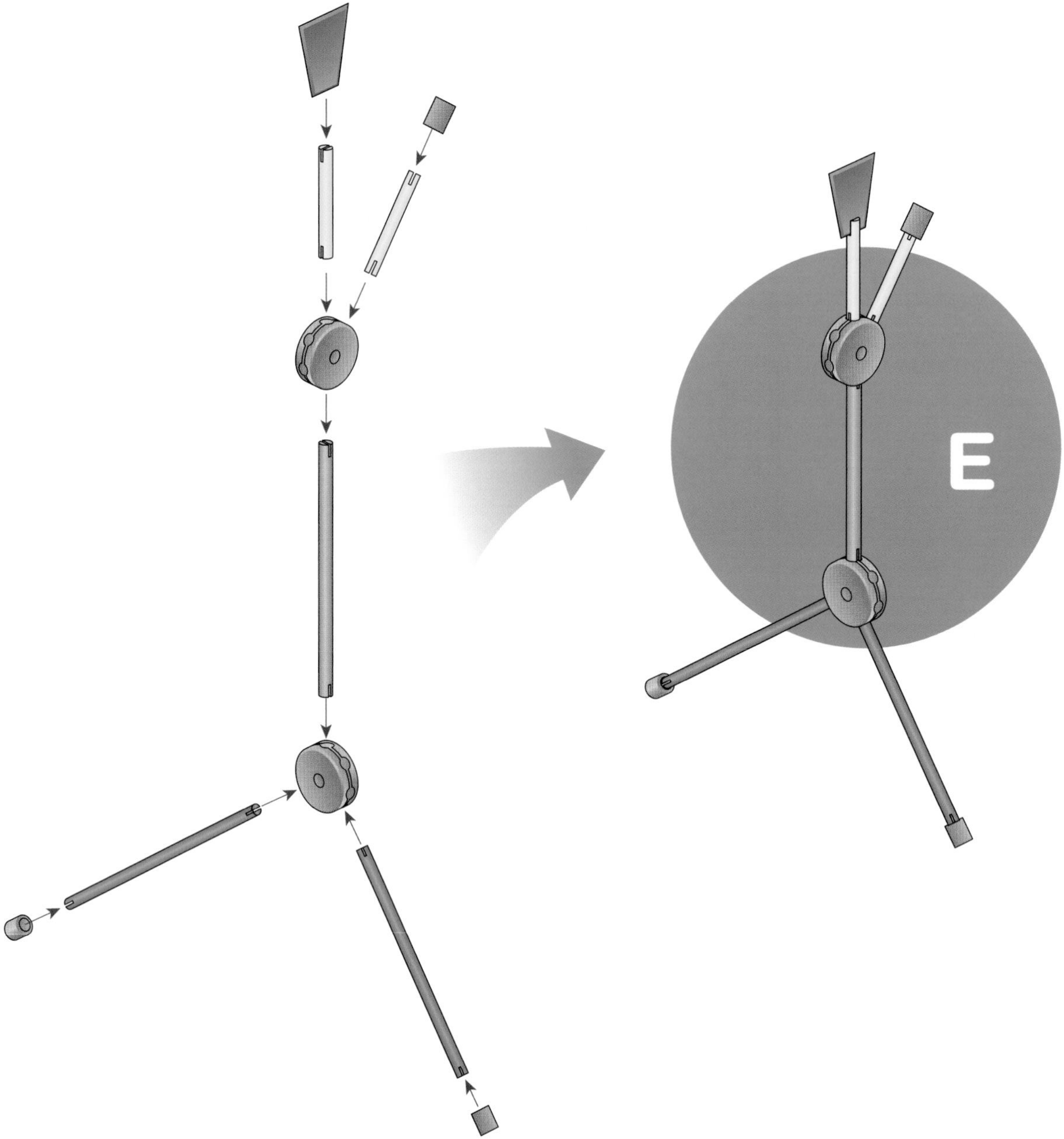
E

Moon Rover

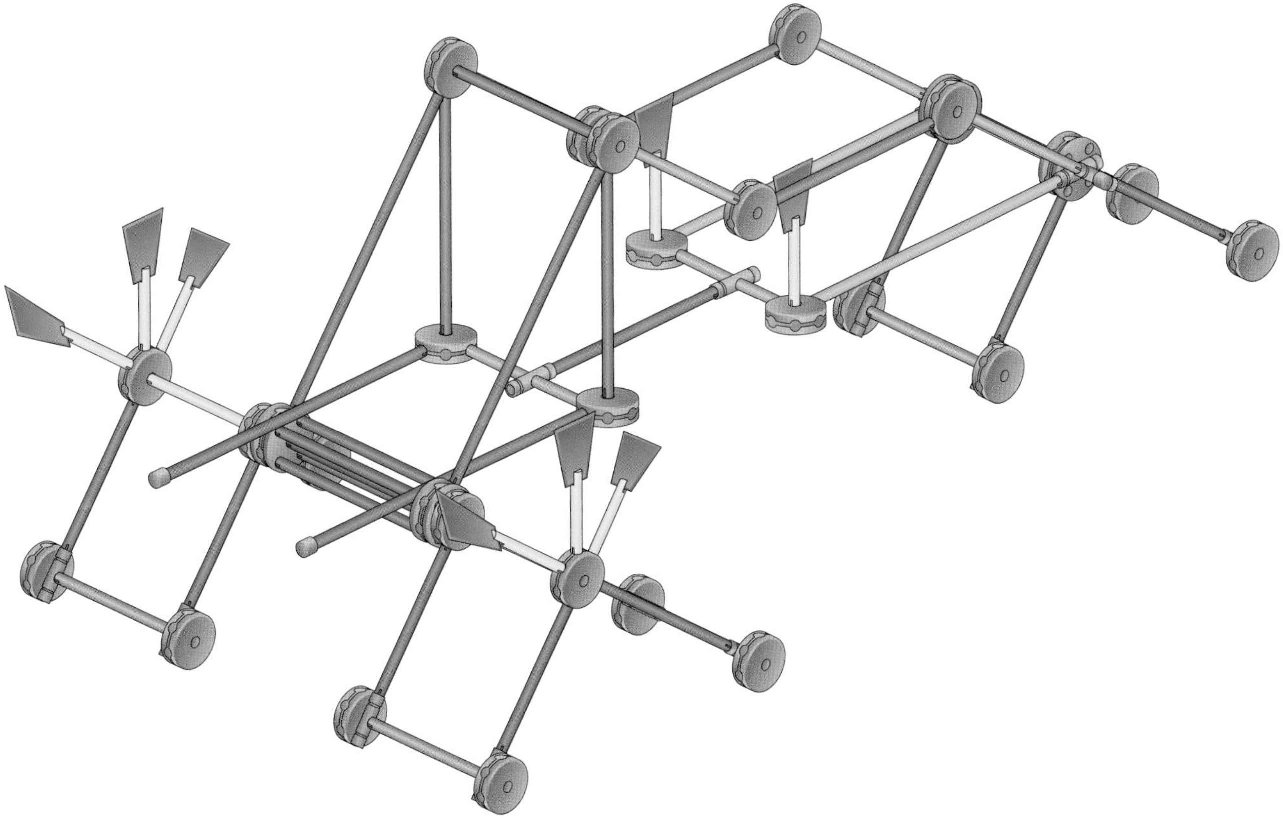

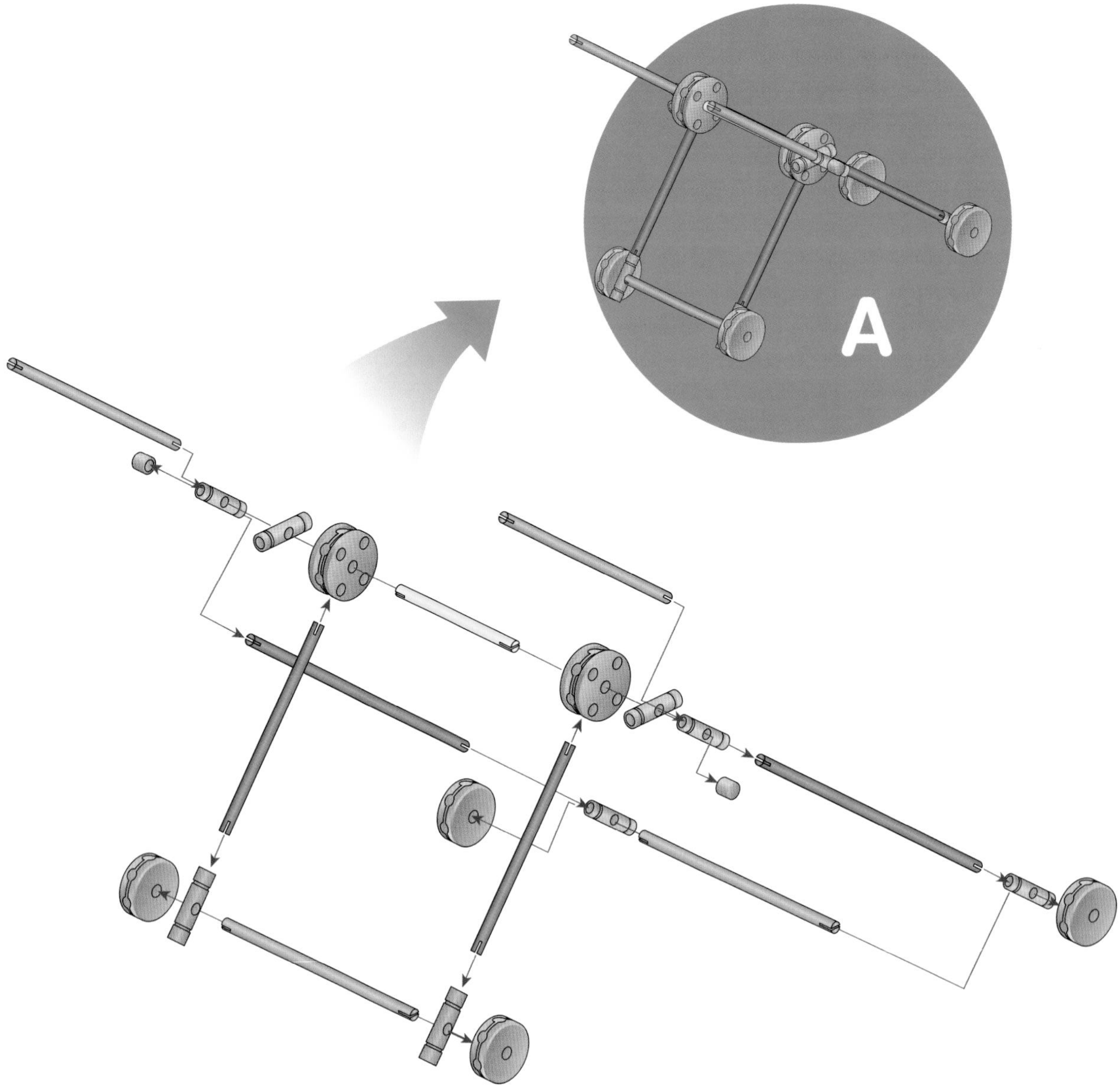
A

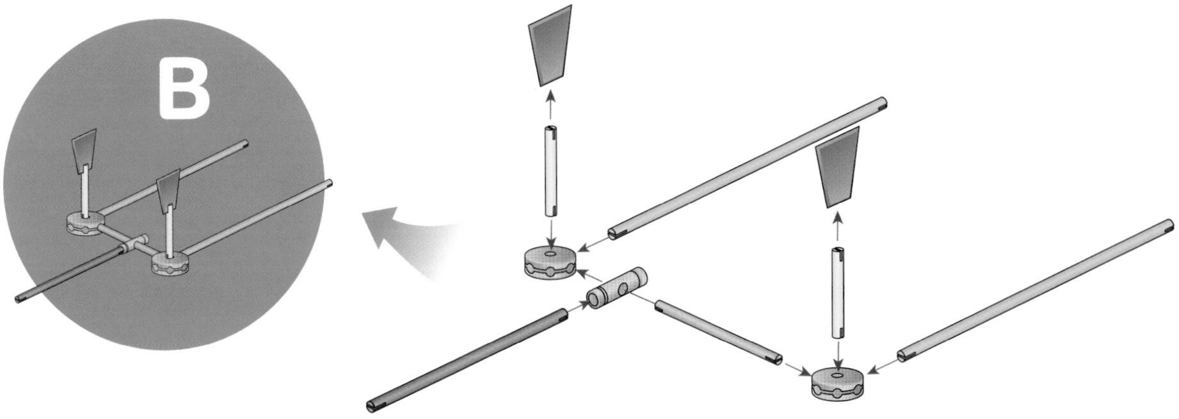
B

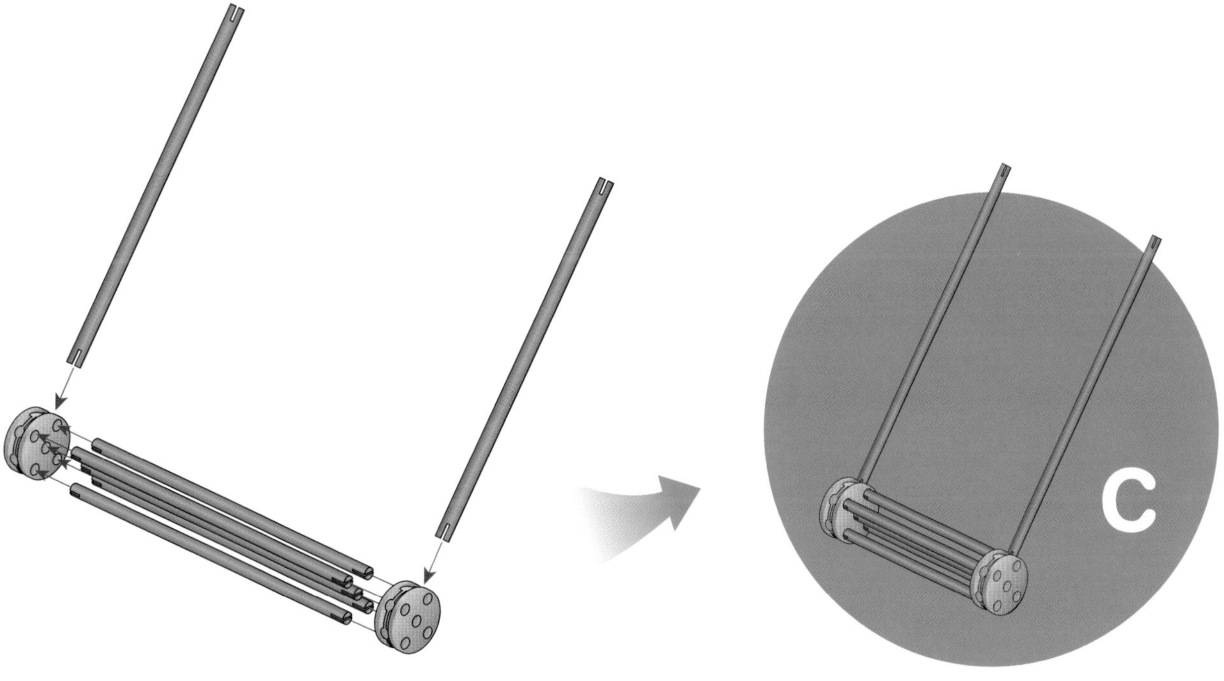
C

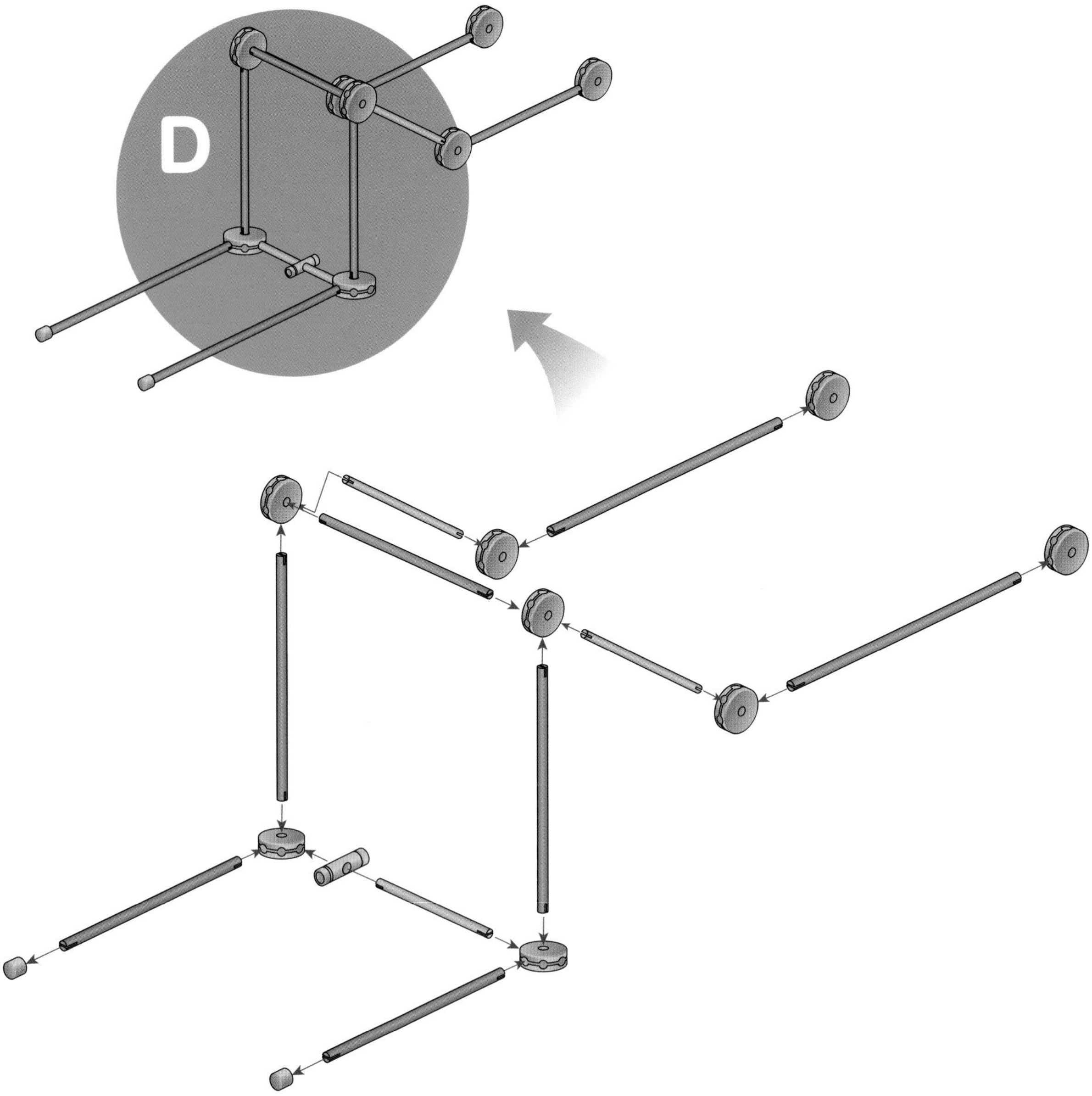
D

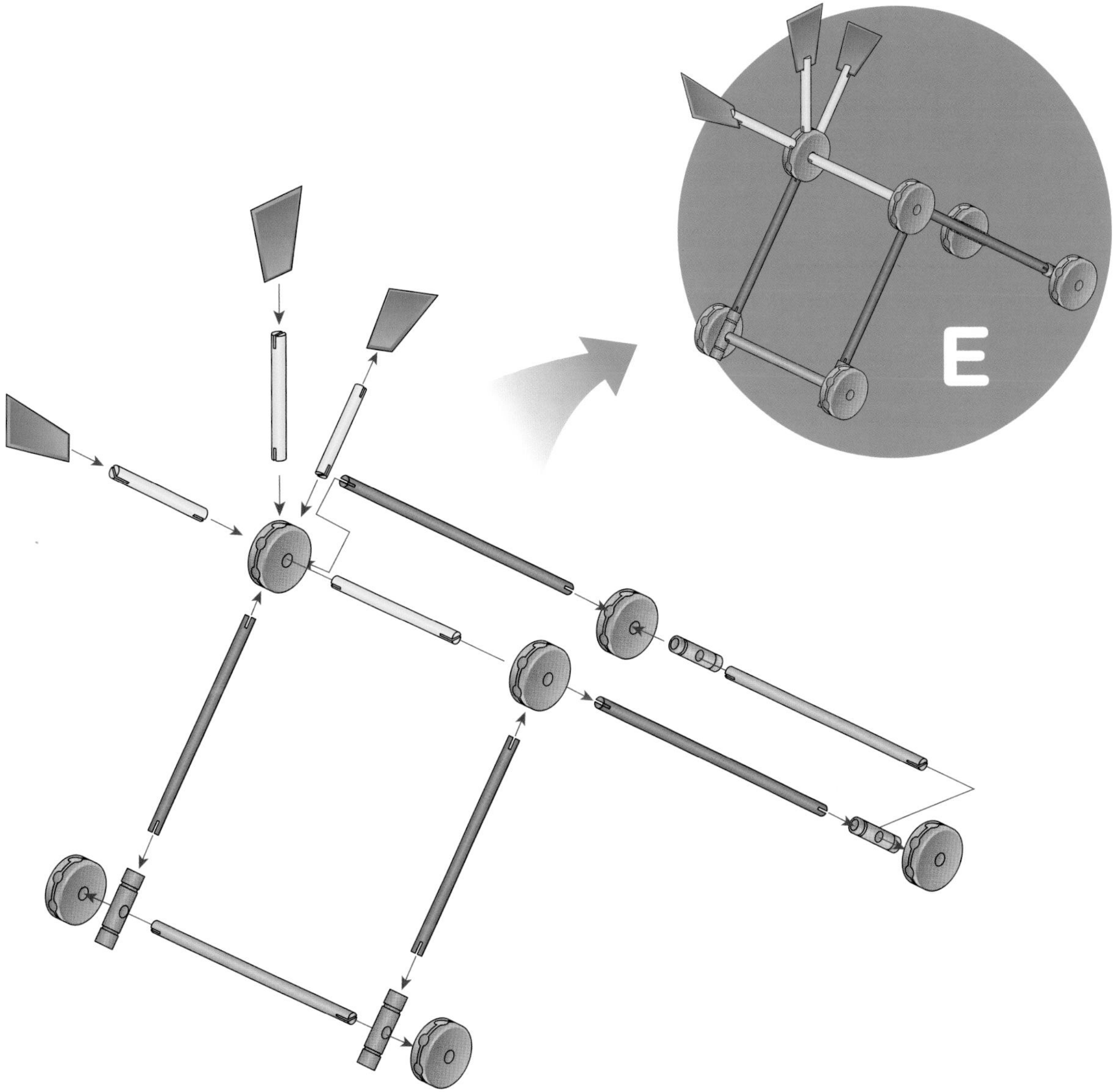
E

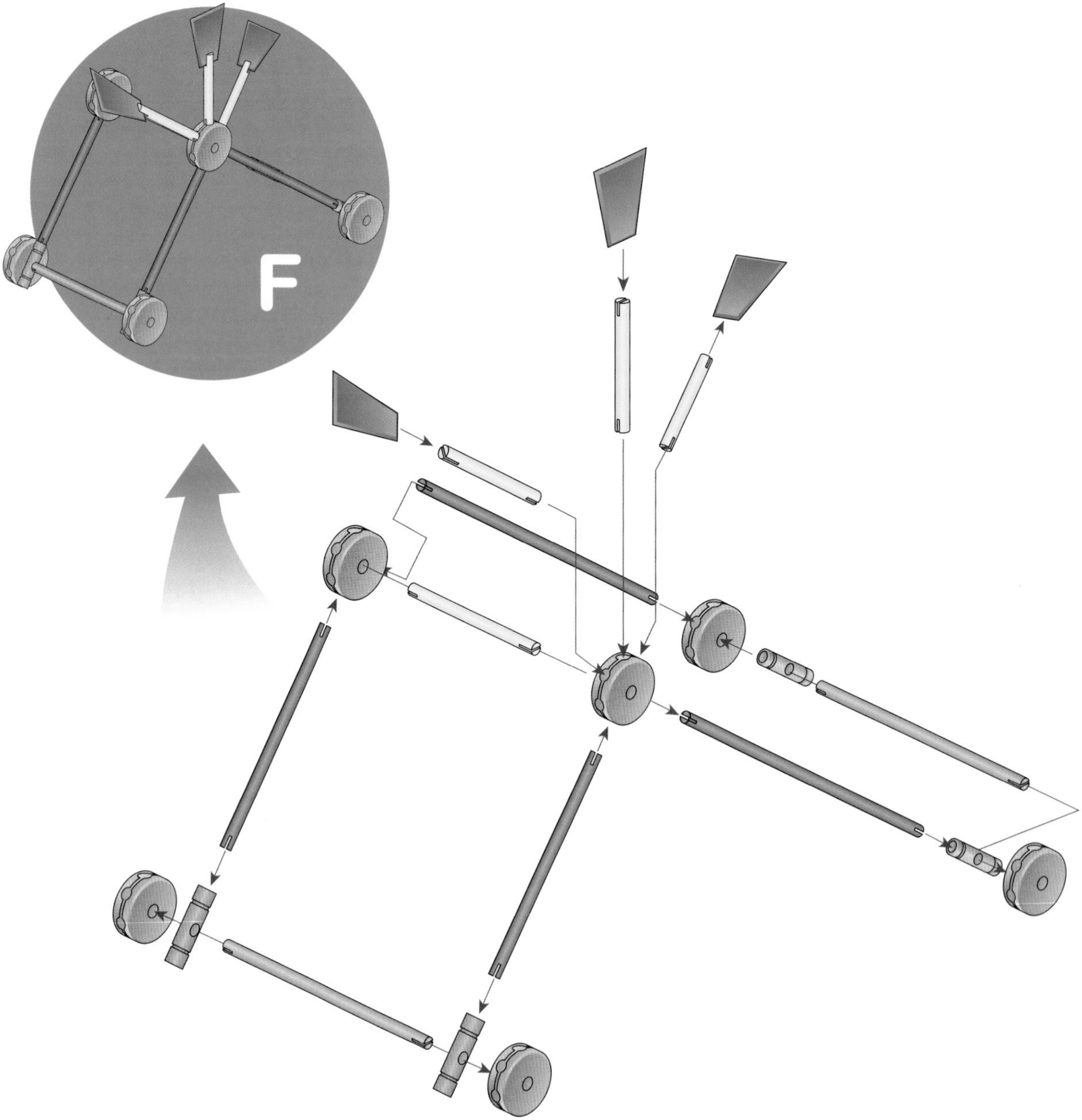
F

Cargo Loader

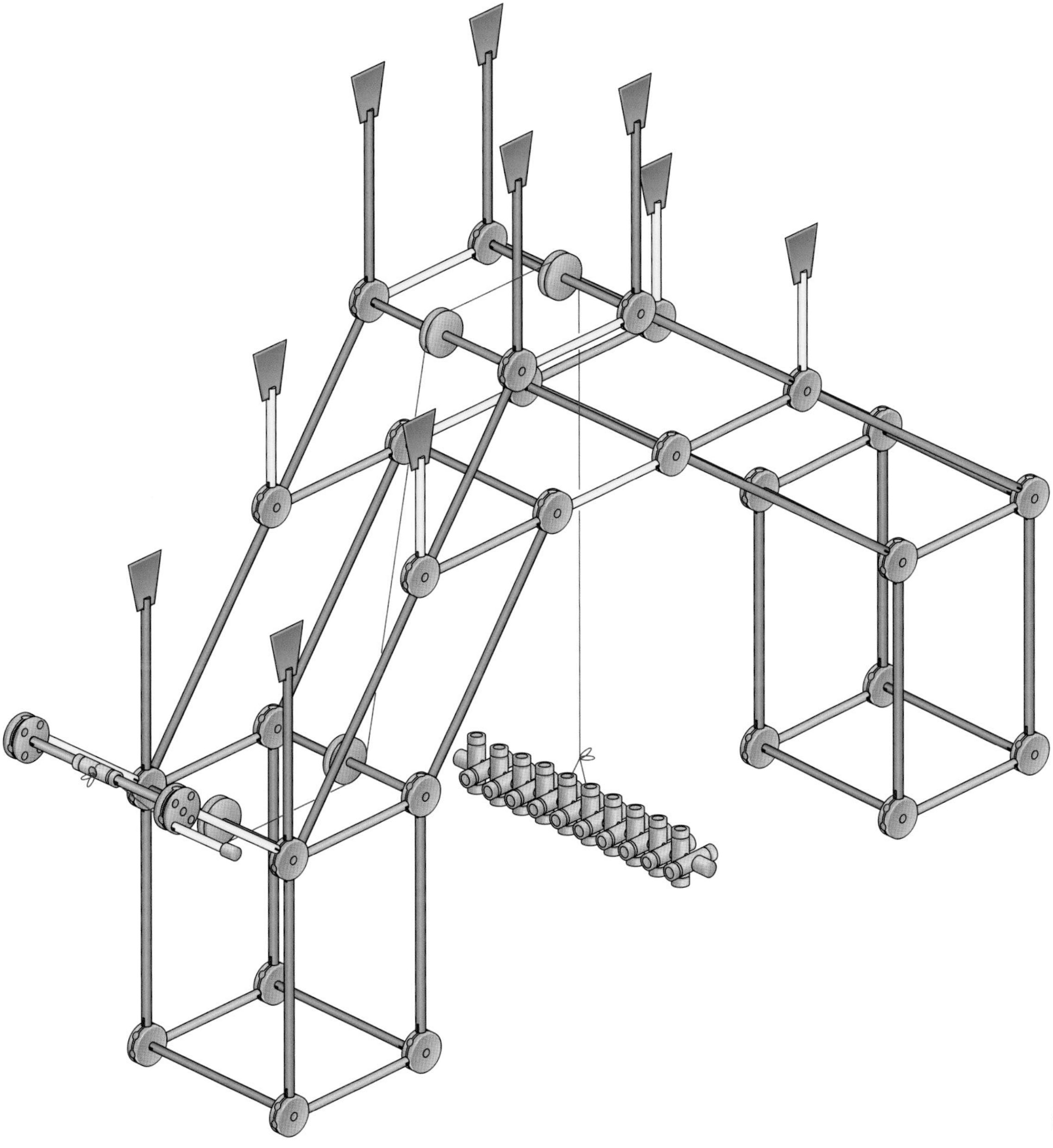

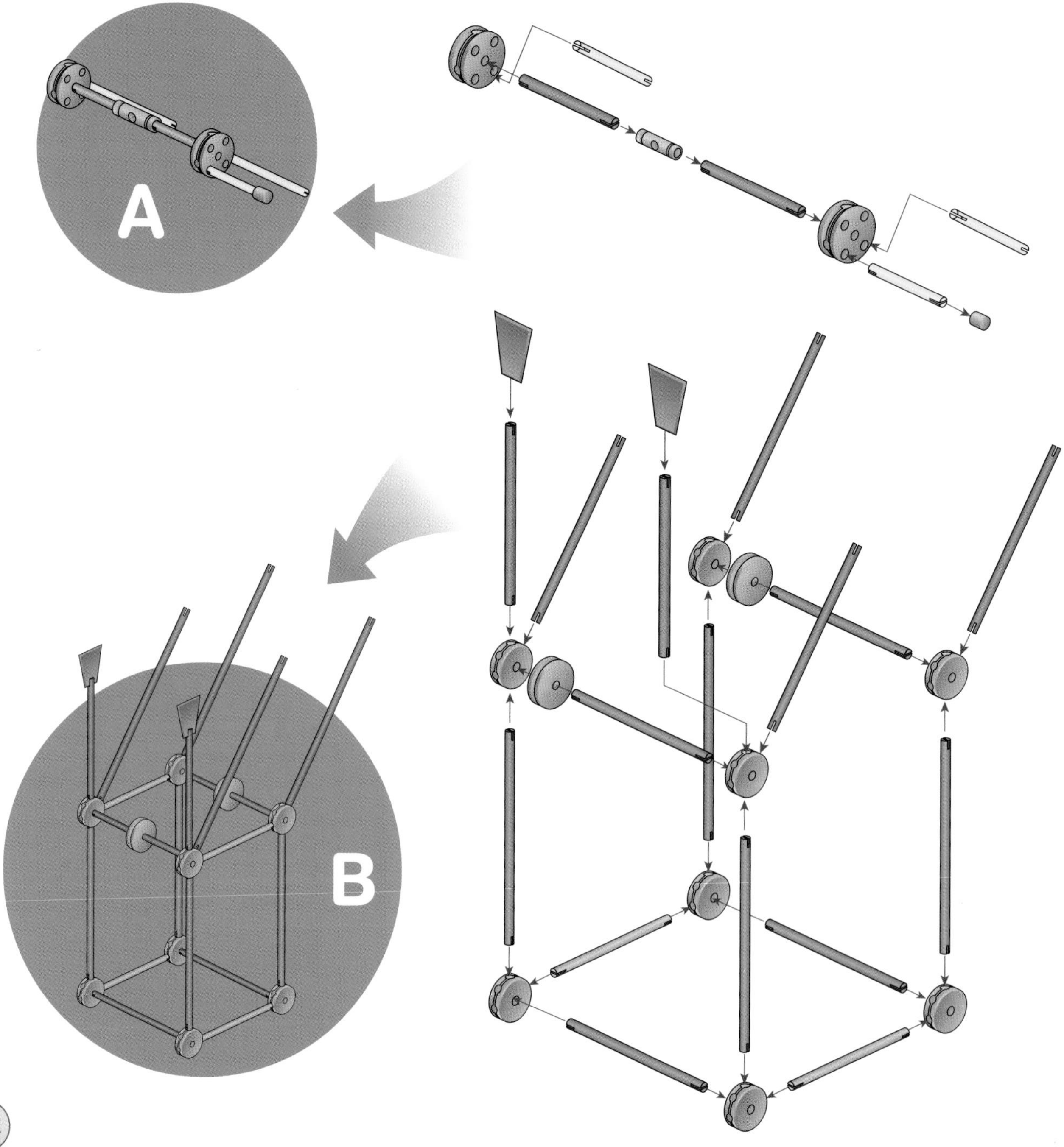
A
B

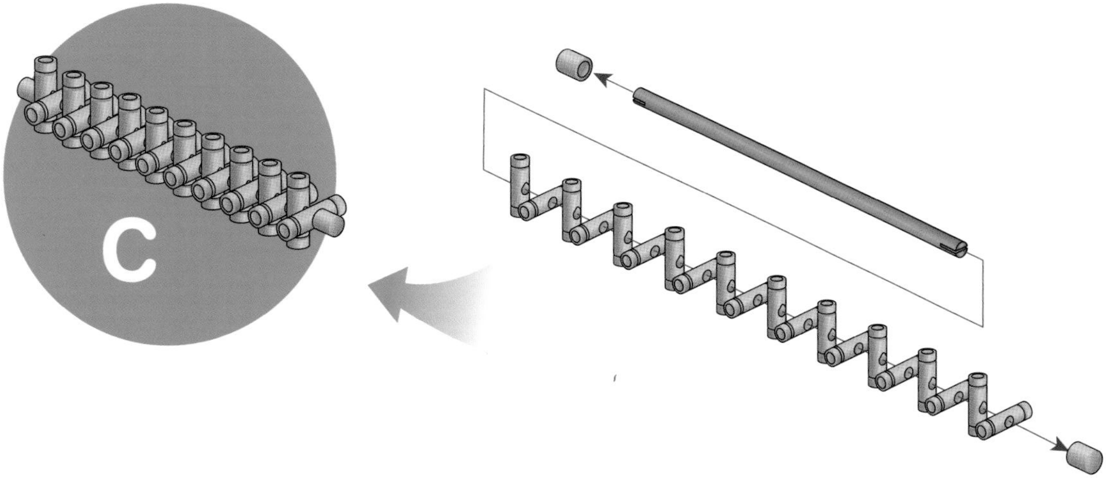
C

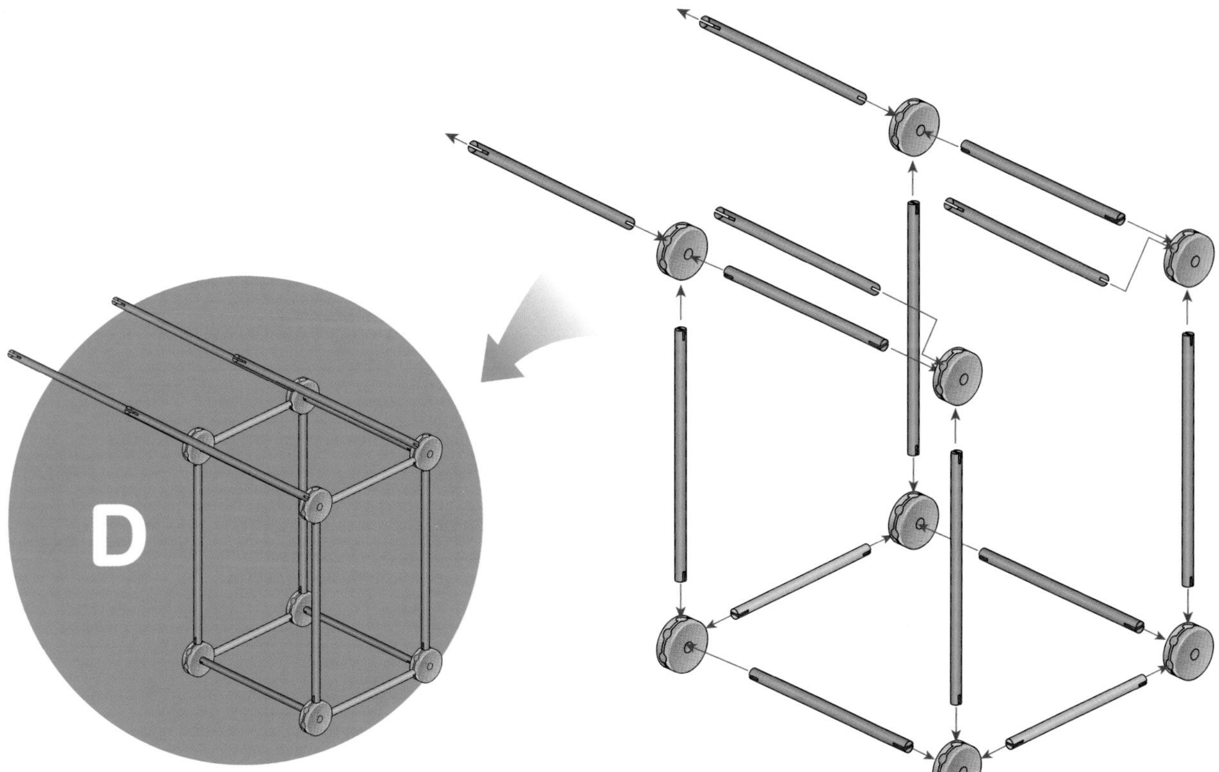
D

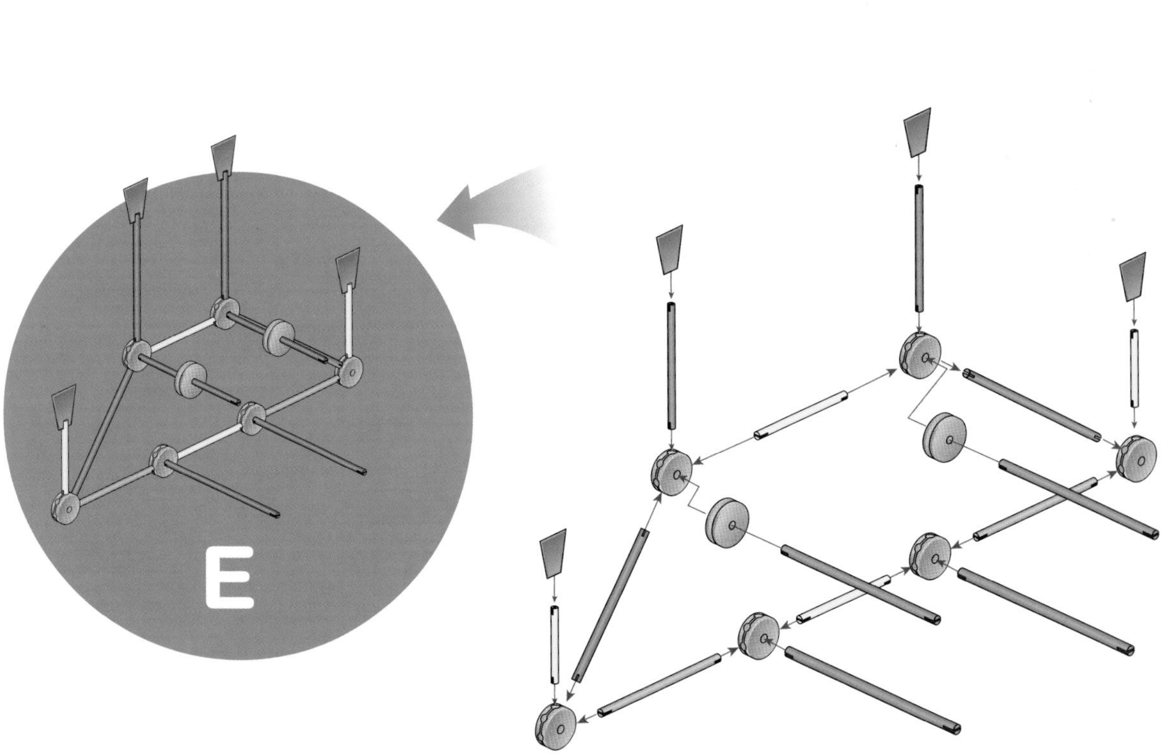
E

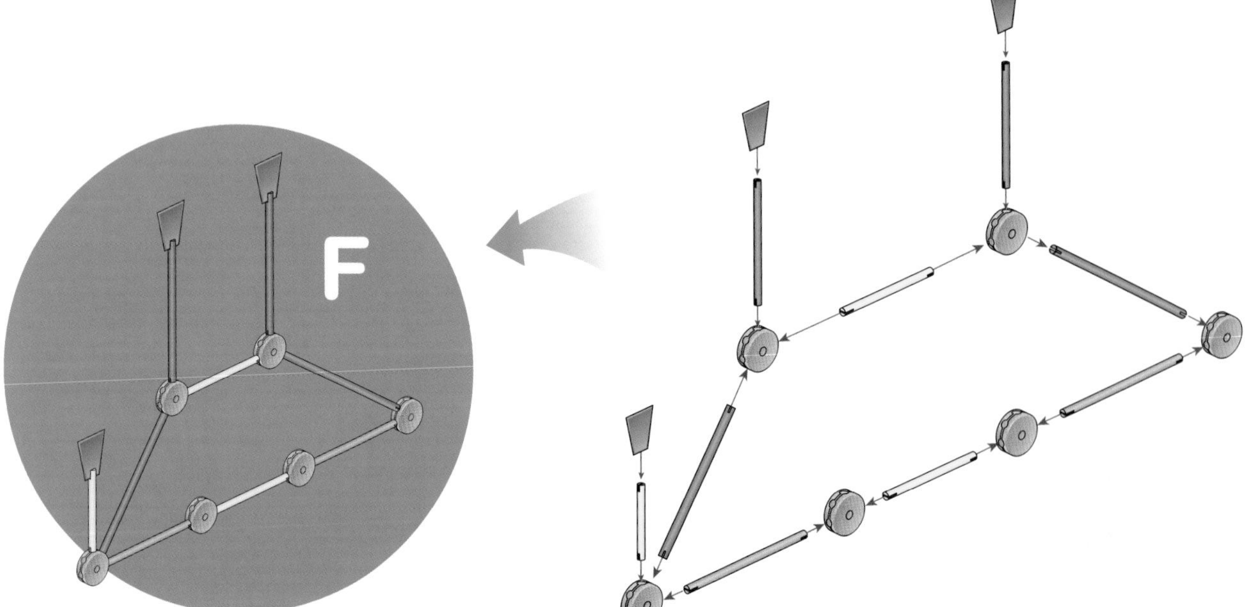
F